Ethnicity and the American Cemetery

Ethnicity and the American Cemetery

Edited by

Richard E. Meyer

Bowling Green State University Popular Press
Bowling Green, Ohio 43403

Material Culture
General Editor
Fred E.H. Schroeder

Library of Congress Catalogue Card No.: 92-74504

ISBN: 0-87972-600-8 Clothbound
0-87972-601-6 Paperback

Cover design by Laura Darnell-Dumm

For Lotte

Jeg elsker dig

Acknowledgments

I owe a large debt of gratitude to those many academic colleagues and administrators at Western Oregon State College who have over the years provided emotional—and sometimes financial—support to my professional interest in cemetery and gravemarker studies. As regards the current volume, I wish to thank in particular the following individuals who, in addition to the contributing essayists, have played separate but equally significant roles in bringing it to pass: Dean and Tracy Blakley, Simon Bronner, Pat and Ray Browne, Ronnveig Ernst, David Gradwohl, Lotte Larsen, Barbara Rotundo, and Brad Taylor. And, finally, those whom this book most directly concerns: for all whose ethnic heritage—in death as in life—has touched and enriched American culture, may what lies between these covers be a special *in memorium.*

Contents

Strangers in a Strange Land: Ethnic Cemeteries in America

Richard E. Meyer

The title of this brief introductory essay alludes, as many will recall, to those plaintive words of Moses uttered during his sojourn in Midian (*Exodus* 2:22). Several millennia later they appear as an epitaph chiseled upon the small, white marble, early Victorian style gravemarker of Alexander Smith (d. 1850), "Belonging to Benton Co., Oregon Territory," who died unexpectedly amidst strange people and unfamiliar circumstances and lies buried in the Oahu Cemetery, Honolulu, Hawaii (Fig. 1:1). This sentiment, inscribed upon the marker of a man who undoubtedly knew much of sojournment—at such an early date he could not have even been resident in the Oregon Territory for very long—provides, I feel, a most appropriate metaphorical context for the present volume's scope and purpose, which is to explore, through a series of original, individually commissioned essays by knowledgeable scholars in a variety of academic disciplines, the manner in which representative ethnic groups in America (like Moses and Alexander Smith, strangers in a strange land) have made their cemeteries—the sites themselves, the material objects found therein, and the customary practices bound to both—a most powerful and eloquent voice for the expression of values and worldview inherent in their self-conscious awareness of their own special identity.

It is certainly no secret that the past several decades have witnessed an enormous flourishing of interest in ethnic studies in America. Several factors, one largely retrospective and the other essentially prospective, may be driving this interest simultaneously. On the one hand, the general emergence of revisionist history and the use of formerly neglected source materials as respectable methodologies have produced such highly significant works as Lawrence W. Levine's *Black Culture and Black Consciousness: Afro-American Folk Thought from Slavery to Freedom.*[1] At the same time, the dawning understanding that the America of the twenty-first century might well be a place where multiculturalism will come to replace the "melting pot" metaphor as the desired and accepted societal norm has provided new impetus to the long-standing debate between theories of ethnicity based upon assimilation vs. pluralism.[2] Whatever the case, one highly visible result of this heightened interest in the role of ethnicity in American life has been an outpouring of

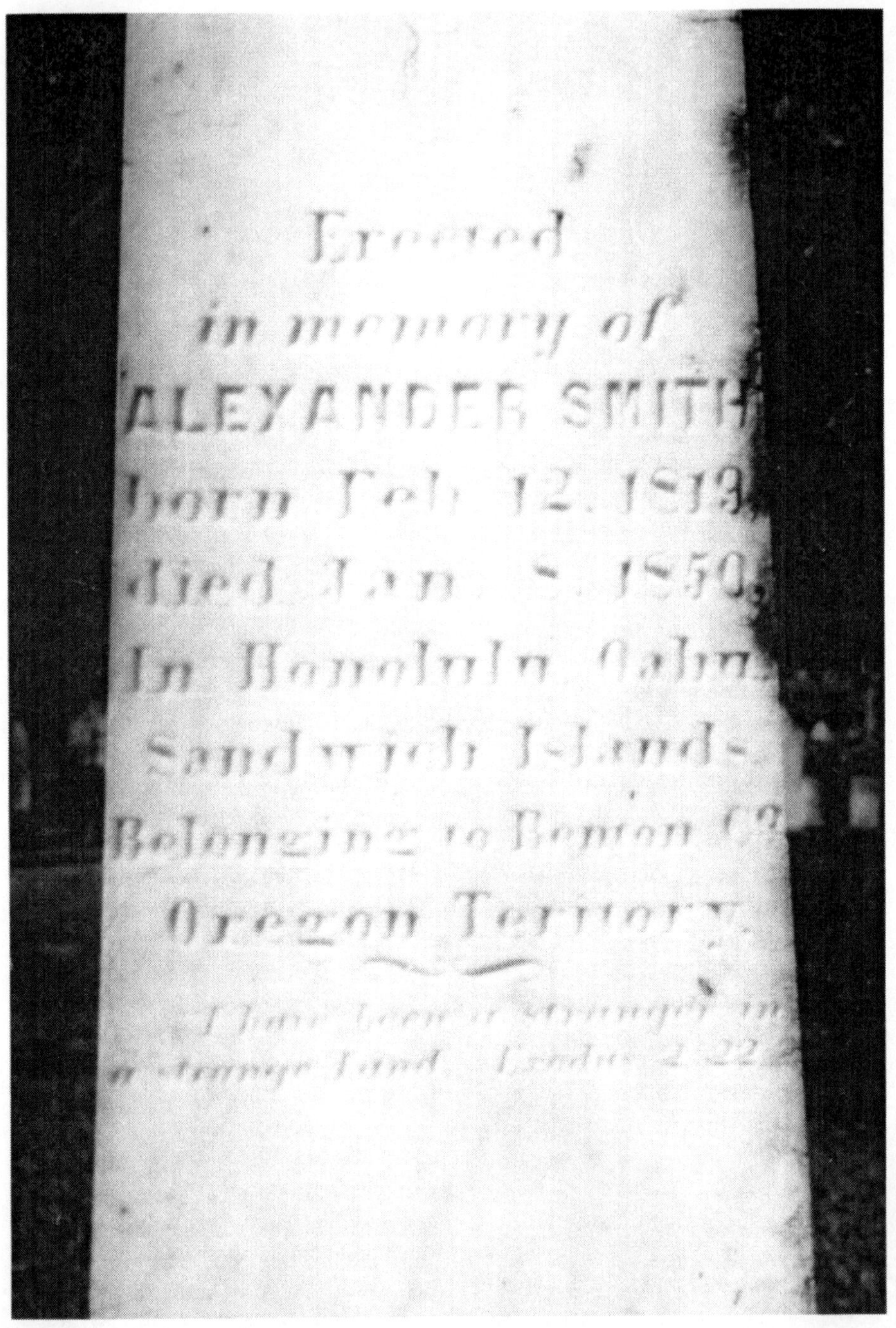

Fig. 1:1. Gravemarker and epitaph—"I Have Been a Stranger in a Strange Land"—of Alexander Smith. Oahu Cemetery, Honolulu, Hawaii.

scholarly studies from an exceptionally wide variety of disciplinary perspectives. Indeed, the quantity of such output has been so vast that it has prompted one observer to note that "To attempt a bibliography of the immigration and ethnicity literature at this time is like taking a snapshot of an avalanche. It inevitably will be dated before it appears."[3]

The best of these examinations of ethnicity in American culture, I would maintain, have been those which have enhanced our understanding not only of the various ethnic groups themselves but of the essential dualities and opposing pressures which are at work within any pocket of minority surrounded by the larger, democratized forces of "mainstream" life—continuity and change, tradition and innovation, retention and assimilation. The discipline of folklore has been particularly effective in achieving this synthesis, and recent years have seen a number of excellent studies devoted to various elements of ethnic folklife in America ranging from music to foodways and from conversational genres to material culture.[4]

As I have argued elsewhere on a number of occasions,[5] cemeteries are far more than merely elements of space sectioned off and set aside for the burial of the dead: they are, in effect, open cultural texts, there to be read and appreciated by anyone who takes the time to learn a bit of their special language. Put another way, architectural historian Michel Ragon notes that "...in the tissue of urban and rural space, death forms a network of places and objects, with its allegories and symbols, its signs and its reference points, forming a specific course."[6] Nowhere is this more apparent than in matters of ethnicity, and yet ironically these are the very chapters which few have taken the opportunity to read.[7] Collectively, America's ethnic cemeteries represent largely untapped resources for the study of evolving patterns of ethnicity in American culture, and it is this potential, more than anything, which the present volume hopes to make clear.

The various essays which comprise this book address the broad topic of ethnic cemeteries in America from a number of disciplinary perspectives. Folklore is represented here, but so are the fields of cultural history, archaeology, landscape architecture, and philosophy, plus several other areas which stand outside traditional academic nomenclature. While striving to bring a certain normalcy of style and organization to these separate efforts, particularly as regards documentation procedures, I have attempted insofar as possible to leave intact the sometimes disparate methodologies and mind sets which distinguish these various approaches, for to do so, I feel, is to acknowledge and indeed emphasize the fact that the study of cemeteries and gravemarkers, not to speak of that of ethnicity, belongs properly within no one area of knowledge but is truly best served through the encouragement of multidisciplinary inquiry.

Taken as a whole, *Ethnicity and the American Cemetery* emphasizes diversity in a number of other respects as well. A noticeable geographic spread shifts the foci of location treated in individual essays from North to South, from coast to coast (and even beyond in the case of Hawaii), and in several cases emphasizes elements which cut across regions. The approaches of the various authors strike a balance between those emphasizing site and/or artifactual analysis and those which lean toward customary practice (though in point of fact they all, to one degree or another, include both). Finally, the ethnic groups represented in these essays, though by no means an all-inclusive listing, do nonetheless constitute a representative selection of immigrant and indigenous peoples often neglected in mainstream studies of American life—Czechs, Native Americans, Ukrainians, Hispanics, Jews, Italians, Gypsies (Scottish, Irish and Rom), Chinese, Japanese and Polynesians.

What can we hope to learn from the study of ethnic cemeteries? Many avenues of insight are possible, as you will shortly discover, but perhaps of paramount importance is the issue, previously mentioned, of the ongoing tension between cultural retention and assimilation, a tension often dramatically revealed by the study of particular ethnic cemeteries over a period of several generations. On the one hand, the ethnic cemetery (indeed, any cemetery) represents one of the most culturally conservative focal points in the community. As historian Kenneth T. Jackson points out, "...for immigrants, cemeteries fostered a sense of identity and stability in a new country characterized by change."[8] This desire for continuity is largely responsible for some of the most immediately noticeable and frequently commented upon features of ethnic cemeteries in America, such as the heavy use of native languages and national symbolism upon individual gravemarkers (Figs. 1:2, 1:3) and the preference for unusual marker shapes and materials among certain groups (Fig. 1:4).[9] In some instances the tendency to display visible ethnic identifiers may be as much inspired by a desire for revival of cultural traits as retention of them; such would seem to be the case in an increasing number of contemporary Native American gravemarkers, where one or more culturally relevant symbols are often worked into the design (Fig. 1:5).[10]

At the same time, funerary practices, like other areas of ethnic folklife, may come over time to lose elements of their distinctiveness as part of the general process by which groups become acculturated into dominant mainstream life. Though less frequently studied, these patterns are also among the significant cultural lessons which ethnic cemeteries can teach us, and they form important elements in several of the essays featured in this collection.

One of the more interesting phenomena to observe in contemporary ethnic cemeteries, standing somewhere between the polarities of retention and assimilation, is the occasional readiness to incorporate newer materials or techniques into ongoing traditional practices. In certain areas of the Mexican-American Southwest, for instance, where families have traditionally followed the practice of decorating gravesites with colorful fresh flowers on religious and secular holidays, the trend in recent times is to supplement these displays with large greeting cards, mylar balloons and a host of other commercially produced materials (Fig. 1:6).[11] In a like vein, the traditional practice much favored amongst southern Mediterranean, eastern European, and Asiatic groups of placing small photographs of the deceased upon their gravemarker, made possible by a process—virtually unchanged since the latter portion of the nineteenth century–of baking photographs on enamel or porcelain and then

Fig. 1:2. Nineteenth century German language gravemarker for six-month old child. Blooming Cemetery, near Cornelius, Oregon.

Fig. 1:3. Contemporary gravemarker featuring flag and map of Vietnam, dual language inscription. Lakeview Cemetery, Seattle, Washington.

Fig. 1:4. Early twentieth century German wrought iron marker. Mt. Angel Cemetery, Mt. Angel, Oregon.

Fig. 1:5. Contemporary Native American gravemarker in the shape of an arrowhead with eagle emblem. Calvary Cemetery, Austin, Nevada.

Fig. 1:6. Decorated Mexican-American gravesite. Easter, 1991. San Fernando Cemetery No. 2, San Antonio, Texas.

Fig. 1:7. Granite etching technique on contemporary Chinese husband/wife gravemarker. Woodlawn Memorial Park, Colma, California.

affixing them to the surface of the monument, is currently undergoing a significant expansion of possibilities through the increasing use of greatly enlarged, less fragile, and intensely lifelike representational images produced by such new technologies of the monument industry as granite etching and photoblasting (Fig. 1:7).[12]

We often tend to think of cemeteries in terms of what they can tell us about the past. "The American cemetery," David Charles Sloane reminds us in his recent study, *The Last Great Necessity: Cemeteries in American History*, "is a window through which we can view the hopes, fears, and designs of the generation that created it and is buried within it."[13] This is certainly a valid approach, and one particularly useful in studying the history of ethnic groups in this country, for written boldly across the face of America's ethnic cemeteries is a vivid chronicle of these groups' struggles, aspirations and shared values. Here we may find, in the words of cultural geographer Terry G. Jordan, "...obvious and subtle reminders from our ancient past and distant, diverse homelands."[14] Less appreciated, perhaps, but equally true, is the fact that cemeteries are constantly evolving, dynamic features of the cultural landscpae, and their value in interpreting the past is clearly matched by their ability to provide remarkable insights into the trends and values of contemporary society. Here again they provide a most intensive focal point for the ongoing study of ethnicity in the fabric of American life. Inextricably connected to that most profound and mysterious of life's rites of passage, these sites of meaningful interaction between the living and the dead bear continual material testament to the most deeply held beliefs and values of any group. And this, for any one of us truly interested in understanding our culture in its broadest and most inclusive sense, is a fitting legacy from those who have become, once again, strangers in a strange land.

Notes

All photographs in this essay are by Richard E. Meyer.

[1](New York: Oxford UP, 1977).

[2]For a general overview of this theoretical debate see Werner Sollors, "Theory of American Ethnicity, or: '? S Ethnic?/Ti and American/ti, De or United (W) States S1 and Theor?", *American Quarterly* 33:3 (1981), pp. 277-281. Additional consideration is provided in Ronald A Reminick, *Theory of Ethnicity: An Anthropologist's Perspective* (Lanham, MD: UP of America, 1983).

[3]Rudolph J. Vecoli, quoted in Sollors, "Theory of American Ethnicity," p. 257. Such frustrations aside, two somewhat dated but still extremely useful bibliographic and reference works to consult as starting points are the *Comprehensive Bibliography for the Study of American Minorities*, comp. Wayne Charles Miller. 2 vols. (New York: New York UP, 1976) and the *Harvard Encyclopedia of American Ethnic Groups*, ed. Stephan Thernstrom, Ann Orlov, and Oscar Handlin (Cambridge: Harvard UP, 1980). Also of

particular value are Anya Peterson Royce, *Ethnic Identity: Strategies for Diversity* (Bloomington, IN: Indiana UP, 1982) and Werner Sollors, *Beyond Ethnicity: Consent and Descent in American Culture* (New York: Oxford UP, 1987). For a somewhat specialized examination of the role ethnicity plays in matters concerning death and dying in America see Richard A. Kalish and David K. Reynolds, *Death and Ethnicity: A Psychocultural Study* (Farmingdale, NY: Baywood Publishing Co., 1981).

[4]Here too the sheer magnitude of the published literature precludes comprehensive listing, and the interested reader is encouraged to consult the relevant portions of such indexes as the annual *MLA International Bibliography* or the bibliographic notes appended to the various chapters of Jan Harold Brunvand's *The Study of American Folklore: An Introduction*, 3rd ed. (New York: Norton, 1986). For a brief but useful overview of this area of folklore studies see Barbara Kirshenblatt-Gimblett, "Studying Immigrant and Ethnic Folklore," In *Handbook of American Folklore*, ed. Richard M. Dorson (Bloomington, IN: Indiana UP, 1983), pp. 39-47. Somewhat more extensive is the treatment offered by Elliott Oring in his chapter, "Ethnic Groups and Ethnic Folklore," in *Folk Groups and Folklore Genres: An Introduction*, ed. Elliott Oring (Logan, UT: Utah State UP, 1986), pp. 23-44. Barre Toelken provides a valuable contextual methodology for the study of ethnic folklore at numerous points in his *The Dynamics of Folklore* (Boston: Houghton Mifflin, 1979). An exciting recent work which surveys ethnic lore from a multi-genre approach is *Creative Ethnicity: Symbols and Strategies of Contemporary Ethnic Life*, ed. Stephen Stern and John Allan Cicala (Logan, UT: Utah State UP, 1991). Though not explicitly linked to ethnic considerations, the broad spectrum of death-related folklore is thoroughly examined within a regional context in William Lynwood Montell's classic study, *Ghosts Along the Cumberland: Deathlore in the Kentucky Foothills* (Knoxville, TN: U of Tennessee P, 1975). A collection of brief but exceptionally enlightening essays on one aspect of ethnic material culture—the primary generic reference point for this volume as well—is found in *America's Architectural Roots: Ethnic Groups that Built America*, ed. Dell Upton (Washington, D.C.: Preservation P, 1986).

[5]For example, " 'So Witty as to Speak'," in *Cemeteries and Gravemarkers: Voices of American Culture*, ed. Richard E. Meyer (Ann Arbor, MI: UMI Research P, 1989; rpt. Logan, UT: Utah State UP, 1992) pp. 1-6; and "Image and Identity in Oregon's Pioneer Cemeteries," in *Sense of Place: American Regional Cultures*, ed. Barbara Allen and Thomas J. Schlereth (Lexington, KY: UP of Kentucky, 1990), 88-102.

[6]*The Space of Death: A Study of Funerary Architecture, Decoration, and Urbanism*, trans. Alan Sheridan (Charlottesville, VA: UP of Virginia, 1983), p. 21.

[7]Which is not to say that studies of ethnic cemeteries and gravemarkers are nonexistent, only that the majority of such approaches have tended to be piecemeal and insufficiently dedicated to a fuller understanding of the ethnic groups themselves. A selection of relevant sources is presented in the annotated bibliography found at the conclusion of this book.

[8]In Kenneth T. Jackson and Camilo José Vergara, *Silent Cities: The Evolution of the American Cemetery* (New York: Princeton Architectural P, 1989), p. 60.

[9]One must exercise caution in the latter area, however. The tendency for members of an ethnic group to opt for use of non-standard materials may be owing more to necessity and matters of economy than to preference and cultural retention, a case in point being the frequent use of home-fabricated concrete markers amongst southern rural Afro-Americans and other groups.

[10]For another striking example of these contemporary Native American markers see Kathryn Cunningham's photograph of a hand-painted Zuni stone, in Keith Cunningham, "Navajo, Mormon, Zuni Graves: Navajo, Mormon, Zuni Ways," in *Cemeteries and Gravemarkers: Voices of American Culture*, ed. Richard E. Meyer (Ann Arbor, MI: UMI Research P, 1989; rpt. Logan, UT: Utah State UP, 1992), p. 209.

[11]This activity is extensively discussed in Lynn Gosnell and Suzanne Gott's essay, "San Fernando Cemetery: Decorations of Love and Loss in a Mexican-American Community," in *Cemeteries and Gravemarkers: Voices of American Culture*, ed. Richard E. Meyer (Ann Arbor, MI: UMI Research P, 1989; rpt. Logan, UT: Utah State UP, 1992), pp. 217-236.

[12]For detail on the process of granite etching, or granite engraving as it is alternately called, see Lawrence Sanata, "Granite Etchings," *Stone in America* 98:11 (1985), pp. 38-43. Photoblasting is discussed in "Photoblast's Technique Reproduces Photograhpic Images on Granite," *MB News* 41:8 (1984) pp. 34-35.

[13](Baltimore: The Johns Hopkins UP, 1991), p. 6.

[14]*Texas Graveyards: A Cultural Legacy* (Austin, TX: U of Texas P, 1982), p. 126.

Windows in the Garden: Italian-American Memorialization and the American Cemetery

John Matturri

In the last of a series of international cemetery travelogues published in the trade journal *Park and Cemetery* during the late 1920s, landscape architect Ray F. Wyrick summarized the difference in ideals between Latin cemeteries and those of the United States by noting that in Havana, as in Italy and France, he had found:

> ...another example of the Latin lack of quiet lawns, natural groupings of trees, or subordination of monuments to the restful green of our better cemeteries. Their ideal seems to be to try to keep alive the fame or the wealth of those who have died, whereas ours is to make the living forget the trials of death in contemplation of the present beauty of our earth. They seem to try to keep grief alive for a long time, and we try to soften grief and think of the graves of our dead as melted into the peace of a quiet landscape.[1]

The Latin cemeteries, that is, acted to elicit thoughts of particularized ongoing relations between the living and the dead whereas North American cemeteries encouraged at most a vague sentimental attachment to the deceased.[2]

The differences that Wyrick identifies are quite real and are critical not only for the comparative study of burial practices, but also for understanding the accommodation of ethnic diversity within the American cemetery. Although the American cemetery has at times been portrayed as a symbolic ground where the diverse population of the nation is united in "a sacred unity,"[3] an examination of actual memorialization practice reveals the cemetery to be as rent with social fissures as any other institution of American life. Immigrant groups have rarely, if ever, entirely given up the traditions and values of their homelands, and these traditions have frequently helped determine the way they bury their dead.

In this essay, I will examine the memorialization practices of Italian-Americans and the ways these practices cut across the dominant tradition of American cemetery design. In doing so, I will place special emphasis on the cultural roots of the differences between the traditions and the very different attitudes towards the relationship between the living and the dead that they embody, as well as the implications that these differences have had for the ability of the American cemetery ideal to meet the needs of a pluralist nation.

The American Memorialization Tradition

The slab tablets of the colonial churchyards of New England present to their beholders a vivid reminder of human mortality and the utter separation of the realms of the living and the dead. In the medieval era, the doctrine of purgatory had provided an intermediary realm which allowed a continuing relationship between the living and dead, but with the rejection of this doctrine the only possible channel of contact with the dead was severed. Although the Puritans did not necessarily oppose the secular commemoration of the dead, their official beliefs denied that familial and other earthly relationships lasted beyond the grave. Aside from their purely commemorative role, therefore, burial grounds acted more as mirrors of mortality than conduits of continuing relationships between the two realms. The primary didactic message of the churchyard for the Puritan is well conveyed in the following directive from a seventeenth-century English sermon:

> Go to the graves of those that are gone before us, and there see; are not their eyes wasted, their mouthes corrupted, their bones scattered? Where be twin ruddy lips, lovely cheeks, sparkling eyes, comely nose, hairy locks?[4]

From this perspective, a churchyard visit serves more to throw back to the visitor a reflection of his or her own upcoming death than to allow a consoling image of a continuation of the earthly identity of the deceased.[5]

The attitudes toward death proposed by strict Calvinist theology were, however, never fully assimilated into the popular culture, and in some contexts the psychological tensions that resulted as the dead were cut off from the living may have actually been responsible for an increase of ghostly apparitions within communities whose official belief system no longer provided a basis for contact between the living and the dead.[6] However, as the strict Puritan religious culture gradually declined during the seventeenth and eighteenth centuries, beliefs in the total separation of the living and the dead were ameliorated, as is indicated by the development of a mourning culture that encouraged the living to retain a consoling sentimental attachment to their dead. A major manifestation of this culture can be found in the development of the ideal of the burial place as a landscape of emotional reconciliation.

The rural and lawn plan cemeteries that embody this ideal seek to engender this reconciliation not through maintaining a strongly particularized memory of the dead but rather through subduing that memory–and its associated grief—by eliciting contemplation of the integration of the dead into what was seen as a beneficent natural order. Although memorials are not necessarily excluded from the park-like settings of these cemeteries, discreet family monuments designed to harmonize with the landscape are most in accord with their emotional and aesthetic norms. The consolatory function of these grounds was described early in the twentieth century by O.C. Simmonds:

> Cemeteries serve families by serving as beautiful places where loved ones who have died may be left in peace. Mankind has always been fond of imagining the continued existence of those who have departed this life, of imagining their spirits enjoying places which we call "Heaven," and which the Indian called the "Happy Hunting Ground," and of imagining also that sometimes these spirits return and hover about the haunts of the living. We can think, therefore, of cemeteries ministering in a certain way to the satisfaction of departed individuals. We can imagine the spirits getting some pleasure from the beauty of the morning concerts of the birds and consider the music a personal tribute, or, we may think of their going peacefully to the sweet music of the woodtrush which continues long after sundown. The beauty of a cemetery, therefore, should be its chief attribute–that quiet, restful beauty which nature seems to provide without effort.[7]

This ideal allowed a sentimental imagining of a continuing relationship between the living and the dead, but one effected only through depriving the dead of their specific identity. Although many plot owners in rural and lawn plan cemeteries have resisted this loss of particularized remembrance, this tradition of American cemetery design has remained the dominant ideal to the present day.[8]

Memorialization and Italian-American Culture

It is this ideal of a landscaped cemetery that Wyrick contrasts so sharply with the ideals exemplified by the cemeteries of countries whose burial practices have been dominantly influenced by Catholic beliefs concerning death. Catholicism retained the doctrine of purgatory as an intermediary realm of personal existence after death and has thus allowed and encouraged continuing imagined interaction between the living and the dead.[9] Under this doctrine, those who die in a state of sin not serious enough to warrant eternal damnation must undergo a spiritual cleansing through punishment received during a passage through the state of purgatory. The prayers and good works of the living can facilitate this passage, and, in establishing the opportunity and obligation to intercede into the fate of the dead, purgatory established what Natalie Zemon Davis has called a "mutual economy of salvation."[10] Intercessionary deeds and prayers could not only be enacted by a survivor but also purchased on an institutionalized marketplace whose goods and currency opened up lines of social exchange between the earthly and spiritual realms. Within Catholic religious culture, particularly that of Mediterranean countries, the realm of the spirit is not utterly transcendent to the world, and social and familial relationships and obligations do not end with death. To ignore or forget one's dead is to violate basic norms and expectations. It is this value system that provides the underpinning for the Latin cemeteries that Wyrick finds so different from the "better" American cemeteries.

The continued belief in purgatory in Catholic countries also allows the maintenance of popular traditions—many of which predate the twelfth century institution of the doctrine of purgatory—of a type that had been (at least officially) suppressed in Protestant countries. These traditions were often retained within immigrant communities in the United States.[11] For some time after the prime immigration period of the late nineteenth and early twentieth centuries, Italian-American funeral customs often involved the participation of a female eulogist who performed a ritual chant that affirmed the goodness of the deceased, promised continued due respect and the performance of the obligations due to the dead, and asked him or her to be benevolent to those who lived on.[12] These promises made at the wake and funeral were maintained as many families continued in subsequent years to place memorial advertisements, often with photographs of the deceased, on the anniversary of the death and to put out in the home a plate of spaghetti for the deceased family members on All Soul's Day.[13] Where appropriate behavior toward the dead was not possible—when, for example, the death had occurred in a hospital—the passage of the soul to purgatory was said to be subject to interference.[14] The imagined relationship between the living and the dead was uneasy and often fraught with anxiety in this culture, but the interconnection of the two realms was among its central features.

As Italian-Americans became increasingly assimilated into American culture during the second and subsequent generations, many of these practices were lost or modified. Home vigils over the body of the deceased were replaced by funeral parlor wakes, and such customs as leaving offerings of food on All Soul's Day and taking a photograph of the corpse died out. This adoption of American customs does not, however, necessarily indicate a total loss of the old traditions and customs. As late as the mid-1970s, Carla Bianco reported that her informants did not like the new customs and felt that they "endanger the journey of the dead to the other world."[15] Moreover, neighborhood events such as the annual feast for a local patron saint—which often attract those who have moved away from an Italian or formerly Italian community—serve to reaffirm the continuing communion between the living and the dead.[16] It is true that many traditional values and customs have been eroded or lost among many members of the third and subsequent generations, but even where customs regarding death have been Americanized, they often continue to be suffused with characteristics that are quite foreign to the mainstream culture.

Beliefs and practices concerning memorialization are strongly intertwined with the central importance of the family in Italian, particularly Southern Italian, culture. Persons living within Italian communities have social existence only within the context of their families, and without a connection to a family they lack a major source of their values and personal support.[17] Continued respect for dead ancestors and relatives thus provides a way of affirming the continued strength of a central social institution upon which one's own identity and well-being depends. The weight of this responsibility is indicated by Rudolph M. Ball's observation that during the period of Italian immigration one can find in death registers "frequent and poignant testimony about the efforts of family members...to locate burial places and obtain assurances that they were suitably marked."[18]

These cultural attitudes toward the dead could not but be reflected in memorialization practices and inevitably often conflicted with the desires of cemetery superintendents who wished to maintain the norms of the landscaped cemetery model. For Italian-Americans who retain their ethnic identity, the cemetery plot is a site of highly particularized communion with the dead, not one where the dead are to be imagined as having melted into natural surroundings. The distinction between the two ideals is certainly moot in many cases; many of the Catholic cemeteries that served the early generations of Italian-Americans did not yet accept the landscaped ideal and, in any event, immigrants and members of the second generation often could only afford gravesites in the single plot sections of the cemeteries that inevitably were difficult to integrate into a landscape design. However, even where these constraints are not present, Italian-Americans have often chosen to not conform to the dominant American ideal of memorialization.

Because of these traditions and beliefs, Italian-Americans, like members of several other non-Protestant American ethnic groups, have continued to maintain the cemetery as an active site of ritualized communion with the dead at a time when the American cemetery has been seen by many to have become a purely functional site of interment.[19] This has been verified by the author on several occasions during the past several years by holiday period visits to several locations where Catholic and non-denominational/Protestant cemeteries are located in close proximity to each other: on each occasion, the Protestant cemetery was virtually empty and bare of decoration whereas the Catholic cemetery was quite crowded with visitors to graves that were often elaborately decorated. Moreover, even when extensive decorations are found on graves within non-Catholic cemeteries, the name on the grave quite often indicates membership in a Catholic ethnic group.[20]

Thus, for Italian-Americans, weekend visits to the plots of family members are frequent, and plants, flowers, and other ornaments are routinely placed on the grave and often maintained for decades after a death. Not only do special visits take place during holiday periods, but these periods are often marked by placing highly elaborate decorations on the graves (Fig. 2:1). In many cases, the relationships between the living and dead are expressed in even more direct terms: frequently elderly family members will be seen standing before the grave engaged in deep and serious conversation with a dead spouse, parent or child. In other cases, holiday greeting cards will be placed on the grave with personal inscriptions of love and continued emotional affiliation. Iconic displays are also an important part of many of the mausoleums that are popular among wealthier members of the community: within the mausoleums are often found photographs and such personal memorabilia as wedding announcements, religious articles and displays of holiday decorations. These customs serve not so much to "keep grief alive," as Wyrick assumes, but to keep the relationship between the living and dead alive.

Of particular interest is the rather common practice of surrounding the front area of a small gravesite with a miniature fence.[21] While this practice may in part be due to the need to protect plants and flowers from destruction by

Fig. 2:1. Holiday grave decoration with Christmas card. North Arlington, New Jersey.

lawnmowers, it also contributes to establishing even a single-lot plot as a distinct gravesite identifiable with a particular person. Both the plants and the fencing serve to isolate an area of ground that is closely associated with the deceased, and that thus can serve to elicit imaginings of a continued relationship with the deceased. This marking out of a private territory provides a clear contrast with the ideal of a communal ground expressed in the dominant tradition of cemetery design.

The values of the community are also reflected in the types of memorials chosen for the gravesites. These frequently include religious imagery and/or inscriptions which at times involve intercessionary themes that can be directly related to the tradition of purgatory.[22] Occasionally, more specific imagery, such as a picture of a local patron saint, is placed on the gravemarker. Although conventional commercial monuments are currently most typical, homemade monuments can be seen and are occasionally produced even at present, particularly when a memorial marks a child's burial (Fig. 2:2). Homemade markers are very often constructed of concrete and frequently incorporate shells or other objects into their designs. Sculptural portraits, the most remarkable of which very realistically portray life-sized full-length figures, were often produced in the past (Fig. 2:3). Less dramatic but far more common than sculptural portraits are the photographs of the deceased that were very frequently placed on gravestones of Italian-Americans up until the 1940s. Because these photographic memorials are perhaps the most distinctive type of memorial device used by Italian-Americans, their character is deserving of rather extensive examination.

Photographic Gravemarkers

After the invention of photography, it was almost inevitable that the new technology would soon be applied to memorialization. Photography not only allowed portraiture to become available to sectors of society for whom painted or sculpted portraits were unaffordable, it did so through a mechanical procedure that established a direct causal connection between the image and the person or object portrayed. This lack of mediation of human intentions seems to give these images a relic-like quality that was even more important than the ability of the technology to provide sharp, objective, realistic images. That is, the photograph appears almost to be a temporally transparent image that allows the viewer contact with people, things and events that may have ceased to exists.[23] Thus, Elizabeth Barrett could remark that what was important about photographic portraits was "not merely the likeness" but the "association and sense of nearness" of an image that was "*the very shadow of the person* lying there fixed forever!"[24] The inherently memorial character of these images is commented upon in an essay on photography by Oliver Wendell Holmes:

> It is hardly too much to say, that those whom we love no longer leave us in dying, as they did of old. They remain with us just as they appeared in life; they look down upon us from our walls; they lie upon our tables; they rest upon our bosoms; nay, if we will, we may wear their portraits, like signet-rings, upon our fingers. Our own eyes lose the

Fig. 2:2. Concrete homemade gravemarker decorated with colored pebbles. North Arlington, New Jersey.

Fig. 2:3. Full-length portrait statue on gravemarker. East Orange, New Jersey.

images pictured on them. Parents sometimes forget the faces of their own children in a separation of a year or two. But the unfading retina which has looked upon them retains their impress, and a fresh beam lays this on the living nerve as if it were radiated from the breathing shape. How these shadows last, and how their originals fade away![25]

Photographs themselves, in other words, act as appropriate memorials to the deceased.

The specific application of photographic images to cemetery monuments was recognized as early as 1851 when Solom Tomkins obtained a patent for "securing daguerreotypes to monumental stones," and by 1855 the Scoville Manufacturing Company of New York, which in 1851 had offered a daguerreotype case designed as a memorial piece, was distributing a catalog for "Monumental Daguerreotype Cases." Throughout the nineteenth and twentieth centuries, daguerreotypes, ambrotypes, tintypes and finally photo-ceramics would be placed on American tombstones.[26] Portraits, of course, have been used on monuments since antiquity, and they began appearing in American cemeteries at an early date, but only with the invention of photography did this form of memorialization became available for those who could not afford to commission a realistic sculpture of the deceased.

Although gravestones with niches for photographs are seen in mainstream nineteenth American cemeteries, most Americans have chosen not to take advantage of this type of memorialization. Given the character of the American cemetery this is not surprising. Gravestones containing photographic portraits inevitably assert themselves against the surrounding landscape and thus are incompatible with the reconciliation with the natural environment that is the dominant ideal of the American cemetery. Although at least five firms offering porcelain portraits advertised regularly in monument industry trade journals during the pre-World War II period, the only illustration of a gravestone from this period incorporating a photograph that has been found in a magazine's editorial content was contained in an article on pet cemeteries. Ray F. Wyrick, in an article that seeks out ways of rekindling interest in cemeteries by compromising the landscape ideal through the use of more personalized memorials, noted that it was good that most families could not afford stone portraits, for if "there was much of this, our burial grounds would become ghostly indeed."[27] This is precisely the point. Such monuments tend to elicit the very sense of the continued presence of the dead that the landscaped cemetery by design is meant to suppress, and they can thus contribute to that lack of "quiet and restful appearance" which Wyrick finds all too characteristic of Catholic cemeteries.[28]

The use of photographs, generally in the form of photoceramics, was (and remains), however, very common in Southern and Eastern Europe, and such markers became a common feature of Catholic (as well as Jewish) cemeteries serving immigrant populations from these areas. That photographic gravestones should be popular among Italians and Italian-Americans should not be surprising in considering the attitude toward the dead in Italian-American culture. If a survivor has a responsibility to maintain a continuing relationship

Fig. 2:4. Photographic montage affixed to gravemarker. North Arlington, New Jersey.

with a dead relative, the most appropriate cemetery monument will be one that can best serve to elicit a vivid memory of the deceased, and the relic-like likeness provided by a photograph is able to fulfill this function in a uniquely appropriate manner. The photograph thus serves as a kind of window of imagination through which one can maintain a relationship with a deceased family member; that is, these monuments serve to summon up precisely those "ghostly" graveyard presences that Wyrick finds distasteful.[29]

By keeping alive the memory of the deceased, the gravestone photograph thus helps maintain the communion between the living and the dead upon which rests central familial values of Italian-American culture. These values are particularly symbolized on photographic gravestones which attempt to smoothly join within their frame images that are widely separated in time, locality and style (Fig. 2:4). Within the disjointed perspectives of these extraordinary photographs there is an attempt to photographically synthesize a space that could overcome generational and geographical barriers and thus affirm the integrity of the family and the traditional household. Whereas the simple presentation of a name in the traditional American family plot affirms a rather abstract familial continuity that transcends individual personality, photographic tombstones provide an opportunity for the concrete personalized communication that is demanded within Italian-American culture.

The gravestone photographs must, moreover, be seen in the overall context of a religious culture that is permeated with images serving as intermediaries between the material and spiritual worlds. Popular Italian-American Catholicism places greater emphasis upon the intercessionary power of the saints and local traditions of the Madonna than upon an impersonally transcendent God, and the channels of communication between the believer and a religious patron are often mediated by the use of vivid images. Religious iconic displays are common in the homes and those displays frequently intermix religious and familial images. In an illustrated iconic display, set up along the path of a street procession for St. Gerard in Newark, New Jersey, one finds religious, secular and familial images brought together freely. The record that was played as the family pinned strands of currency onto a statue of the saint was not a devotional hymn but Connie Francis' recording of "Mama"; the saint and the deceased family members both inhabit a single spiritual world, and gravestone photographs and other images act as imaginary windows into that world (Fig. 2:5).[30] It is, in fact, quite appropriate that one manufacturer of ceramic gravestone portraits took the name "Studio Veronica"; within an image-oriented culture, photographs must almost inevitably be seen in the context of those most sacred of icons that were said to be miraculously produced without the intervention of the human hand.

This is not, however, to say that placing a photographic image on a cemetery monument is exclusively motivated by private religious or familial concerns. In this very concretely-oriented culture, a sharp dichotomy cannot be drawn between the private and public or the sacred and secular realms. Just as the ritual act of placing strands of currency onto a processional statue of a saint is at times accomplished with an ostentatious Las Vegas-like flair,

Fig. 2:5. Iconic street display placed in path of procession during Feast of St. Gerard. Newark, New Jersey.

memorialization practices, as Mathias has noted, frequently are influenced by considerations of social competition. The Southern Italian peasant ancestors of many Italian-Americans would have only been able to afford very simple burials, and with the increased affluence of life in the United States there has been some borrowing from funereal patterns that in the old country would have been reserved for the *signori*, the landowners.[31] This is in accordance with a social norm requiring that one show a "*bella figura*," a "clean, elegant, controlled self to public eyes."[32] Although Italian-American immigrants often continued to perform menial jobs in America, its urban society allowed them to avoid the indignity of exhibiting their low status in a manner that would have been impossible for a Southern Italian peasant. An immigrant to Canada is quoted as saying that:

> ...here, when five o'clock comes round, I clean my fingernails, dress like a king, and I am a king, like everyone else. I am not the son of So-and-So; I am not a hodman; I am just Mr. [name deleted] and I feel a hundred times better than those vagabonds.[33]

This desire to achieve dignity is exhibited in the selection of photographs placed on gravestones. Although informal photographs or those indicating occupation or social class are found, these are not the norm; snapshots are most common in child burials (Fig. 2:6). Most adults are portrayed dressed formally—with displays of medals or other insignia of status not uncommon—and posed according to the conventions of formal portraiture (Fig. 2:7); particularly common are photographs taken at weddings, first communions, confirmations and graduations.[34] Studio photographers in the Little Italies of the immigration period played an important role in allowing members of the community to present a dignified face to the world and, particularly, to those who remained in the old country,[35] and for the most part it was the formal face of their photographs that were chosen to represent the deceased on the grave.

Thus, the practice of placing photographs on the grave is part of a complex social form that served to affirm the dignity of the deceased and the status of the family while, most importantly, acting as a prop that allowed the elicitation of memories and imaginings of a continued relationship between the living and the dead. Like religious images and relics, they served to establish a cultural space in which the earthly and spiritual realms could intersect and to act as windows through which the living could peer through to the dead and the saints.

Ethnicity and the American Cemetery

In the 1940s the use of photographs on the gravestones of Italian-Americans and a number of other Catholic groups suddenly became uncommon. Although the custom may have already begun to lose popularity as the second and third generations became more Americanized, the major reason for the change was the decision to establish regulations against photographic memorialization as a means of making Catholic cemeteries more uniform.[36] This change in memorialization practice can thus be seen as an imposition of the

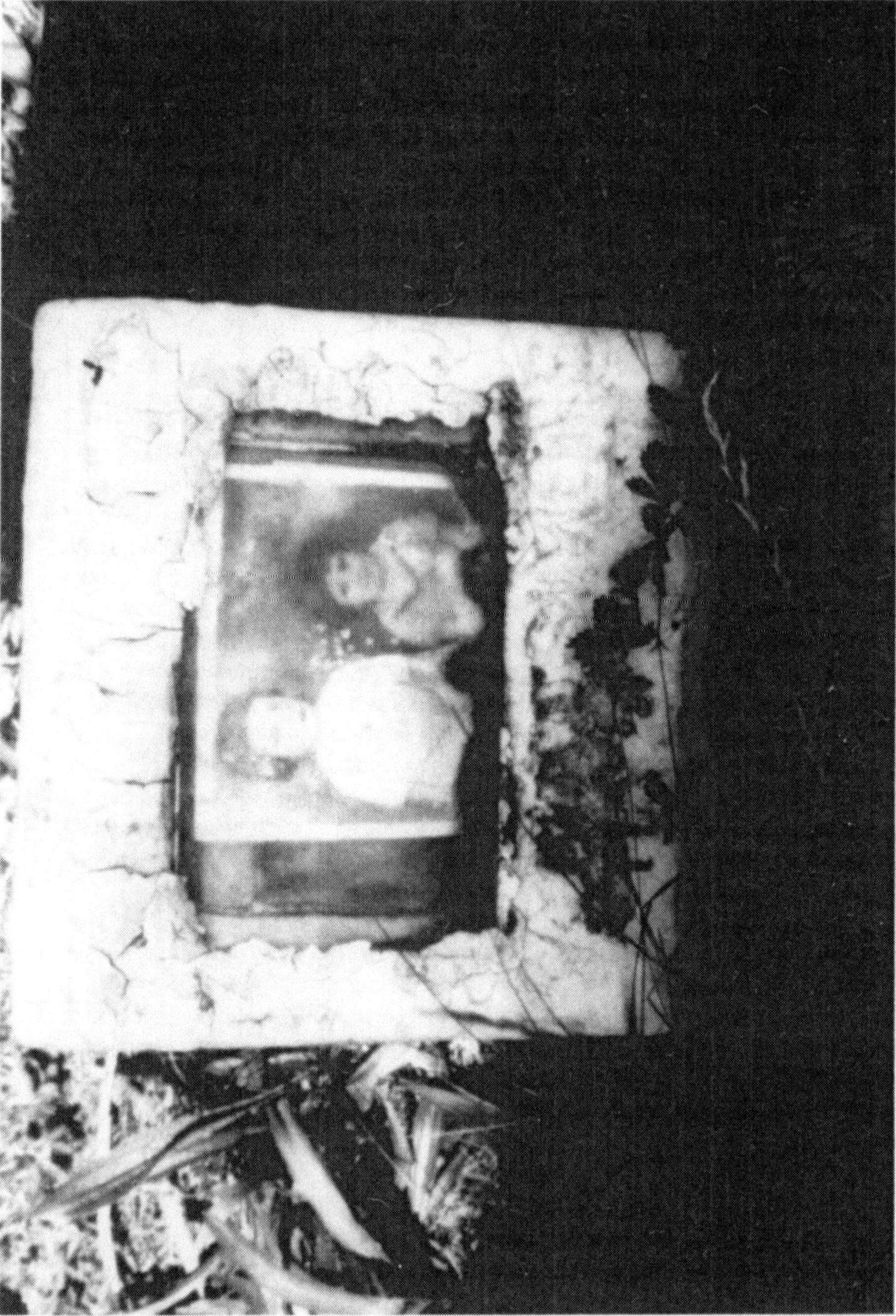

Fig. 2:6. Homemade child's gravemarker with snapshots. East Orange, New Jersey.

Fig. 2:7. Formal photograph on gravemarker. East Orange, New Jersey.

standards of the American tradition of landscaped cemeteries upon a group whose own traditions did not conform to the American ideals. This decision may also be a manifestation of the longstanding disapproval that the predominately northern European American Catholic hierarchy felt toward the popular religion and culture of Southern European immigrants. In a 1932 interview, a Catholic priest and cemetery superintendent expressed sympathy for "elderly foreign people who were accustomed to peculiar treatment of cemetery lots," yet expressed the wish to convince them of "the logic and necessity of our restrictions."[37] By this time, a majority of Catholic cemeteries had generally adopted the norms of the American cemetery and were seeking to impose them on the immigrant groups.

The tension between ethnic memorialization practices and the American cemetery tradition had long been recognized as an issue among cemetery superintendents. In 1896, Matthew P. Brazill of St. Louis had complained that it seemed "morally impossible to get [immigrants] to conform to improved American ideals of cemetery management,"[38] and by 1920 a superintendent of Bridgeport, Connecticut's Mountain Grove Cemetery had found it necessary to require prior design approval of monuments to combat the "weird taste of the foreign element for freakish monuments and such."[39] Although some superintendents allowed various ethnic groups, including Italians, their own sections in a cemetery,[40] more often they had to contend as best as possible with the "diversified number of nationalities...usually represented in a single grave section, every one desiring to care for his particular grave in his own way."[41] The difficulty in reconciling the standards accepted by groups like the American Association of Cemetery Superintendents and the monument industry with the needs of groups wishing to maintain their own ethnic traditions is expressed in the following 1939 statement by a monument dealer:

> How am I going to convince an illiterate foreigner, full of sentiment and emotion, that a 'thoroughly studied composition in the tablet type with the decor in the current modern influence is' better for the grave of the child than the carved Lamb for which the soul of him yearns? Am I supposed to tell him that he is a darn fool and ignorant for being so sentimental? Am I supposed to give him a high school education and intensive course in the appreciation of beauty while my competitor sells him the Lamb?[42]

At the same time that this dealer was expressing his bitterness about the conflict between cemetery norms and ethnic demand, however, leaders of the monument industry ironically enough began looking to Catholic and Jewish cemeteries for suggestions on how to revivify a memorial tradition that seemed rapidly to be dying out among most other sectors of American society.[43] The lawn plan ideal to which the industry had acquiesced early in the century had by this time come to seem to result in a "barren greensward" with "[n]o individuality, no seclusion, no appeal to the imagination, no stimulation of the emotions" and to adversely affect monument sales.[44] The strategy of shifting to a form of memorialization that encourages emotionally significant monuments received great emphasis throughout the 1930s and 1940s and the connection with ethnic practices is brought out clearly in a 1941 *Monumental News-Review* editorial describing a nicely designed gravestone that had been aesthetically compromised by an Italian widow's addition of statuary. The author noted that he and his companion:

> spent a few moments mentally condemning the poor taste of some people, etc., until out of an unnoticed car came an elderly woman in black with some beautiful flowers and in prayer. It was then we realized how right she was and how wrong we all were. Yes, she had purchased what we all agree was a beautiful design, but unfortunately for her, it was not a monument, it did not have meaning for her. For another person, sensitive to the fine proportions, the design might have been adequate; for the woman in black it was not, so she gave it meaning with the statuary; and God bless her and the many others who may have sacrificed esoteric aesthetisms for sincere expressions of Faith and testimony of the Glory of God. So we took our small camera and got this poor picture of a thought which should make us all think![45]

If only most Americans could be encouraged to have the sentiment of this woman, the author implies, business would improve. What he fails to recognize, however, is that the widow belonged to just that cultural and religious tradition against which the originators of the American cemetery had reacted and that it was precisely her sense of an ongoing relationship with the dead that the American cemetery was designed to discourage.

Among the major goals of the American cemetery has been the linking of members of its culturally diverse population into a symbolic unity: "all our ways, however diverse, meet at last," noted John Albro at the dedication of Cambridge Cemetery.[46] A nineteenth-century guidebook to Cincinnati's Spring Grove Cemetery suggested that ethnic diversity could be integrated into the harmonious landscapes of urban cemeteries if in place of "dilapidated marble slabs and toys" foreigners planted trees native to the homelands over the graves of their dead.[47] This aspiration of using the cemetery to establish the symbolic unity of a varied population was, however, as bound to fail as was the plan of monument industry leaders to revive business by following the lead of the Italian widow and her compatriots. The cultural differences that Wyrick recognized on his trips to Europe and Latin America were quite real, and, as manifested within an increasingly pluralistic society, were too deep to admit of simple reconciliation. Ethnic differences have played a critical role in the development of modern American society and the rifts established by such differences have been inevitably manifested in cemetery landscapes that diverge sharply from the ideal of a unified garden that might bring together in death those who lived separately in life.

Notes

All photographs in this essay are by John Matturri.

[1]"Cemetery Travelogues: VIII. Havana," *Park and Cemetery* 38 (Jan. 1929), p. 306.

[2]Kendall Walton's analysis of the function of artistic works as props for imaginative activity provides a suggestive account of the nature of such elicitation. See his *Mimesis as Make-Believe: On the Foundations of the Representational Arts* (Cambridge: Harvard UP, 1990).

[3]Lloyd W. Warner, *The Living and the Dead: A Study of the Symbolic Life of Americans* (New Haven: Yale UP, 1959), p. 249. Richard Huntington and Peter Metcalf also argue for the existence of an American civil religion in which death rituals cut across religion, ethnic group and class. See their *Celebrations of Death: The Anthropology of Mortuary Ritual* (Cambridge: Cambridge UP, 1979), p. 193.

[4]Isaac Ambrose, *Ultima: the Last Things* (London: 1659).

[5]These complex issues were examined in more detail in John Matturri, "Uncommon Grounds: American Burial Memorials and the Relationship between the Living and the Dead." Paper presented to the Annual Meeting of the Association for Gravestone Studies, Byfield, Massachusetts, June, 1989. See also Claire Gittings, *Death, Burial and the Individual in Early Modern England* (London: Croom Helm, 1984). In the Anglican colonies of the South there developed a somewhat different memorialization tradition: see Diana Coombs, *Early Gravestone Art in Georgia and South Carolina* (Athens: U of Georgia P, 1986).

[6]Natalie Zemon Davis, "Ghosts, Kin and Progeny: Some Features of Family Life," *Daedalus* 106 (Spring 1977). See also Keith Thomas, *Religion and the Decline of Magic* (New York: Charles Scribner's Sons, 1971), ch. 19. The Puritan churchyard itself, in its role as a site of secular commemoration, may have functioned to ameliorate some of these psychological tensions.

[7]"Progress and Prospect in Cemetery Design," in *The Cemetery Handbook* (Chicago: Allied Arts Publishing Co., n.d.), p. 90.

[8]The existence of a tradition of resistance to the ideal through the privatization of cemetery plots was examined in detail in John Matturri, "Sentiment or Stone? Death and Emotional Norms in the Modern Cemetery," paper presented at the Annual Conference of the American Culture Association, New Orleans, Louisiana, March, 1988. The nineteenth-century development of spiritualism may also provide an indication of tensions resulting from an increasing alienation of the living from the dead: see Janet Oppenheim, *The Other World: Spiritualism and Psychical Research in England, 1850-1914* (Cambridge: Cambridge UP, 1985).

[9]For the history of the institution of purgatory see Jacques Le Goff, *The Birth of Purgatory*, trans. Arthur Goldhammer (Chicago: U of Chicago P, 1984). It is interesting to note that some speakers at nineteenth-century cemetery dedication ceremonies specifically saw the rural cemetery movement as a reaction against customs established in accordance with the institutions supported by purgatory. For example, in dedicating the Fishkill Rural Cemetery in Dutchess County New York in 1866, Allard Anthony noted that in "the preparation of this rural ceremony we return to the mode which nature prompts, discarding the habits and prejudices which grew out of the corruptions of the papal church.": "Address Delivered by the Hon. Allard Anthony at the Dedication of the Fishkill Rural Cemetery, October 17, 1866," in Tristan Coffin, *Recollections of Allard Anthony* (New York: 1916), p. 13. On the other hand, in revolutionary France, the campaign to move the cemeteries was said by some to be part of a campaign by *philosophes* to destroy the idea of purgatory: see J. McManners, *Death and the*

Enlightenment (Oxford: Claredon, 1981), p. 314.

[10]Davis, "Ghosts, Kin and Progeny," p. 93.

[11]The interaction between the popular and the theological traditions has deep roots in the European cultural tradition. Jacques Chiffoleau found a distinction between the perpetual masses and prayers requested by those in the learned-clerical culture and the popular requests that were oriented toward those anniversaries when the worlds of the living and the dead became reintegrated: cited in James R. Banker, *Death in the Community: Memorialization and Confraternity in an Italian Common in the Late Middle Ages* (Athens: U of Georgia P, 1988), p. 6.

[12]Carla Bianco, *The Two Rosetas* (Bloomington: Indiana UP, 1974), p. 119; Leonard Covello, *The Social Background of the Italo-American School Child* (Leiden: E.J. Brill, 1967), p. 114.

[13]Covello, *The Social Background* , p. 114; Coleen Leahy Johnson, *Growing Up and Growing Old in Italian-American Families* (New Brunswick, NJ: Rutgers UP, 1985), p. 100; Jarre Manginone, *Mount Allegro* (New York: Columbia UP, 1981), p. 97; Elizabeth Mathias, "The Italian American Funeral: Persistence Through Change," *Western Folklore* 33 (1974), p. 38.

[14]Phyllis Williams, *South Italian Folkways in Europe and America* (New Haven: Yale UP, 1931), p. 172.

[15]Bianco, *The Two Rosetas*, p. 119.

[16]Robert Anthony Orsi, *The Madonna of 115th Street* (New Haven: Yale UP, 1985), p. 229.

[17]*Ibid.*, p. 82. The classic description of the Southern Italian roots of this ethos is found in Edward C. Banfield, *The Moral Basis of a Backward Society* (New York: Free, 1958).

[18]*Fate and Honour, Family and Village* (Chicago: U of Chicago P, 1979), p. 161.

[19]For examples of analogous groups see Lynn Gosnell and Suzanne Gott, "San Fernando Cemetery: Decorations of Love and Loss in a Mexican-American Community," in *Cemeteries and Gravemarkers: Voices of American Culture*, ed. Richard E. Meyer (Ann Arbor, MI: UMI Research P, 1989; rpt. Logan, UT: Utah State UP, 1992), pp. 217-236; and Nanette Napoleon Purnell's essay, "Oriental and Polynesian Cemetery Traditions in the Hawaiian Islands," found in the present volume.

[20]The graves of children often provide an important exception to this lack of interest in ongoing memorialization in non-Catholic cemeteries.

[21]For a corollary practice amongst members of another group see Russell Barber's discussion of the *cerquita* in his essay "The Agua Mansa Cemetery: An Indicator of Ethnic Identification in a Mexican-American Community," found in the present volume.

[22]In part, this use of religious themes might be attributed to regulations in many Catholic cemeteries that require imagery to be religious in nature, though in point of fact, such regulations are often minimally enforced.

[23]For a modern account of the photograph as a non-intentionally mediated natural sign see Paul Grice, "Meaning," *The Philosophical Review* 46 (1957), pp. 377-388. Kendall Walton uses Grice's work to argue, on the basis of a philosophical theory of perception that places virtually exclusive emphasis on the causal connection between the perceiver and what is seen, that when viewing photographs we are literally, albeit indirectly, seeing the object photographed. Even if this argument of literal

causal/temporal transparency is rejected, it remains true that the causal relationship operative within photography does tend to elicit an imagined sense of being in contact with the object portrayed. See Kendall Walton, "Transparent Pictures: On the Nature of Photographic Realism," *Critical Inquiry* 11 (1984), pp. 246-277.

[24]Quoted in Patrick Maynard, "The Secular Icon: Photography and the Functions of Images," *The Journal of Aesthetics and Art Criticism* 42 (1983), p. 10.

[25]"Sun-Painting and Sun-Sculpture," *Atlantic Monthly* 8 (July, 1861), p. 14.

[26]Jay Ruby, "Post-Mortem Portraiture in America," *History of Photography* 8 (1984), pp. 201-222; F. Spira, "Graves and Graven Images," *History of Photography* 5 (1981), pp. 325-328; Robert Taft, *Photography and the American Scene* (New York: Dover, 1938), p. 162.

[27]"Personality in Individual Memorials in the Wyrick Cemeteries," *Park and Cemetery* 47 (April 1937), p. 30.

[28]Wyrick, "Improvement of Catholic Cemeteries. I," *Park and Cemetery* 40 (Nov. 1930), p. 238.

[29]The significance of such "windows" is also seen in the belief that if one stares into a pail containing three rings after having gone to confession and communion, he or she could see the dead on All Soul's day. See Covello, *The Social Background*, p. 116.

[30]This interchange occasionally is found on the gravestone itself, when a print of a patron saint replaces, or is put next to, the space usually reserved for the portrait of the deceased.

[31]Mathias, "The Italian-American Funeral," p. 35.

[32]S. Silverman, *Three Bells of Civilization* (New York: Columbia UP, 1975), pp. 40, 189.

[33]Joseph Lopreato, *Peasants No More* (San Francisco: Chandler, 1967), p. 84.

[34]Also occasionally found are photographs of the deceased in a casket, although as early as 1931 it was reported that only very old-fashioned families followed the custom of having post-mortem photographs made. Williams, *South Italian Folkways in Europe and America*, p. 209.

[35]George A. Pozzetta, "The Mulberry District of New York City," in Robert F. Harney and J. Vincenza Scaraci, eds., *Little Italies in North America* (Toronto: The Multicultural History Society of Ontario, 1981), p. 17.

[36]Mathias, "The Italian-American Funeral," p. 44.

[37]Ray F. Wyrick, "Modern Management of a Catholic Cemetery," *Park and Cemetery* 41 (Jan. 1932), p. 322.

[38]James J. Farrell, *Inventing the American Way of Death, 1830-1920* (Philadelphia: Temple UP, 1980), p. 138.

[39]Ernest S. Leland, "Mountain Grove Cemetery in Bridgeport," *Park and Cemetery* 30 (Dec. 1920), p. 258.

[40]F.I. Sloan, "Reviving the Run Down Cemetery," *Park and Cemetery* 34 (Feb. 1925), p. 327.

[41]Elbert A. Hoffman, "Care of the Single Grave Section," in *Prettyman's Composite Catalog for Cemeteries*, no. 1 (Chicago: Prettyman, 1936), p. 116.

[42]"Can We Stop the Slump," *Monumental News* 51 (1939), p. 459.

[43]See, for example, "A Monument is a Prayer in Stone," *Monumental News-Review* 52 (Aug. 1940), p. 15; Ernest S. Leland, "What's to Become of the Mortuary

Crafts?," *The Monument and Cemetery Review* 24 (April 1939), pp. 14-15; Ernest S. Leland, "*Life* Goes to a Memorial Park," Monumental News-Review 56 (March 1944), p. 17; "Religion and the Memorial Idea," *Monumental News-Review* 57 (June 1945), p. 17.

[44]"Can We Stop the Slump in Cemetery Lot Sales," *Monumental News-Review* 54 (Aug. 1942), pp. 19-20. For the history of the conflict between the monument industry and cemetery superintendents in the late nineteenth and early twentieth centuries see Farrell, *Inventing the American Way of Death, 1830-1920, passim.*

[45](Feb. 1941), p. 10.

[46]Quoted in David E. Stannard, "Calm Dwellings," *American Heritage* 30 (Aug. 1973), p. 46.

[47]*Spring Grove Cemetery: Its History and Improvements* (Cincinnati: Robert Clarke, 1869), p. 6.

Keeping Ukraine Alive Through Death: Ukrainian-American Gravestones as Cultural Markers

Thomas E. Graves

"The Testament"

When I shall die, pray let my bones
High on a mound remain
Amid the steppeland's vast expanse
In my belov'd Ukraine:
That I may graze on mighty fields,
On Dnieper and his shore,
And echoed by his craggy banks,
May hear the Great one roar!

When from Ukraine that stream shall bear
Over the sea's blue sills
Our foemen's blood, at last shall I
Forsake the fields and hills
And soar up to commune with God
In His eternal hall.
But till that Day of Liberty-
I know no God at all!

Bury me thus I pray, and rise!
From fetters set you free!
And with your foe's unholy blood
Baptize your liberty!
And when in freedom, 'mid your kin,
From battle you ungrid,
Forget not to remember me
With a kind, gentle word!

Taras Schevchenko (1814-1861)[1]

Ukrainians have been emigrating to the Americas since the late 1800s. Large numbers of the earlier immigrants settled in the anthracite coal region of Pennsylvania. Starting in 1880, Shenandoah, Pennsylvania, was the first Ukrainian settlement in the United States. Shortly after, other mining towns were settled.[2] Later, more immigrants settled in other regions of the state, including Philadelphia and Pittsburgh, and in other states such as New Jersey and New York. Ukrainians also settled in Canada and Latin America. Members of this ethnic group continue to arrive to this day, although not in the numbers of one hundred years ago.

The Ukrainians have a strong, colorful craft tradition which is actively being maintained and transmitted to the younger genration.[3] Well known are Ukrainian *Pysanky*, or decorated Easter Eggs, and Ukrainian embroidery. Less well known are Ukrainian woodwork, including furniture making and carving, leatherwork, beadwork, and food as an art form. Besides the crafts, Ukrainian dance, foodways, literature and language endure in many communities.[4]

After having worked with various Ukrainian craftspeople over the last decade, I decided to visit contemporary Ukrainian cemeteries to see if they carried their culture to the grave. I expected that I would find some use of the Ukrainian language in the epitaphs, some references to Ukraine, and, hopefully, some use of the folk art motifs for decoration.[5] I went to the Fox Chase Ukrainian cemetery in Jenkintown, just north of Philadelphia in Pennsylvania, and to the St. Andrew's Ukrainian cemetery in South Bound Brook, near New Brunswick, New Jersey. What I found not only fulfilled but exceeded my expectations. Rather than isolated examples of ethnicity or remembrances of Ukraine, I found a vibrant constellation of motifs which formed a full picture of Ukrainian culture, history, aspirations and religiosity. The spirit of being Ukrainian shines through these stones, both the longing for their homeland and what is considered to be morally appropriate for life on this earth. Not all Ukrainian cemeteries are filled with such examples of ethnicity, however. Some of the cemeteries, such as the one in McAdoo, Pennsylvania, have stones in the Ukrainian language which date from around 1900. The contemporary stones in McAdoo have epitaphs in the English language and are more representative of mainstream Catholic markers.

This study is based on the Ukrainian cemetery at St. Andrew's Ukrainian Orthodox church.[6] Based on my findings there, I purposely use the term Ukrainian rather than Ukrainian-American for the spirit that shines through these stones. Although Fox Chase is strictly a congregational cemetery, that cared for by St. Andrew's Ukrainian Orthodox Church is a "national" cemetery. The only condition for burial there is Ukrainian origin or descent. In walking through the cemetery, you will see graves for Eastern Rite Catholic and Protestant as well as Orthodox Ukrainians. St. Andrew's calls itself a "Memorial Church." Sitting right out in front is a statue honoring Saint Olha, Grand Princess of Kiev (945-969), who brought Christianity to Ukraine and who, on the monument, is called "Equal to the Apostles" (Fig. 3:1).[7] As this monument was raised in 1987, it was probably part of the celebration of the Millennium of Christianity in Ukraine (988-1988) as well as the millennium of her baptism. The dedications appear in both Ukrainian and in English. The English text reads:

> This monument was blessed on Aug. 16, 1987 A.D. in honor of the baptism of the Holy Princess Olha (957) wise ruler, zealous Christian and Grandmother of the Holy Prince Volodymyr the Great who in 988 A.D. proclaimed Holy Orthodoxy the State Religion of Rus'-Ukraine.
>
> This monument was erected upon the desires of devout Ukrainian women, with the blessings of the Metropolitan of the Ukrainian Orthodox Church of the USA and Diaspora, Mstyslav and by the labors and generous gifts of Ukrainian women dispersed throughout the entire world, especially those incorporated in the United Sisterhoods of the Ukrainian Orthodox Church of the USA.

To the side of the church is a statue of Archbishop Vasyl Lypkivsky, the Metropolitan of Kiev and of all Ukraine of the Ukrainian Orthodox Church from 1921 to 1927, pointing to the church, saying that now you (Ukrainians) have your own church where you can practice your religion in your own language. And tucked up close to the side of the church is a bilingual memorial stone whose English text reads: "In memory of the millions of women and children victims of genocide who died during the famine of 1932-1933 in Ukraine."[8] The present church building, which includes a museum dedicated to Ukrainian history and culture, was built in the 1960s, although the church owned the property and allowed burials there prior to erecting the present structure. The church was designed in the "so-called Kozak-baroque style" by George Kodak (see Fig. 3:1).[9]

Many of the people buried here were born in Ukraine. There are graves of people whose place of death is listed as New Jersey, Pennsylvania, New York, Ohio, Kansas, Canada and Venezuela. Several cenotaphs and memorials for people who died in Ukraine, Germany, Siberia and elsewhere dot the cemetery. Many of the people who are buried here are well-known among Ukrainians and Ukrainian-Americans, making a stroll through this cemetery a lesson in the contemporary cultural and political history of these people.

The Basic Epitaph

The epitaphs found on these Ukrainian stones are highly formulaic and follow conventions typical of Europe and the Americas and which, at least in the United States, were more common before the present century.[10] The language used on over 90 percent of the stones is Ukrainian. Basic biographical information forms the kernel of the epitaph:

Serhij Shchvajkovskyj
* (Born) August 5, 1923
+ (Died) February 25, 1984
Born in Volyn

The name and the birth and death dates are almost mandatory. One

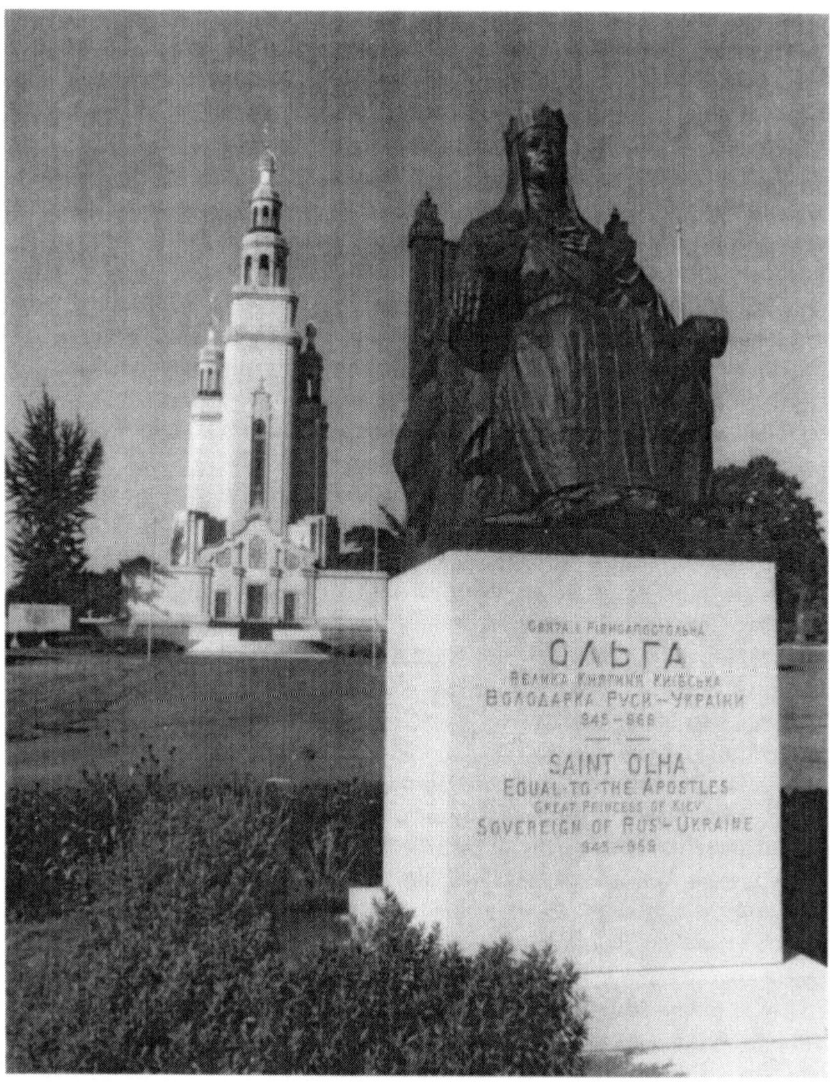

Fig. 3:1. Statue of St. Ohla, with St. Andrew's Ukrainian Orthodox Memorial Church in background.

woman, I was told, wanted her birth date left off her stone and she was told that it was unheard of to leave out the dates. Two other elements found on Serhij Shchvajkovskyj's stone are typical, almost universal. The first is the use of a "sun" or "star" to represent "born in" and the use of a "cross" to represent "died in" (see Figs. 3:2, 3:4, 3:5, 3:10). Secondly, like his, the majority of stones list the place of birth. Parania Woch, for example, was born in Lvivshchyna, or the Lviv region. Her stone also shows that Ukrainians, like most of the European groups, list the wife's maiden name. Ukrainians use the convention "from the family of," usually as an abbreviation. Parania was born in the Datskiv family. Sometimes, the term "Nee" is used.

Mykola and Daria Chymych want it known exactly where they come from, namely the towns of Tatari and Werkuny, which are explicitly pinpointed on their stone with the aid of a map of Ukraine. The stone also mentions that Daria is from the Bardachiwska family. For births in non-Ukrainian lands, the Ukrainian language is sometimes not used, as is the case for Petro Woch, who was born in Jersey City, with "Jersey City" being in English.

In extending the biography, the place of death is often added. Boris Martos was born in the village of Horodishche in Poltavshchyna, the Poltava region, and he died in Irvington, with Irvington spelled phonetically in Ukrainian. This phonetic spelling of non-Ukrainian places is common. Volodymyr Pylypec, for example, was born in Skalat and died in Washington, D.C. (see Fig. 3:2). Maria Palij was born in Lubicha Korolivska and she died in Lawrence, Kansas. These American cities are all spelled phonetically in Ukrainian. Mychajlo Palij, who it is stated was a Doctor of Philosophy, was born in Chrostkiw in Ukraine. Adding the profession is yet another prominent extension to the personal biography Although not as graphic as the map on the Chymych stone, adding "Ukraine" to the place of birth emphasizes the country of origin and this addition is frequently found.

Although Maria Palij has died, her husband Mychajlo, who shares the same stone, is still living. Many people, however, are buying plots and erecting "pre-need" markers before anyone is dead. Both the Krils are still alive, as is Ivan Hrynko, who was born in the village of Selo Luka in the Kiev Region of Ukraine. I noted this trend in the Fox Chase cemetery as well. With these cemeteries filling up, people are buying plots and putting their markers on them in advance of their deaths. The Fox Chase cemetery is so full, as a matter of fact, that families are buying plots in the adjacent public cemetery and they are buying lots which are as close to the church cemetery as are available. This latter practice is reminiscent of the time when people who could not be buried in the church, either because they could not afford it, for example, or because the church was filling up, wanted to be buried as close to the side of the church as possible.[11]

The next common feature on these stones is that on about 60 percent of them the surname is transliterated into English on the reverse of the stone. It is sometimes possible to trace a family's movement in Europe and elsewhere from these transliterations. As one example, Ukrainians who spent time in Austria or Germany will often have a "w" in the transliteration of their name whenever

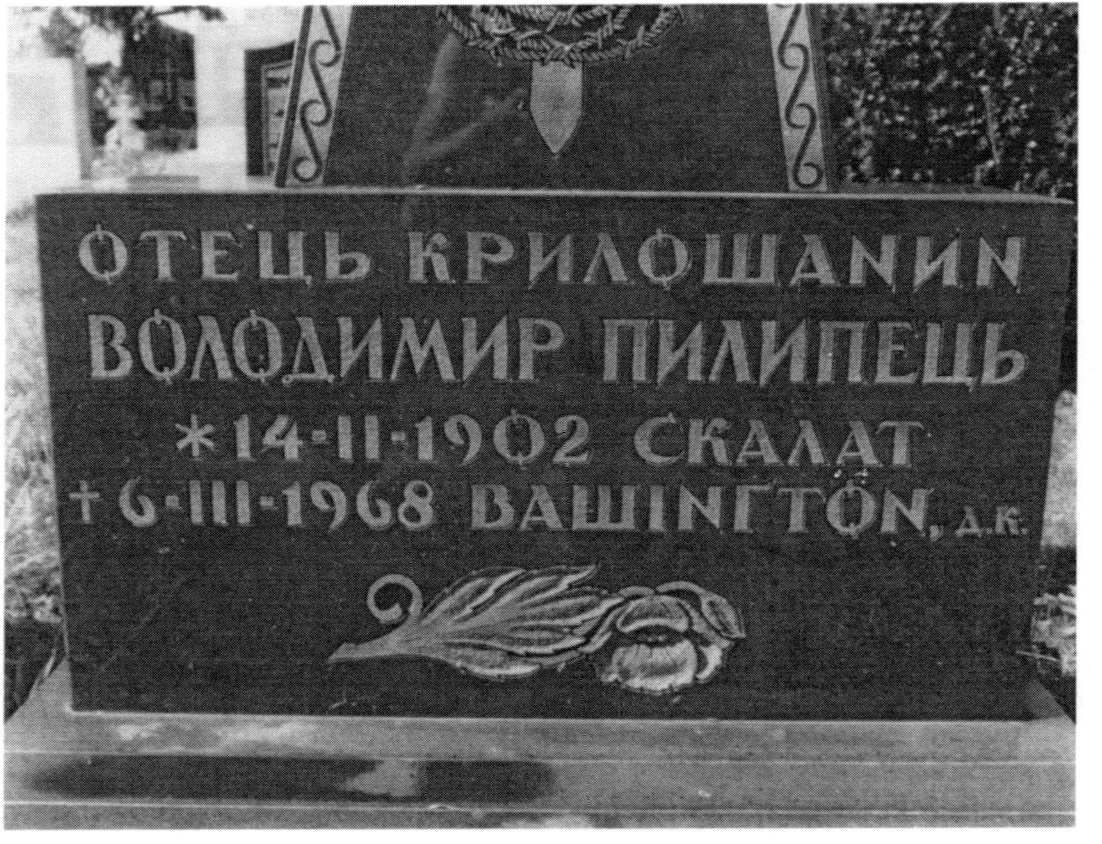

Fig. 3:2. Inscription on marker for Volodymyr Pylypec.

there is a "v" sound in their name. Although the majority of stones have the Ukrainian text on the obverse and the transliteration on the reverse, the opposite is sometimes found, such as on the stone for Nina Haluszczak. Completely bilingual stones on which the text is given in both Ukrainian and English, such as the one for General Petro Grigorenko, are rare, although partially bilingual stones, such as the one for Boris Martos which has his name and profession in English but not the rest of his biography, are more common.[12]

Ethnic Markers

Many artistic motifs with ethnic and nationalistic symbolism are used to highlight the fact that these are Ukrainians buried here. Although several motifs can be found on any one stone, we will examine each in turn.

The *tryzub*, which literally means "trident," is the Ukrainian national symbol and is by far the most common design found on the stones. It may be found alone or in combination with other motifs (see Figs. 3:4, 3:10). There are several variations of the *tryzub*. The *tryzub* on a stone memorializing Simon Petlura, one of the leaders of the Ukrainian National Republic during the late 1910s and early 1920s and who was killed by Soviet Agents in 1926, consists of the Ukrainian letters which form *Volia*, the Ukrainian word for "freedom."[13] Other *tryzubs* have an upward pointed sword for the central part of the trident. The most common form of the *tryzub* is made of intertwined lines forming a never-ending loop. Many *tryzubs* are part of various emblems, such as the emblem for the Ukrainian National Republic of 1918 and emblems for various Ukrainian military divisions.[14]

Several designs from the fund of Ukrainian folk art occur sporadically, such as Ukrainian confrontal birds, or, for those familiar with twentieth century Pennsylvania German art, Ukrainian *distlefinks*. An occasional tree-of-life makes its appearance. Birds and trees-of-life are motifs common among all the Indo-European groups, but they have specific regional flavors, and it is the Ukrainian adaptation of these designs that is present on the gravestones.[15] Traditional candelabras can be found. Some of the candelabras are more than generic Ukrainian designs; they are specifically patterned after those from the Hutzul region of the Carpathian Mountains in southwestern Ukraine.[16]

Ukrainian folk art varies considerably from region to region and many craftspeople strive to continue to keep these differentiations alive in this country to the extent that many of the designs on the stones can be placed in a regional context. Among the most common of the regionally derived forms on the stones are patterns taken from Hutzul wood carving.[17] This style is easily adapted to stone and a very similar effect is achieved.

The next most commonly derived regional form comes from a form of Hutzul embroidery called *nyz* or *nyzynka* (Figs. 3:3, 3:4).[18] The geometry is similar to the carving patterns, but the embroidery patterns are placed as strips embellishing a stone rather than as part of an object such as a cross. The embroidery designs are also less deeply cut into the stone. There does not seem to be a necessary relationship between a person's place of birth and the design on the stone. Ivan Vedmid, for example, has a Hutzul *nyzynka* design on his

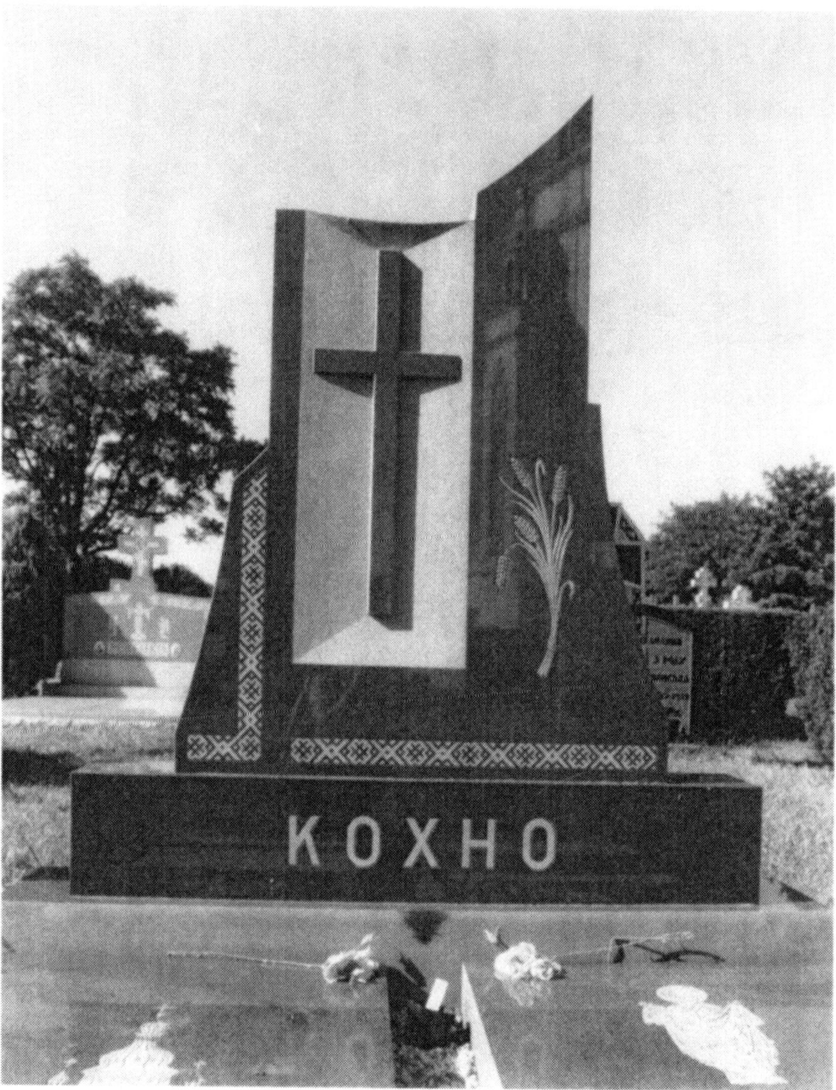

Fig. 3:3. Marker for Archpriest Mykyta and Panimatka Vira Koxno. Note wheat and *Nyz* embroidery design.

Fig. 3:4. Marker for Ivan and Maria Vedmid. Note *Tryzub* (trident) and *Nyz* emroidery design.

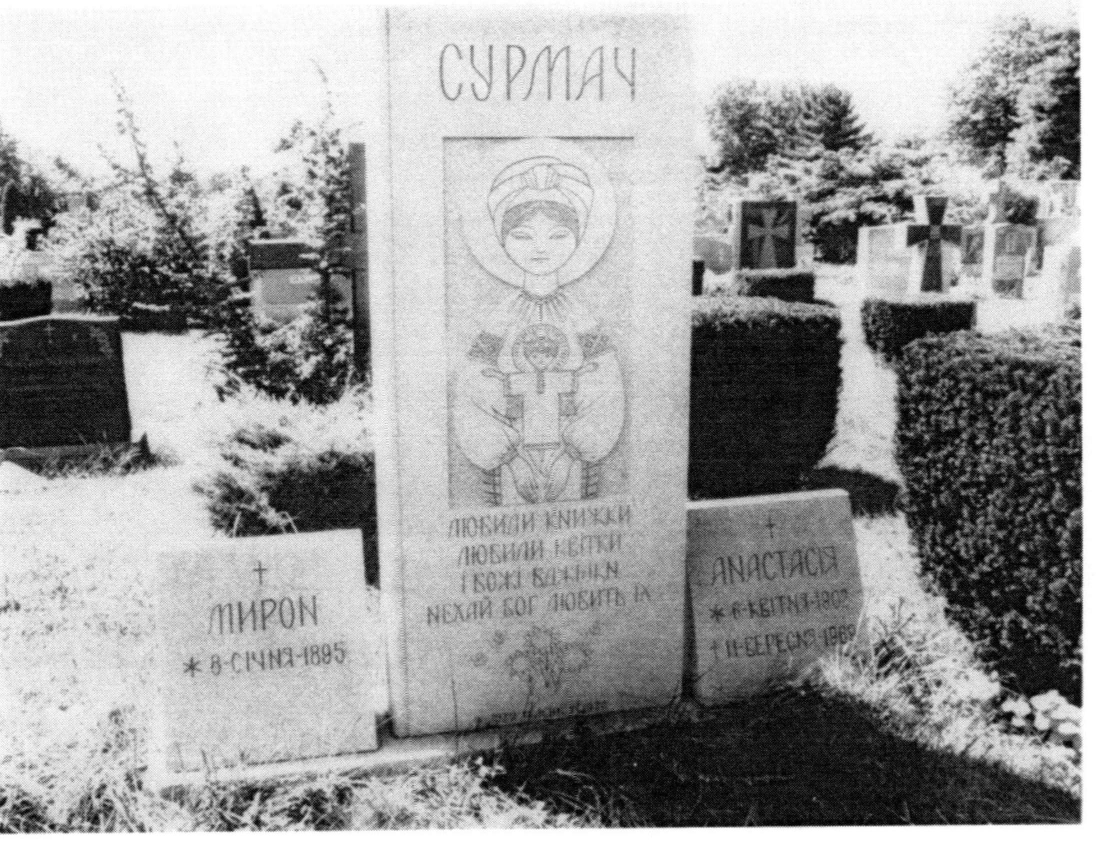

Fig. 3:5. Marker for Miron and Anastasia Surmach, with design of "Ukrainian Madonna" by their daughter, Yaroslava Surmach Mills.

Fig. 3:6. Marker for Basyl Krychevsky, with Potlava oak leaf design.

stone, but he was born in the Poltava region in northeastern Ukraine (Fig. 3:4). Speaking of embroidery, there is a Madonna and Child on one stone that is irresistible with the figures all dressed up in traditional Ukrainian embroidered costume (Fig. 3:5).

The Hutzul designs, with their straight lines, are easily adapted to stonework. The other region to have a degree of visibility is Poltava, with a mixture of curvelinear forms, such as meanders around borders, and straight lines, such as oak leaves and grape vines.[19] The stone for Basyl Krychevsky is interesting for several reasons (Fig. 3:6). It has Poltava oak leaves. It has the transliteration of his name on the same side as the Ukrainian rendering, it states that he was a well known artist and architect, and it mentions that he was born in Ukraine and died in Venezuela. The stone has *Ucrania* for Ukraine. *Ucrania* is one of the forms the word Ukraine took in Latin and it has been adopted by some languages, such as Spanish, Portuguese and Flemish.[20] Like the variant transliterations of last names into English on some of the stones, the term *Ucrania* helps to identify Krychevsky's travels, even if we did not already know where he had lived. Although he died in Venezuela in 1952, the epitaph says that both he and his wife, who died in 1964, were buried here, at St. Andrew's, in 1975. The implication is that he and his wife's bodies were transported from Venezuela to this country and reburied in this cemetery. That this marker is a cenotaph or a memorial is ruled out by the epitaph, which specifically states that the couple are buried at this site.

Other ethnic designs appear as well, often with several on the same stone. Several stones have a carving of a bandura, called by many the national instrument of Ukraine.[21] Roman and Nadia Ishchuk have a stone patterned after a Ukrainian wayside shrine. And there are two or three sculptural representations of Kozaky (Cossacks) (e.g., Fig. 3:7).

Five plants having symbolic meaning appear frequently on Ukrainian stones. The most common is wheat, a nationalistic symbol for "the breadbasket of Europe" (see Figs. 3:3, 3:14). Although wheat is not a political, national symbol, it has taken on nationalistic connotations in Ukraine and has become an ethnic symbol for Ukrainians who have emigrated to other lands. Wheat appears standing tall and proud, waving in the breeze, and bent over, sad, and in mourning. As a nationalistic symbol, it is often found with the *tryzub*. Wheat is often draped over a cross, but it can also become the cross, in either case taking on additional connotations of the Eucharist. A cooked form of wheat, *kolyvo* (wheat, or barley, cooked with honey), was sometimes left on the grave in Ukraine.[22] A wreath of wheat, held fast against the wind by a stone, was placed on one grave at St. Andrew's. Wheat is the only Ukrainian nationalistic symbol worked into the seal of the Ukrainian Soviet Socialist Republic.[23] It is interesting to note that Soviet historian Boris Rybakov refers to Kievan Rus as "the kernel from which a spike of wheat with several new grains-principalities grew."[24] Kievan Rus, also known as Rus'-Ukraine, was the state centered around Kiev from c. 800 to c. 1300 A.D. which grew to include most of eastern Europe and from which sprang modern Ukraine as well as Byelorussia and Russia.[25]

Fig. 3:7. Cossack marker for artist Mykola Muchyn.

Fig. 3:8. Symbolically rich combined marker for Ostap and Volodymyra Sawchinski and memorial for their family members killed during World War II.

The second most common plant to appear is the *kalyna*, also known as the guelder-rose and a relative of the hawthorne (Fig. 3:8). Where wheat stands for Ukraine tall and proud, the *kalyna*, always drooping even in real life, stands for Ukraine sad and mournful. A famous song from the period of Ukraine's wars for liberation at the end of the first world war says that Ukraine can never be happy because the *kalyna* is sad[26] The *kalyna* also stands for the Ukrainian soldier, and, with its red berries, for spilt blood. Known sometimes as the wayfaring tree, it becomes particularly appropriate for people who have wandered from their homeland. Additionally, the *kalyna* has ritualistic significance. In Ukraine, it was one of the plants given by the midwives—not the mother—to guests at baptismal parties and it was one of the plants used in the ritual washing and purification of the new mother and the midwife.[27] Further, on a newlywed's first night was practiced a ritual called "breaking the guelder-rose" (*lamannia kalyny*) in which, among other things, proof of the consummation of the wedding (actual or symbolic) was produced. In this case, instead of *kalyna* actually being present, there is probably a symbolic relationship between the red color of the berries and the blood on the bride's shirt or the red banners hung on the house.[28] One of the most common plantings at grave sites, including those at St. Andrew's, is *kalyna*, which, with its green leaves and red berries, highlight the representation of this plant on the stones themselves. There is a song about the death of a cossack and the planting of *kalyna* on his grave:

"Oi U Vborodi (In the Fields)"

Oh, in the fields a tragedy occurred
Oh, in the fields a cossack was killed
Oh, they buried him
They buried him in a wide valley
And they planted, oh, they planted
A Guelder-rose on his grave.
With mourning voices they sang:
"Oh, young widow, awake and arise
People say my beloved is no longer alive."
When the widow this mourning heard
She cried bitter tears.[29]

This song brings together the cossack, the *kalyna*, the grave, and mourning. The appearance of the *kalyna* on the gravestones can be seen as a symbolic planting as well as an ethnic indicator. Additionally, could the *kalyna* ritualistically help the dead into their new world just as it helps the newborn and newlywed into theirs?

Three other plants occur sporadically. There is the *volosky*, or corn-flower, after which is named one of the finest Ukrainian-American dance ensembles; there is the daisy; and there is the poppy. In the Hutzul region, the coffin, once it was lowered into the grave, was often strewn with poppy seed.[30] The Ukrainian encyclopedia says this practice was done so that the dead would not later "walk" and thereby disturb the living.[31]

The romantic mournfulness graphically rendered by the *kalyna* is echoed on several stones which show a flight of birds (see Fig. 3:8). On the first marker discovered with this motif, the stainless steel monument for John and Nadia Romanczuk, the birds looked like sea gulls and it was thought that maybe one of the two people came from the coast, but that is not the case. Both people were born inland, although Nadia was born in a river town. The immediate reaction from a small audience of Ukrainians viewing slides made on the first field trip to the cemetery was that the birds refer to a funeral song sung at the end of the service at the gravesite which mentions lines of cranes disappearing in the distance:

"Chuyesh, Brate Miy? (Do You Hear, Brother?)"
Hear, my brother, my friend,
The cranes are leaving,
Flying in a grey line,
Calling: croo, croo, croo!
On foreign land I will die
Ere I cross the ocean
My wings will chafe.
In the horizon glimmers
An endless path,
In the blue clouds
The cranes slowly vanish
Calling: croo, croo, croo!
On foreign land I will die
Ere I cross the ocean
My wings will chafe.[32]

Later, two more stones with this motif in which the birds look more like cranes were found. This mournfulness for Ukraine is explicitly verbalized in some of the epitaphs. On one stone, rather than saying that the people come form Bukovina, it says "Zelena Bukovyna," Green Bukovina. Radekhiv Dmytriv, who left Ukraine on June 4, 1945, says:

And so I bid farewell
to my parents, my mother and brothers
but why I did not know at all,
it seems that God guided me.

The stone for Vasyl and Pawlina Lucaky says:

Traveler, someday when you arrive in Kiev
tell that we, faithful to the commandments
of our fatherland, are resting here.

Nationalism

The previous two sentiments express a longing for the homeland and faithfulness to the culture. Other sentiments are more nationalistic, such as the stone which reads: "Pray for Ukraine, pray for your nation, pray for your beloved church." Another nationalistic statement proclaims: "In unity the strength of a nation, God give us unity."

These stones state the importance of remembering Ukraine, of striving to keep Ukraine alive, and of working to make Ukraine whole again. Such sentiments rise above the ethnic statements expressing identification with the culture of the homeland: they express active participation in the continuation of not just their culture, but their nation. Also to be noted is the religiosity of Ukrainians. God guided Radekhiv Dmytriv, we are asked to pray for Ukraine and her church, and we are again asked to pray for the unity of Ukraine. These epitaphs state that although these people are no longer in Ukraine, they are still a part of it.

Until 1991, Ukraine was a nation outlawed at home and in exile abroad. As early as 1863 the Ukrainian language was outlawed and Ukrainian publications and literature were suppressed by the czarist government.[33] Although this suppression was relaxed somewhat during the early part of the twentieth century, the Czarists and then the Soviets returned to active suppression not just of the language, but of the culture as well.[34] Ukrainians were not allowed to practice their culture or religion within Ukraine and there were two governments in exile. Similar troubles existed in those parts of Ukraine once ruled by Poland. Ukraine and Ukrainians wanting their freedom is nothing new, as Dmytro Doroshenko points out: "All readers of Voltaire know his words in his *History of Charles XII of Sweden* about Ukrainians, the allies of the King of Russia: 'Ukraine has always desired to be free.' "[35]

On the surface it may appear that Ukrainians were reaping the gains of the contemporary movements toward democracy and the loosening of the Soviet yoke in Eastern Europe, but such advances were superficial at most. For example, the Soviet press publicized the legalization of the Russian Orthodox Church in Ukraine; however, the Ukrainian Autocephalous (Independent) Orthodox Church, which proclaimed its reestablishment in 1990 and wants its independence from the Russian Church, remained outlawed.[36] Additionally, Ukrainians, especially in the north, are in the middle of the worst medical disaster since the Stalinist pogroms of the 1930s due to the combined effects of the 1986 Chernobyl nuclear power station explosion and the subsequent handling of that explosion by the Soviet authorities.[37] This disaster was so bad that Mikhail Gorbachev used it as an example of why the world should never have a nuclear war.[38] According to *Newsweek*, in the Spring of 1990 Ukrainians were sending mixed signals concerning recent events in Eastern Europe. Ukrainian Prime Minister Vitaly Masol said his country would "stand firm in opposition" to Moscow's economic reforms.[39] As far as any moves toward independence go, people in the west were seen to be strongly separatist while people in the east were seen to be more apatheic.[40] It can be noted that eastern

Ukraine has been under Russian and Soviet rule longer than the west, which was taken into the Soviet Union at the start of the second world war with the 1939 Molotov-Ribbentrop Pact.[41] However, more was happening that was overshadowed by more dramatic events in Lithuania. There were repeated rallies of support for Lithuania, the creation of independent political parties, the election of non-aligned people to office, the resignation of some Soviet officials, including Masol, and the recall of delegates from the 28th CPSU Congress.[42] On August 28, 1990, Ukraine declared itself a sovereign state with its own state power and citizenship and with the intent of creating its own banking, customs and military systems.[43] Ukraine declared itself an independent, neutral, non-nuclear state on August 24, 1991.

Beyond expressing general concern over the fate of Ukraine is the recognition of personal involvement in her struggles. Showing allegiance to Ukraine in St. Andrew's cemetery is most commonly done by depicting one of the crests indicating membership in one of the various Ukrainian army units, or one of the crests indicating participation in particular campaigns or battles. At least one marker has a ceramic photograph of the deceased's medals.

At the crossroads within the cemetery lies a large cross dedicated to those who fought for a free Ukraine. Around the base of the cross are crests from several of the Ukrainian Army units, crests which are also prominently displayed on many of the gravestones. At the base of the cross is the stone for Simon Petlura which was mentioned earlier. This memorial to the freedom fighters reinforces the statues of St. Olha and Archbishop Lypkivsky and the stone dedicating the church to those who died in the Stalinist pogroms. The church and cemetery together become a marker for Ukraine and her people, truly fulfilling the name of a "Memorial Church."

Many of the people who struggled against oppression, whether that of the Nazis or the Soviets, lived, and many of those people emigrated to the United States or elsewhere, but many also died in the struggle for freedom. The sacrifices these people made are not forgotten; the stories are retold in stone:

> Archpriest Mykyta Koxno
>
> The symbolic grave of unforgotten memory of a priest of the Ukrainian Autocephalous Orthodox Church who was tortured and murdered in Siberia; a husband and father whose imperishable remains no one knows where rest.
>
> (Fig. 3.3 shows part of this marker)

The stone for Ostap and Volodymyra Sawchinski brings the ethnic, national and sacrificial elements together into a single statement (Fig. 3:8). The design depicts the flight of cranes, flying off to distant lands. The Carpathian Mountains rise in the back. The Iron Cross, representing the Ukrainian military order of the Iron Cross, stands boldly in the front with four graves standing next to it, each marked with a cross with an initial in it. In the center of the Iron Cross is the symbol for the Ukrainian scouts, a fleur-de-lis intertwined with a *tryzub,* and at its base lies a sprig of *kalyna*. On the base of the monument is a memorial for members of the family, highlighted with oak clusters, which reads:

> Here symbolically we host Lev, the tortured-to-death father; Olga, the suffering mother; and Peter and Yarema, the two brothers, shot-to-death while bound with barbed wire.

That the stone is as much a memorial for those who died in Europe as it is a memorial for Ostap and Volodymyra is shown by the four graves, each with an initial for one of the four dead relatives along with the other symbols denoting Ukraine. Both Ostap and Volodymyra were born in 1908 but both are still alive at the time of this writing.

The poem by V. Simonenko on the stone for Jacob Struk and his wife captures the feeling of many Ukrainians concerning the past, now history, and the future, which exists only as potential:

> O Earth, cruel and dear, You swallowed all their days-
> Everything that they loved give back to me to finish loving.
> Everything that they did not dream, let enter into my thoughts,
> Because I do not live just for myself,
> I must also live for them.

The verse on the stone for Ivan and Maria Hnid explicitly states why sacrifices are necessary:

> Don't cry but win—if only for your sons if not for self—a better fate in battle.

Another area of service to Ukraine is the political and diplomatic. Many people who held political and diplomatic positions in the Ukrainian government are buried in this cemetery. Among these are Andrij Livitzki, President of the Ukrainian Democratic Republic and Professor Boris Martos, Prime Minister of the Ukrainian National Republic. Several people held multiple roles:

John Prince of Tokary
Tokarzewski Karaszewicz
Knight of Malta etc.
Born in Czabaniwka Ukraine
June 24th, 1895
Died in London November 18th, 1954
Minister Plenipotentiary
Foreign Minister of Ukraine
****
Col. Vladimir Kedrowsky
*Kherson, 1890 - + 1970

Colonel Ukrainian National Republic Army
Under-Secretary of War 1917, Chief Inspector
Of Army 1919, U.N.R. Ambassador to Latvia 1920-1921

Chief, Ukrainian Service, Voice of America, 1955-1963

Vladimir Kedrowsky was also a member of the Ukrainian Central Rada, or parliament.[44]

The hoped-for outcome of all the struggles and sacrifices of Ukrainians is present in the vision on the stone for Zakhar Ivasishyn, who was an officer in the army of the Ukrainian National Republic. On his stone is a *tryzub* "sunburst" with the word "*Tryzub*" in bold letters underneath. This sunburst is beside the cross with *tryzub* and sword which is a mixed symbol of religion and freedom-fighters. Down below is a crown with a cross on top and a *tryzub* inside. And there is a necklace of military crests surrounding a cross. The verse says: "This is a renewed crown of a Ukrainian nation in the east of Europe."

Occupations

St. Andrew's cemetery is laid out by occupation, with priests buried in one section, medical doctors in another, artists in yet another. Although there are exceptions, this plan holds true through most of the cemetery. Men are usually buried with their occupational group and their spouses with them rather than separating the couple because of differing occupations. This pattern is in contrast to cemeteries which are laid out by family or even those cemeteries, typical of the Moravians in the 1700s and 1800s for example, which bury people by sex and marital status. What someone was, what someone did in life, is given an important role in memorializing the dead, and occupational identification is often placed on the markers. One example simply has *mystets*, the Ukrainian word for "artist," underneath a bird motif. The bird may well be by that particular person.

The mixing of verbal and visual identifiers occurs frequently. Volodymyr Kiveliok was an artist, as is both stated by the word "artist" and shown by the palette on his marker. Sometimes, the only hint is visual, as with the feather pen on one stone. In some cases, the occupation is worked into the entire stone: such is the case with the one for author Halyna Zhurba, whose stone has been fashioned to represent a closed book, complete with a title, *Daleki Svit*, or "Distant Land" (Fig. 3:9). This title has dual connotations. First, it is the title of Zhurba's book of memoirs published in 1955.[45] I find it interesting to note that this, her most famous book, is her memoirs concerning her life in Ukraine and that, according to the Ukrainian encyclopedia, one of the connotations of the word "Ukraine" in the nation's folklore is "a distant land" or "a foreign land," something Ukraine had become in reality for Zhurba once she had emigrated to the United States.[46] Secondly, as this title appears on her gravestone, it could be interpreted as representing the place in which she now resides, especially by those unfamiliar with her work.

Professor Dr. Volodymyr Sichinsky was an architect who specialized in churches, and his stone is a stylized steeple. Mykola Zaborsky was an Engineer of Bridges. A large suspension bridge dominates his marker. That religion was also important in his life is implied by the fact that the supports for the bridge are not normal bridge piers, but rather Christian crosses.

Music plays a prominent part in Ukrainian life, and musician's markers

Fig. 3:9. Marker for in shape of book for author Halyna Zhurba.

are often overflowing with musical motifs, as with the stone for concert cellist professor Ludmilla Timoshchenko Polewska. Part of her epitaph is a listing of the various schools of music at which she taught: Moscow, Carciew, Vienna, Rome and the Ukrainian Musical Institute in New York. The stone for maestro Juri Holovko and his wife Lydia has a line from a hymn with its tune. The line says: "In your kingdom remember us Lord." Did Maestro Holovko write this hymn, or did someone chose it knowing that he was a musician?

Dr. Ivan Rozhin's marker has the symbols of his veterinary trade, while his wife's vocation, that of a graphic artist, is also listed, but without any visual representation:

Ivan Rozhin, D.V.M., D. Sc., Professor
of Pathology; A Graduate of the
Veterinary College of Kyiv 1929;
Participated in the Ukrainian
Liberation War of 1917-1920. Born
September 18, 1897 in Kumaniv,
Podilla, The Ukraine.

Eugenia Rozhin, Born Turkalo, Artist Graphic,
A Graduate of the Kyiv Art Institute 1929;
Polygraphic Arts Supervisor of the "Knyhospilka"
Publishers in the Ukraine; Born March 26,
1895 in Velyki Nemyrenci, Podilla, the Ukraine.

The graves of clergymen are easily recognizable because of the visual symbolism used. The stone for Archbishop Igor has his photograph and miter. More common are paired symbols representing the Eucharist, either a chalice and wafer, or grapes and wheat. Some stones have both sets of symbols. Wheat, therefore, appears in at least two contexts and it is the appearance of other elements which helps to render meaning to the overall design. Wheat surrounding a *tryzub* makes a strong ethnic statement, but the person could well have had any number of occupations. Wheat alongside of, or intertwined with, a grapevine or a bunch of grapes denotes that the person buried there is a priest, not necessarily Ukrainian, although other elements on the marker may well, indeed, highlight his nationality. The wives of Ukrainian Orthodox priests sometimes have *Panimatka* ("Mrs. Mother"), as on the stone for Panimatka Vira, the wife of Archpriest Mykyta Koxno.

Priests also have had opportunities to serve their country, usually as chaplains in the armed services:

Archbishop Iov
*1.1.1914 -+ 18.11.1974

Chaplain of Ukrainian Resistance
Chaplain of the First Ukrainian Division, Ukrainian National Army
Chief Chaplain of Ukrainian Military Chaplains (Fig. 3:10).

Fig. 3:10. Cross-shaped marker for Archbishop Iov. Note also use of the *Tryzub* (trident).

Occasionally, you will find a complete vita on a stone, as on the one for Dr. Wasyl Pluschtsch and his wife Nadia:

Prof. Wasyl Pluschtsch, M.D.
Docent, Prof., Director of
Kiev T.B. Research Inst., 1931-43
Med. Dir., T.B. Hosp., Silberg, Germany
Author of Scholarly Works and the First History of Ukrainian Medicine.
President-Central Representation
of Ukrainian Emigration, Ger., 1949-52.
Editor-Ukrainian Ency., Med. Sect.
Shevchenko Scientific Society.
Ukr. Acad., of Arts and Sciences.
* 12 . 28 . 1902, Warsaw
+ 11 . 16 1976, Munich

Nadja Pluschtsch, M.D.
Nee Kotlyar
City Hosp. No. 2 Kiev
T.B. Hosp. Silberg, Ger.
* 8 . 14 . 1918, Kiev

On the front of this monument is a caduceus to highlight the Pluschtsches' profession. Dr. Pluschtsch was also a member of *Plast*, as is indicated by the symbol for the Ukrainian Scouts between his bust and biography. Being a scout, the scouting experience, is important enough that many gravestones, such as Dr. Pluschtsch's and the one already mentioned for the Sawczynskys, sport the scouting emblem. Scouting is taken seriously by Ukrainians and the attitudes instilled by the scouting experience often last a lifetime.[47] Dominating the stone for Yaroslav Luchkan, an engineer, is the symbol for the Ukrainian sea scouts, which is the basic scouting symbol with wings and an anchor, but the wings have other connotations as well when combined with the verse on his stone which says: "And with the flight of wings of Scouting under the clouds I will soar." This epitaph opens further possibilities because the Ukrainian word translated as "scouting," *Skob*, is really an anagram for the Ukrainian version of the scout's law, so that the epitaph in fact says that he will fly with the wings of Scouting and of all that Scouting stands for, with the wings of strength, of beauty, of caution, of keenness.

Besides occupational attributes, other personal attributes are sometimes commemorated. Scouting has been mentioned. Interest in sports is sometimes depicted, as in one stone which sports a soccer ball. Several markers have family crests on them.

Contemporary Art

Contemporary Art also plays a large part in the lives of Ukrainians, and this interest is reflected in their gravestone art. Ethnic symbolism is often a springboard for modern adaptations, as may be seen on one stone where a traditional tree-of-life, cross, and border form a design which has reminded some viewers of a *ryshnyk*, the "ritual" towel used to honor marriages, welcome guests, adorn icons, and sometimes, I've been told, to wrap the dead. In the Hutzul region, a *ryshnyk* was sometimes hung in the house or in a window as one of the signs stating that the deceased was lying within, awaiting burial; and a red *ryshnyk* was often tied around the gates of a deceased landowner's stabling area so that the farm animals would not follow the funeral procession.[48] But this marker is not an exact replication of a *ryshnyk*; it is the signed work of art of a particular artist, S. Timoshenko. This stone is also signed by the person who actually made the stone from Timoshenko's design, John Rudnetski. The use of ethnic designs appears throughout the cemetery, as in a Hutzul cross made large and used as a marker for Dr. Voyevidka.

Yaroslava Surmach Mills, a contemporary Ukrainian artist, adapted one of her prints, called "Ukrainian Madonna," for the marker for her parents (Fig. 3:5). This marker, mentioned earlier, depicts Mary holding the Christ child in front of her. Both Mary and Christ are wearing embroidered Ukrainian dress. At the bottom, she has added some bees buzzing around a flower, for her father is a beekeeper. Her parents also ran a book store in New York, and the central section of the marker has also been made to represent a book, complete with a spine on the left. The smaller sections on either side bearing her parent's names could well be interpreted as bookends. All three of these visual elements—the bees, the flowers, and the book—are echoed in the verse, which says:

They Loved books,
They Loved flowers,
And God's Honeybees.
May God love them.

Dmytro Tkachuk designed for himself and his wife a marker showing his homelands in the Hutzul Mountains (Fig. 3:11). Maestro Tytla was the artist who executed Tkachuk's design. Dmytro Tkachuk was born in the village of Sheshory. His first wife, Berta, is buried here. She was born over the political border from Ukraine in the Slovensko region of Czechoslovakia. The scene, with two people praying at a wayside shrine, is captioned "Farewell Hutsulshchyno, Beloved Country of my Ancestors..." On this stone, against the backdrop of the Black Mountains, we have accurately portrayed the regional costume and wayside shrine, the saddle and Hutzul axe, and representations of Ukrainian churches and farms. I suppose it is a compliment, but just a few rows behind this stone, and in sight of it, is another one which has about half of the design, the part with the people and the shrine, reproduced almost exactly. In another instance, an interpretation of the Virgin Mary on a stone is copyrighted by the artist and has a plaque stating: "All copy rights reserved V. Staruch." However, this design, too, has been used on another stone. These are the only two cases I know about in which someone has explicitly copied another's

Fig. 3:11. Symbolically rich marker for Dmytro and Berta Tkachuk.

Fig. 3:12. Richly decorated marker for artist Mykola Butovych.

original design.

Mykola Butovych was an artist, and his stone is decorated with his own designs, including a tree-of-life at the top and various floral designs (Fig. 3:12). I have not been able to determine if he actually designed his own stone or if someone else designed it using his art work.

There is a fair amount of sculpture in the cemetery. One example is a bust of what I thought at first was a Cossack with a streaming headpiece that stuck out three feet behind his head. On closer inspection, a World War I uniform appears, complete with medals on the figure's left breast, epaulets on his shoulders, and a leather belt crossing his chest diagonally. On his collar is the star and *tryzub* of the Ukrainian National Army. It turns out that this is the marker for Brigadier General Petro Diachenko (1895-1965) who led the Chornoslyznyky Division, an elite Ukrainian cavalry unit who were so feared that it was said that if the Russians knew they were in the area they would go the other way. Diachenko, given the rank of General after the war, was a Colonel when he led the Chornoslyznyky Division and was on the General Staff of the Army of the Ukrainian National Republic. *Chornoslyznyky* means "black slick" and stands for the hats they wore, which included the long streamer. These hats appear to be modeled somewhat after a cossack hat. At the bottom of the marker, typical of many of the stones which are signed, is a full list of credits:

Sculptor-V. Simiancew (the creator of the original model)
Architect-A. Timoscenko (the designer of the monument)
Text & Design-P. Mehyk (the author of the epitaph and designer of the lettering)
Executed By-A. Bilokur (the person who actually produced the monument)

Simiancew, the sculptor, was a fellow member of the Chornoslyznyky Division. Professor Petro Mehyk was the founder of the Ukrainian Art Studios in Philadelphia and is currently the editor of *The Ukrainian Art Digest*. I have noticed Bilokur's name on other stones in the cemetery.[49] The list of credits on signed stones is in addition to the label placed on the marker by the monument company.

Another sculpture is of a life-sized cossack standing with arms folded and sword ready, sculpted by the contemporary artist Mykola Muchyn for whose grave it is used (Figure 3:7). Muchyn was famous for his sculptures of cossacks. The particular cossack standing guard over his grave could possibly represent his namesake, a medieval cossack leader.

Not all people visually display their occupations. Petro Kapschutschenko is an artist and sculptor who goes by the professional name of "Enko." He is the creator of the statues of St. Olha and Archbishop Lypkivsky, as well as many other well known pieces of Ukrainian art. His marker, however, is one of the plainest stones in the cemetery. Although his stone does mention that he is an artist and a sculptor, his professional name is not listed and there is no decoration on the stone. Neither he, nor his wife Zoia (a chemist), nor his daughter Ludmilla (a Doctor of Philosophy) have died, but they have their plot all laid out and marked in preparation for the inevitable.

Sculptures of the deceased appear on a few stones, as on the one for scholar and publicist Victor Domanyckyj and the one for Professor Yaroslav Paladij, a sculptor. Paladij's stone is unique in that each of the Ukrainian letters forming his name was designed to include a scene depicting some aspect of Ukrainian culture, history, or literature:

P = Prometheus tied to the Caucasus Mountains and being tortured.[50]
A = An Angel holding a cross and a shield, with a *tryzub* in the shield.[51]
L = A man with a rifle entering the woods in which are some deer (probably *Lovy*, to go on a hunt, or *Lis*, the woods).
A = Another angel, a near duplicate of the first.
D = Oleksa Dovbush, the Ukrainian " Robin Hood."[52]
I = Ihor.[53]
J = A frozen cross representing the feast of Yordan (Epiphany), the end of the Christmas celebrations and the beginning of the Ukrainian New Year.[54]

More common than busts of the deceased are the ceramic oval photographs which may also be found in the cemeteries of a number of other ethnic groups.

Gravesite Coverings

As well as having interesting shapes for the gravemarker, the gravesite itself is most often covered, either with another stone, a border around the edges, with sand or small stones, or some other treatment (see Figs. 3:3, 3:10). Often, for husband and wife plots where only one has died, the deceased person's half will be covered while the still-living spouse's half will remain in grass. This treatment correlates with the entering of birth and death dates for the spouse who has died and only the birth date for the other. When the grave is covered by a solid piece of stone, this piece is often decorated and frequently contains part of the epitaph. The vertical and horizontal surfaces are sometimes treated as a single unit such that the epitaph flows from the vertical to the horizontal and the designs on the two surfaces either complement each other or else relate in two different ways to the deceased in such a manner that the two surfaces do not clash visually. The covering of the surface of the grave may be related to the custom in Ukraine of raising a mound over the grave. These grave mounds were originally meant to keep the dead from rising up and bothering the living.[55] At least one marker at St. Andrew's, the Pyziur monument, was designed by Jakiw Hnizdovskyj with Ukrainian grave mounds consciously in mind.[56]

Religious Symbolism

Religious themes occur regularly within St. Andrew's cemetery. Already mentioned are the symbols of the Eucharist which appear on markers for priests. Other religious themes that appear with some frequency are the cross, the church, Christ, and Mary.

The cross is one form that has many artistic interpretations in the graveyard. Crosses in the cemetery have been made from a large variety of materials. Besides granite crosses (Polished black granite is a favorite material on all types of markers in St. Andrews), there are ones made from metal, concrete, wood, and granite made to look like wood. Two crosses, presumably made by the same person, are fashioned out of railroad spikes. At least one of these crosses is signed by V. Doroshenko. Another cross looks like you are supposed to picture a full rectangular image of the crucifixion, and then remove all but a cross-shaped section. This cross, done for a priest, is rendered in tile. In the other direction is the cross made by creating a void in a granite block. Many crosses include a sunburst image around the cross-pieces. One stone has a Roman Catholic cross standing next to an Orthodox cross. Did someone convert, or does this represent a mixed marriage?

Wooden crosses are scattered throughout the cemetery. Some of these crosses are temporary markers on graves waiting permanent ones made from stone. Other wooden crosses, however, are meant to be permanent and usually have a plaque attached with the deceased's name and dates. Most of the wooden crosses are plain and painted white. One has a sun-burst around the cross-piece and has been stained, rather than painted. Wooden crosses were often used in Ukraine, at least in the Carpathian region.[57]

A few crosses are made from birch logs (see, for example, Fig. 3:13). One stone cross has been made to look like birch. Birch crosses on graves were also used in Ukraine, especially for soldiers who died in battle, and they have been used among other ethnic groups as well.[58] Traditionally, in the Carpathian regions the house in which the deceased was lying was marked with birch branches.[59] The use of the birch to represent death is trans-European. In "Sweet William's Ghost," a Scottish ballad, the listener is implored to:

'But plett a wand o bonnie birk
An lay it on my breast,
An drap a tear upon my grave,
An wiss my saul gude rest.[60]

In "The Wife of Usher's Well," another Scottish ballad, a woman's three drowned sons return to her wearing hats "o the birk."[61] In that ballad, the birch grows at the gates of Paradise. One last Scottish Ballad, "Prince Robert," in which a birch tree grows out of the grave, has a White Russian and a Ruthenian variant.[62] One Ukrainian song, "Ya Bachyv Yak Viter Berekzu Zlomyv" ("I saw the wind break the birch tree"), makes the connection between the birch and death very plain. The emphasis comes in the first and last verses (the middle two verses sing of the death of a deer and a butterfly):

I saw the wind, a birch tree break
Its branches crushed, its roots upturned
But its leaves were fresh, they did not fade
Till behind a mountain the sun did hide.

Fig. 3:13. Pair of wooden crosses on a single grave, one a traditional birch cross and the other made of wooden boards painted white.

In life, all have their own little sun;
As long as there's sunshine, living is fun
But when the sun fades, there's no hope for life
For without sunshine, nothing will thrive[63]

In pre-Christian times among the Slavic tribes who would become Ukrainians, according to Boris Rybakov, young birches were decorated on June 4th in honor of Yarilo, the god of the vital forces of Nature. Rybakov also states that the houses were decorated with branches but does not mention if these were birch.[64] Yarilo, as it turns out, is the god of springtime and the regeneration of spring, of planting and of sexual passion. The main festivals in his honor, held into the eighteenth century in Ukraine, were celebrated in the spring, at the time of planting, and in the summer, to mourn his death.[65] Among the Baltic Slavs, the birch was used to celebrate the death of Kupala, a god of joy as was Yarilo, but also a god of bathing, health and cleanliness, and of healing. Kupala's festival was held on June 24th, the summer solstice, and was celebrated into the nineteenth century.[66] Women, who had sole ritual responsibility in this matter, would select a birch in the forest. The birch was cut down and taken to the place of festivities and stripped of all the top branches, creating a "crown" effect which could easily become a "cross" effect.[67] The birch was then decorated with garlands of flowers. From this description of the Kupala festival, it sounds as if Rybakov is describing the death of Yarilo, as he says that the June 4th festival occurred after the spring festivals celebrating the first sprouts held on May 1st and 2nd. Both Yarilo and Kupala were cyclical gods, being born anew each year only to die once again. The birch in the connection of these gods seems to be somewhat equivalent to the Germanic use of the evergreen and may well be related to the birch growing at Paradise's gate. In the above song, then, the birch represents the vital force of life cut off in the bud, similar to the use of tree trunks and cut roses popular on mainstream American gravestones of the Victorian era. Could the birch branches used to mark houses and the birch crosses used to mark graves represent the life force of the deceased and the promise of renewed life?

The Birch has additional functions as well. A symbol of death on the one hand, it also affords an effective means of protecting against evil on the other. In several regions of Europe, Birch rods are used to rid a place of evil and the Devil.[68] Without stating what country or region they are discussing, Sophie Lasne and Andre Pascal Gaultier state that, besides the protective properties of carrying birch bark, a cross of birch placed on the front door will protect the house from the Devil.[69] Thus, a birchen cross on a grave might not only symbolize the dead, but also serve to protect the dead from being misused by evil spirits.

In addition to these varying depictions of crosses, churches appear fairly often on gravemarkers (see, for example, Fig. 3:14). Some churches are on markers for priests, but this does not account for all instances. At least one church appears to be a direct representation of St. Sophia in Kiev. All of the

Fig. 3:14. Church and wheat on marker for Mr. and Mrs. Satsevych.

churches have three domes, some of them "onion" domes, and represent the Orthodox Church and, through that representation, the homeland.

Depictions of Christ are common, but most are samples of everyday twentieth-century western Christian art and have nothing special about them. A few, however, are unique. Already mentioned is the Christ child of the "Ukrainian Madonna" and the tile crucifixion. Another marker that stands out is a tile mosaic of Christ that seems to glow, even when backlit and in the shade.

Like Christ, Mary appears in several non-distinct generic scenes. A few, like the Virgin Mary by Staruch and the Madonna by Mills, are excellent examples of contemporary Ukrainian art.

Proper Way of life

When the epitaph on a marker at St. Andrew's includes a sentiment about the person, it is rarely of the impersonal frozen kind found on many contemporary non-Ukrainian stones ("Asleep in Jesus," "At Rest," etc.); rather, the sentiment describes how the person lived. After viewing several of these sentiments, it becomes apparent that the same kinds of behavior are praised over and over, reflecting how the community believes people should act while they are alive. We have already seen several examples of these sentiments, namely the couple who wanted people to know they remained true to their homeland and the engineer who would soar on the wings of "scouting." The epitaph for Olana Movchan Skybicka says that "To help the other was her will. To help the needy was her greatest avocation." One stone states that "Life is short, good deeds are without death, may his memory be eternal." Daria Jaroslavska, a writer, has on her stone "My steadfastness and my song is with God and words my strength." Being helpful and compassionate, having courage and strength, putting your trust in God—this is the way someone should go through this life. But quality of life is also important, and this is reflected in the occupations which are continually featured on the stones. Priests, doctors, veterinarians—people who try and make the world a better place to live—are frequently marked, but so are the creative people, those who are authors, actors, musicians, artists, even engineers, people who, in their way, also make the world a better place. And then there are all the people who fought for freedom from oppression and foreign rule, people who fought to make their world a safer place to live. There is a definite selection in marked occupations: the entire realm of possible job descriptions does not make an appearance. Between what is said about how people lived and what people did while alive, the aspirations of this Ukrainian community can be felt.

The Non-Ukrainian Section

Off to the side of the cemetery is the original family cemetery dating from the American Revolution when this property belonged to the Fisher family. About a dozen stones remain standing. Starting as an American bicentennial project, the congregation has fenced in and is continuing to maintain this plot. A sign has been erected listing those known to be buried here. The sign makes it clear that, besides honoring the dead, a freedom fighter from another time and place, namely of the congregation's adopted home, is here being honored:

In Memory
Of
Hendrick Fisher
Born: 1697 Died: 1779
Patriot of the American Revolution
Herald of the Declaration of Independence

And his family (the individual people are then listed)

Conclusions

As with a few other realms of contemporary gravemarker design, the cemetery at St. Andrew's Orthodox Church demonstrates that the decoration of, and the use of extended epitaphs on, markers is still being practiced in the twentieth century. Many people, used to seeing nondescript granite blocks or surface-mounted plaques, are not aware that pockets of ornate gravemarkers still exist, that the fashion did not completely go out of style at the turn of the century. This cemetery, this community, goes in the other direction. Going beyond the simple decoration of the markers, they are erecting statuary and works of art, a practice not generally done in most places in this country since the Victorian era of the mid to late 1800s.

Beyond what this cemetery says about contemporary monuments is what it says about the community who erected the markers. The Ukrainian cemetery at St. Andrew's Ukrainian Orthodox Church is an entryway into contemporary Ukrainian culture. More than simply the markers of ethnicity and use of language which I expected to find here, there are glimpses of the struggles of Ukraine, stories from her past—as well as the actual people from her history books—and hopes for her future. Many of the themes which arise on the stones echo the thoughts of Taras Shevchenko in his poem "The Testament," quoted at the beginning of this essay. A living continuity from Shevchenko to the present exists, a continuity which could be traced back even further, back to the earliest Ukrainian literature, including "A tale of Ihor's armament." These themes continue to be important in contemporary Ukrainian writings, including, for example, the articles in the *Svoboda* daily newspaper and the work of Clarence A. Manning.[70] This cultural continuity is also seen in the use of specific regional designs and motifs and in the dominant use of the Ukrainian language. A continuity of place also exists in that the majority of stones list the person's place of birth, thereby connecting that place with this spot in New Jersey which is their final resting place.

Beyond the continuities of time, culture and place, these markers highlight those ideals which should be held by the living, the attitudes that should guide one through life. And, with the magnificent art work in the cemeteries and with those occupations which are continually emphasized, the quality of life becomes equal in importance to the continuity of the culture and the manner in which life is lived.

If definitions of ethnicity did not already exist, one could easily be derived from the material in this cemetery, for most of the points commonly accepted in such definitions are readily apparent here.[71] In fact, most of the eleven attributes of ethnicity generally agreed upon by theorists can be deduced directly from the material in St. Andrew's cemetery.[72] The people buried here all have a common national and geographical origin, as is evidenced by so many of the places of birth being listed as Ukraine and surrounding geographic environs. Some, born elsewhere, are buried in family plots where others in the family were born in Ukraine. The people share a similar culture and customs, as is evidenced by the repetition of the folk art motifs, the designs of the markers, the layout of the gravesite, and the decoration of the graves. They share a common religion in that the beliefs and rituals are similar even though there are two main institutions, namely Ukrainian Orthodox or Eastern Rite Catholicism. Ukrainian is the dominant language. Being buried in St. Andrew's underscores the fact that they have a "we feeling," a sense of loyalty to their "peoplehood." Many Ukrainians want to be buried in this cemetery and one has to belong to the group in order to be buried here. The epitaphs make it clear that the community has a common *gemeinschaft*, a common worldview, as well as a common set of values. The markers highlight several of the shared institutions, such as the military, Ukrainian literary and scientific societies, and Ukrainian scouts. The markers also make it clear that Ukrainians see themselves as subordinate and oppressed in relation to their homeland. And the epitaphs, in referring to their homeland and the deaths in a foreign land, make it abundantly clear that this is an immigrant group. Only two of these attributes of ethnicity—one and a half, really—are not readily apparent at St. Andrew's. First is that the markers do not make it clear that the people share a similar race or that they have a common set of physical characteristics. The other—the half attribute—is that, while it is clear that Ukrainians see themselves as having a subordinate status in their homeland, nothing in the cemetery would make one think that they have such a feeling in regards to their adopted home. In fact, if St. Andrew's were the only cemetery you visited, you might very well think the Ukrainians were the dominant group. Outside of listing the places of death, there are few references to the United States or to the rest of the Americas. I do not mean to define ethnicity all over again with this discussion or to prove that the Ukrainians are an ethnic group. What is important here is that based solely on the material found at St. Andrew's, it is possible to gain significant insights into the cohesiveness of the Ukrainian community, the importance they place on their ethnicity, and how Ukrainians view themselves as a people. Knowing that this information is available here, the reasonable expectation exists that it can be found elsewhere. Researchers looking at other graveyards and cemeteries should be on the lookout for similar clues to the ethnic or cultural makeup of the community using that site and to the importance, or lack thereof, of ethnic or nationalistic feelings to that group.

St. Andrew's cemetery is more than a memorial to Ukraine—it is a living part of Ukrainian culture.

Notes

Portions of this essay were given in presentations at the American Culture Association annual meetings for 1989 and 1990, the Association for Gravestone Studies annual meeting for 1990, and the American Folklore Society annual meeting for 1990. All photographs are by Thomas E. Graves and depict monuments at St. Andrew's Ukrainian Cemetery, South Bound Brook, New Jersey.

[1]Translated by C.H. Andrusyshen and Walter Kirconnel. From C.H. Andrusyshen and Walter Kirconnel, *The Ukrainian Poets 1189-1962* (Toronto: U of Toronto P, 1963); reprinted in *Taras Shevchenko Memorial Book* (Washington, D.C.: The Shevchenko Memorial Committee of America, Inc., 1964), p. 25. This poem is better known as "The Testament." However, the title is translated as "My Legacy" in the above work. See also Alexander Jardine Hunter, *The Kobzar of the Ukraine, Being Select Poems of Taras Shevchenko* (Teulon, Manitoba: by the author, 1922).

[2]Alexander Lushnycky, editor-in-chief, *Ukrainians in Pennsylvania: A Contribution to the Growth of the Commonwealth* (Philadelphia, Ukrainian Bicentennial Committee: Philadelphia, 1976), pp.17-28.

[3]See, for example, Thomas E. Graves, "Ethnic Artists, Artifacts, and Authenticity: Pennsylvania German and Ukrainian Folk Craft Today," *Pioneer America* 15:1 (1983), pp. 21-34; and *Ukrainian Canadiana* (Edmonton: Ukrainian Women's Association of Canada, 1976). Several annual Ukrainian festivals help to foster continuity and to pass on the traditions. In the study area, the annual Ukrainian festival held the first weekend of each October by the Ukrainian Heritage Studies Center of Manor Junior College in Jenkintown is a major event.

[4]See, for example, *Ukrainian Canadiana*; Lesia Danchenko, *Folk Art from the Ukraine* (Leningrad: Aurora Art Publishers, 1982); *Continuity and Change: The Ukrainian Folk Heritage in Canada* (Ottawa: National Museum of Man, 1972); Anne Kmit, Loretta L. Luciow, Johanna Luciow, and Luba Perchyshyn, *Ukrainian Easter Eggs and How We Make Them*, (Minneapolis: Ukrainian Gift Shop, 1979); Tania Diakiw O'Neill, *Ukrainian Embroidery Techniques* (Mountaintop, PA: STO Publications, 1984).

[5]The correct reference for the country is "Ukraine" and not "the Ukraine." Many Ukrainians see the reference to "the Ukraine" as pejorative and belittling, making a region out of their homeland rather than a nation (something Russians—both Czarist and Soviet— have been trying to do for centuries), as well as being incorrect.

[6]I would like to thank Christine Izak, curator of the Ukrainian Heritage Studies Center, Manor Junior College, Jenkintown, Pennsylvania, her husband Zenon Izak, and Dmytro Tkachuk for accompanying me on field trips to St. Andrew's Church, in helping with translating the epitaphs into English, and for their comments. I would also like to thank Professor Petro Mehyk and the staff of Manor Junior Collage for their comments on some of the stones and their backgrounds. Finally, I would like to offer special thanks to Christine Izak for opening up the museum of the Ukrainian Heritage Studies Center so I could use their collections to help compare and identify motifs.

[7]"Olha" and "Ihor" are the Ukrainian forms of these two names. "Olga" and "Igor," the forms more commonly recognized in the United States, are the Russian forms. Ukrainian and Russian are both Slavonic languages, but they are not the same and are considered to be separate rather than dialects of a common language. You will find

reference to both St. Olha and St. Olga (and Prince Ihor and Prince Igor) in the literature in reference to the same person. This difference is apparent in other common terms, including Halych/Galich and Novhorod/Novgorod. Other differences are seen in the variations in the name of the city of L'viv (Lvov in Russian) and in the name Volodymyr (Vladimir in Russian). The Ukrainian forms will be used throughout this essay unless another form is explicitly used on a marker or in a quote.

[8]For a description of this artificially induced famine, which followed not far on the heels of a naturally induced famine, see Rev. Isidore Nahayewsky, *History of Ukraine*, 2nd ed. (Philadelphia: "America" Publishing House of "Providence" Association of Ukrainian Catholics in America, 1975), pp. 291-295.

[9]*Ukraine: A Concise Encyclopedia*, vol. 1 (Toronto: U of Toronto P, 1963), pp. 1116,1144. An article in Ukrainian on St. Andrew's church and cemetery was called to my attention at the very end of this study. See E. Andrievych, "Monumenty," *Terem 5* (1975), pp. 55-8. This latter article was graciously translated for me by Bodhan Pastuszak.

[10]For examples of epitaphs of the English settlers of the United States see, for example, Dickran and Ann Tashjian, *Memorials for Children of Change: The Art of Early New England Stonecarving* (Middletown, CT: Wesleyan UP, 1974), pp. 235-285; and Patricia A. Miller, *CT 18th Century Epitaphs: Language-Love-History* (New Milford, CT: Connecticut Gravestones, 1988). For examples of the early German settlers of Pennsylvania, see Thomas E. Graves, "Pennsylvania German Gravestones: An Introduction," *Markers* 5 (1988), pp. 60-95.

[11]See, for example, Philippe Aries, *The Hour of Our Death* (New York: Borzoi, 1981), pp. 29-92.

[12]For a brief biography of Grigorenko and a photograph of his gravemarker, see Jan Leibovitz Alloy, "The Monument and the Story," *Stone in America* 104:8 (1991), p. 43.

[13]Petlura's name is also transliterated as Petlyura by some authors. See Charles A. Manning, *Twentieth Century Ukraine* (New York: Bookman Associates, 1951), pp. 54-70; 107; 125; 177.

[14]*Ukraine:: A Concise Encyclopedia*, plate 1, op. p. 32.

[15]Uses of these motifs in Ukrainian art can be found throughout the illustrations found in Danchenko, *Folk Art from the Ukraine.*

[16]For traditional Hutzul candelabras, see, for example, Danchenko, *Folk Art from the Ukraine*, plates 106-108; and *Ukraine: A Concise Encyclopedia*, pp. 388; 408-9.

[17]Danchenko, *Folk Art from the Ukraine*, plates 90-120; *Ukraine: A Concise Encyclopedia*, pp. 385-89.

[18]See O'Neill, *Ukrainian Embroidery Techniques*, pp. 25-31, 70-71; and *Ukrainian Canadiana*, p. 5

[19]Danchenko, *Folk Art from the Ukraine*, plates 137, 141, 193, 195, 198.

[20]*Ukraine: A Concise Encyclopedia*, p.11.

[21]See *Ukraine: A Concise Encyclopedia,*, p. 379; and *Ukrainian Canadiana*, pp. 41-43.

[22]*Ukraine: A Concise Encyclopedia*, p. 340.

[23]*Ibid.*; plate 1, fig. 7 (opposite p. 32).

[24]Boris Rybakov, *Kievan Rus* (Moscow: Progress Publishers, 1989), p. 246.

[25]*Ibid..;* Paul Robert Magocsi, *Ukraine: A Historical Atlas* (Toronto: U of Toronto P, 1985), maps 7-8.

[26]Zenon Izak, personal communication.

[27]*Ukraine:: A Concise Encyclopedia*, pp. 334-335.

[28]*Ibid.*, pp. 337-8.

[29]Translation by Magda Surmach. "Monitor Presents YKPAIHA." Monitor Records, MF 315.

[30]*Ukraine: A Concise Encyclopedia* , op. cit., p. 339.

[31]*Ibid.*

[32]*Ibid.*

[33]Manning, *Twentieth Century Ukraine*, p.169.

[34]See Nahayewsky, *History of Ukraine*; Manning, *Twentieth Century Ukraine*; and *Ukraine: A Concise Encyclopedia*, pp. 667-917

[35]"Taras Shevchenko, Bard of Ukraine," *Svoboda* (27 June 1964), p.9.

[36]Christine Izak, personal communication; see also "Organizational Council of the Ukrainian Autocephalous Church," *The Current Digest of the Soviet Press*, 42:23 (11 July 1990); John Kohan, "Breakaway Breadbasket. A Kremlin Nightmare: the Ukraine Seeks Sovereignty," *Time* (30 July 1990), pp. 44-5.

[37]See Steven Goldstein, "The Second Chernobyl Disaster," *The Philadelphia Inquirer Magazine* (14 Jan. 1990), pp. 18-27. See also Carroll Bogert, "Chernobyl's Deadly Legacy," *Newsweek* (7 May 1990), pp. 30-1; and R. Monastersky, "South Pole's 'Hot' Snow': Chernobyl source?," *Science News*, 137: 19 (12 May 1990), p. 295.

[38]"Speech by M. S. Gorbachev on the Results of the Discussion of the CPSU Central Committee's Political Report to the 28th Party Congress," *The Current Digest of the Soviet Press* 42: 34 (26 Sept. 1990).

[39]Harry Anderson and Carroll Bogert, "Too Little and Too Late?" *Newsweek* (4 June 1990), p. 22.

[40]"The Soviet Empire: The Center Cannot Hold," *Newsweek* (4 June 1990), p. 20.

[41]"Breakaway Breadbasket," *Ukraine: A Historical Atlas*, maps 22 and 23.

[42]See relevant articles in the following issues of *The Current Digest of the Soviet Press*: 41:51 (17 Jan. 1990); 42:13 (2 May 1990); 42:14 (9 May 1990); 42:20 (20 June 1990); 42:27 (8 Aug. 1990); 42:28 (15 Aug. 1990). See also *Newsweek* (29 Oct. 1990), pp. 51-52.

[43]See relevant articles in *The Current Digest of the Soviet Press*: 42:30 (29 Aug. 1990); and 42:31 (5 Sept. 1990). See also "Breakaway Breadbasket," pp. 44-45.

[44]*Taras Shevchenko Memorial Book*, p. 13.

[45]*Ukraine: A Concise Encyclopedia*, p. 1082a.

[46]*Ibid.* , p. 6.

[47]Christine Izak, personal communication.

[48]*Ukraine: A Concise Encyclopedia*, pp. 338-39.

[49]The information on General Diachenko and his Division was supplied to Christine Izak by Professor Mehyk in Ukrainian. She then supplied me with a translation of Professor Mehyk's comments.

[50]The theme of Prometheus was brought to the region by the Greeks who settled on the gulf of the Black Sea. The Ukrainian poet Taras Shevchenko used Prometheus in "The Caucausus" as "the symbol of the sufferings of mankind and its aspirations of the

divine fire of human liberty—for which so many unsung heroes have given their lives." Quoted in *Taras Shevchenko Memorial Book*, p. 23 (the beginning of the poem is quoted on p. 25).

[51]This angel is probably the Archangel Michael, who appeared in early heraldic devices representing Ukraine, but it could be Gabriel, who is also important in Ukrainian thought. See *Ukraine: A Concise Encyclopedia*, vol. 1, p. 32. The information on St. Gabriel is from Zenon Izak, personal communication.

[52]*Ibid.*, p. 364.

[53]There are two possibilities here. The first is Ihor, Grand Prince of Kiev from 914-946, husband to St. Olha, and grandfather to St. Volodymr the Great (see *Ukraine: A Concise Encyclopedia*, vol. 1, pp. 585-587). The second is Ihor Svyatoslavich, Grand Prince of Novhorod-Siversky and of Chernihiv (1151-1202), whose campaigns against the Polovtsi (Cumans) in 1185 were immortalized in the epic "Slovo o polku Ihorevi" ("The Tale of Ihor's Armament"). The title of this epic has also been translated as "The Tale of Ihor's Campaign" and "The Tale of Ihor's Host." See *Ukraine: A Concise Encyclopedia*, vol. 1, pp. 985-986. See also Rybakov, *Kievan Rus*, in which this epic is woven through the author's discussion of the history of this region (Ihor's biography is found on pp. 265-280). This epic was also an appeal for Ukrainian unity. Because the figure is shown on horseback, in armor, and raising a drawn bow rather than as a figure sitting on a throne, this representation is probably that of Ihor of Novhorod-Siversky.

[54]On this day the old rites of holy water blessing are performed. The solemn blessing of the waters takes place on the river: in preparation, the community's young men erect a cross of ice blocks cut from the river and dyed with beet 'kvas.' " See *Ukraine: A Concise Encyclopedia*, pp. 321-324.

[55]*Ibid.*, pp. 340, 345.

[56]Andrievych, pp. 55-58 .

[57]*Ukraine: A Concise Encyclopedia*, p. 340.

[58]Zenon Izak, personal communication, for the Ukrainian usage. It is interesting to note that a birch cross was used recently to mark the grave of one of the defenders against the August, 1991 anti-Gorbachev coup in the Soviet Union. For an illustration of this grave see *Newsweek* (2 Sept. 1991), p. 32. An example from the American Southwest may be found in Anthony S. Cannon, *Popular Beliefs and Superstitions from Utah* (Salt Lake City: U of Utah P, 1984), p. 307 (item #9819) .

[59]*Ukraine: A Concise Encyclopedia*, p. 338.

[60]Child Ballad #77g; Frances James Child, *English and Scottish Popular Ballads*, ed. Helen Child Sargent and George Lyman Kitteredge (Boston: Houghton Mifflin, 1932), p. 167.

[61]Child Ballad #79a: *Ibid.*, p. 168.

[62]Child Ballad #87: *Ibid.*, pp. 183-185. Only a synopsis of the White Russian/Ruthenian version is given in this edition, not the whole text.

[63]"Monitor Presents YKPAIHA."

[64]*Kievan Rus*, p. 161.

[65]*Larouse Encyclopedia of Mythology* (New York: Prometheus Press, 1959), pp. 305-306.

[66]Rybakov, *Kievan Rus*, pp. 161-162.

[67]*Ibid.*, pp. 306-307. Although mentioning that the death of Kupala was celebrated

in several different ways, it is not specifically explained how the Slavic tribes in the Ukrainian region practiced this ritual. This brief description of the relation of the birch to death and the otherworld only scratches the surface. The birch, for example, played an important role in shamanism.

[68]Maria Leach, ed., *Funk & Wagnalls Standard Dictionary of Folklore and Mythology* (New York: Funk & Wagnalls, 1972), p. 141.

[69]*A Dictionary of Superstitions* (Englewood Cliffs, NJ: Prentice-Hall, 1984), p. 78.

[70]*Svoboda* is a bilingual daily newspaper for Ukrainians published in New Jersey. For Manning, see the previously cited *Twentieth Century Ukraine*, and his Foreward to Volodymyr Sichynsky, *Ukraine in Foreign Comments and Descriptions From the VIth to XX Century* (New York: Ukrainian Congress Committee of America, Inc., 1953), pp. 9-15.

[71]For an overview on the theories of ethnicity, see Ronald A. Reminick, *Theory of Ethnicity: An Anthropologist's Perspective* (Lanham, MD: UP of America, 1983).

[72]*Ibid.*, pp. 11-12.

Czech Cemeteries in Nebraska from 1868: Cultural Imprints on the Prairie

Karen S. Kiest

While the settlement of the Great Plains by the sodbusters arriving in their "prairie schooners" has become a part of American lore, a majority of the sodbusters themselves were not American, but European immigrants, traveling instead on the new rail lines that traced paths of settlement across the region in the late 1800s. Arriving in great numbers, they quickly translated their cultural goals and forms to an empty landscape and a modern American system of land development. One of the first institutions established that reflected these goals was the cemetery.

Willa Cather, growing up in Red Cloud, Nebraska, chronicled this immigrant settlement of the Great Plains in several of her writings. In *My Antonia*, her best-known work, Cather demonstrates the poignancy of the Czech immigrants' difficult transition from Europe to the United States in the suicide of Antonia's father. The pathos of the situation is heightened by the family's attempts to provide for him a traditional burial, with the chosen location mocked by the placelessness of the prairie, his open grave only a "very little spot in that snow-covered waste."[1] Yet the irony of the situation, Cather writes, is ultimately reversed by the endurance of the graveplot on the changing landscape:

> Years afterward, when the open-grazing days were over, and the red grass had been ploughed under and under until it had almost disappeared from the prairie; when all the fields were under fence, and the roads no longer ran about like wild things, but followed the surveyed section-lines, Mr. Shimerda's grave was still there, with a sagging wire fence around it, and an unpainted wooden cross.[2]

The Czech cemeteries that Willa Cather described remain as significant features on the Nebraska landscape.[3] Today, the cemeteries appear as frail against the scale of surrounding agricultural development as they once did against the infinite prairie, but they have outlasted almost all other remnants of the pioneer landscape—the sod houses, the wagons, the windmills, the prairie itself. Within, they continue to conserve the evolving cultural heritage of the community. In an area where practicality determines preservation, the endurance of the cemetery indicates its necessary though quiescent role within the community.

This essay examines the development of a significant Czech immigrant community in eastern Nebraska after 1865 and the resultant creation of a distinctive cemetery type with associated traits as represented by 55 Czech cemeteries established throughout the state. Three phases of evolution can be seen in these Czech cemeteries in Nebraska, roughly corresponding to the historical periods through which this cultural group passed.[4] The first period, the "pioneer phase," which coincided with the first waves of immigration of the 1870s and immediately following, saw the establishment of the majority of Czech cemeteries without the surrounding context of other Czech cultural forms. As soon as the initial period of hardships had passed, the Czechs, with a community fervor, set out to improve those hastily developed cemeteries. This second period, the "improvement" phase, paralleled the flowering of Czech culture in Nebraska, and lasted until World War I. The third and final period, the "modern" phase, describes the time from World War I to the present, during which many Czechs examined and changed their cultural goals.

A study of the Great Plains presents a clear picture of patterns of cultural settlement. Settlement of the area was rapid, and the product of a few evident factors. While the cultural study of cemeteries in most areas of the country is complicated by the overlay of histories, in the rural plains states the original settlement patterns have not been disrupted. The population number has remained essentially the same since 1890, and although there has been a shift of population from rural to urban areas, the original pattern of development is still easy to discern.

The rapid settlement of the Great Plains, including Nebraska, was made possible by the coincident occurrence of streamlined land development practices and transportation improvements. The establishment of a national survey grid of ranges, townships, and sections for lands acquired in the Louisiana Purchase permitted the quick survey of vast areas. By 1857, the survey of eastern Nebraska was completed—a necessary step before land there could be offered for settlement by the government. The Homestead Act, passed in 1862, gave further impetus to settlement by offering up to 160 acres of free land to those willing to live and make improvements on the property for a period of five years. Parcelling of land along section lines made homestead claims and other land transactions fast and simple.

These developments in land subdivision and distribution coincided with the western extension of the railroads. The first transcontinental line, the Union Pacific, had been laid by 1869; Omaha, Nebraska, was its eastern terminus. Railroads like the Union Pacific were major agents of immigration, advertising widely and offering low fares to encourage settlement. The railroads had been given alternate sections for ten miles on either side of their tracks which they promptly offered for sale to the settlers they delivered.[5]

In Nebraska, as elsewhere, these developments coincided with a large influx of European immigrants from Germany, from the Scandinavian countries and from central European provinces like Bohemia and Moravia—the lands that are now part of the country of Czechoslovakia.[6] Nebraska received more of these Czech immigrants than any other state in the Union; by 1910 they constituted 13 percent of the state's immigrant population.[7] Most of the Czechs were concentrated in a band of five counties—Douglas, Saunders, Butler, Colfax and Saline—in the eastern third of the state where some towns, like Wilber, Prague, Bruno, Dwight and Abie were and remain almost entirely Czech (see Fig. 4:1).

Czechs came to the United States to escape political, religious and economic repression. Nationalist sentiments, particularly in Bohemia, arose in the mid-1800s in reaction to three centuries of authoritarian Hapsburg rule. Resentment of the Catholic Church for having supported the Hapsburgs and earlier helping to crush religious reform efforts, beginning in 1415 with the burning of John Hus, leader of the first reformed church in all of Europe, encouraged a nationalism that saw cultural heritage as paramount over religion and so was labeled "Freethought." Freethinkers espoused a progressive view of humanity and expected that reason and scientific inquiry would overcome belief in a supreme being. Their political objectives dated from the Revolution of 1848 and included the growth of civil liberties, complete separation of church and state, universal suffrage and the emancipation of women.[8]

Bohemians were most closely associated with the Freethinker movement, while immigrants from Moravia remained more firmly tied to the Catholic church. With more Bohemians immigrating to the United States than Moravians, over 55 percent of the Czech immigrants called themselves Freethinkers.[9] In Nebraska, in the early 1890s, 95 percent of the Czechs in Saline County were from Bohemia, while to the north, the majority of the Czechs were from Moravia: Moravian immigrants accounted for 54 percent of the Czech immigrants in Butler County, 47 percent in Saunders County and 31 percent in Colfax County.[10]

In Nebraska the Czechs saw the opportunity for a flowering of Czech culture. Even though immigrants were challenged by the demands of homesteading and the rigors of the prairie during their first few years in Nebraska, they were quick to establish strong community ties with other Czech settlers. While they strove to become prosperous American citizens, they resisted assimilating into the larger American culture. Language, literary, musical, social, athletic and political associations were organized to serve and preserve the Czech community. Generally established by Freethinkers, these associations together provided the local social, political, cultural and moral leadership for the community instead of the Church or State.

The period of initial settlement corresponds to the pioneer phase of cemetery development. In most towns, Czech cemetery associations were immediately established as an integral part of the cultural support system. While the challenges of homesteading and the poverty of immigrants postponed the development of other cultural institutions, the necessity of burials saw the establishment of cemeteries in every settlement. While there is no indication the

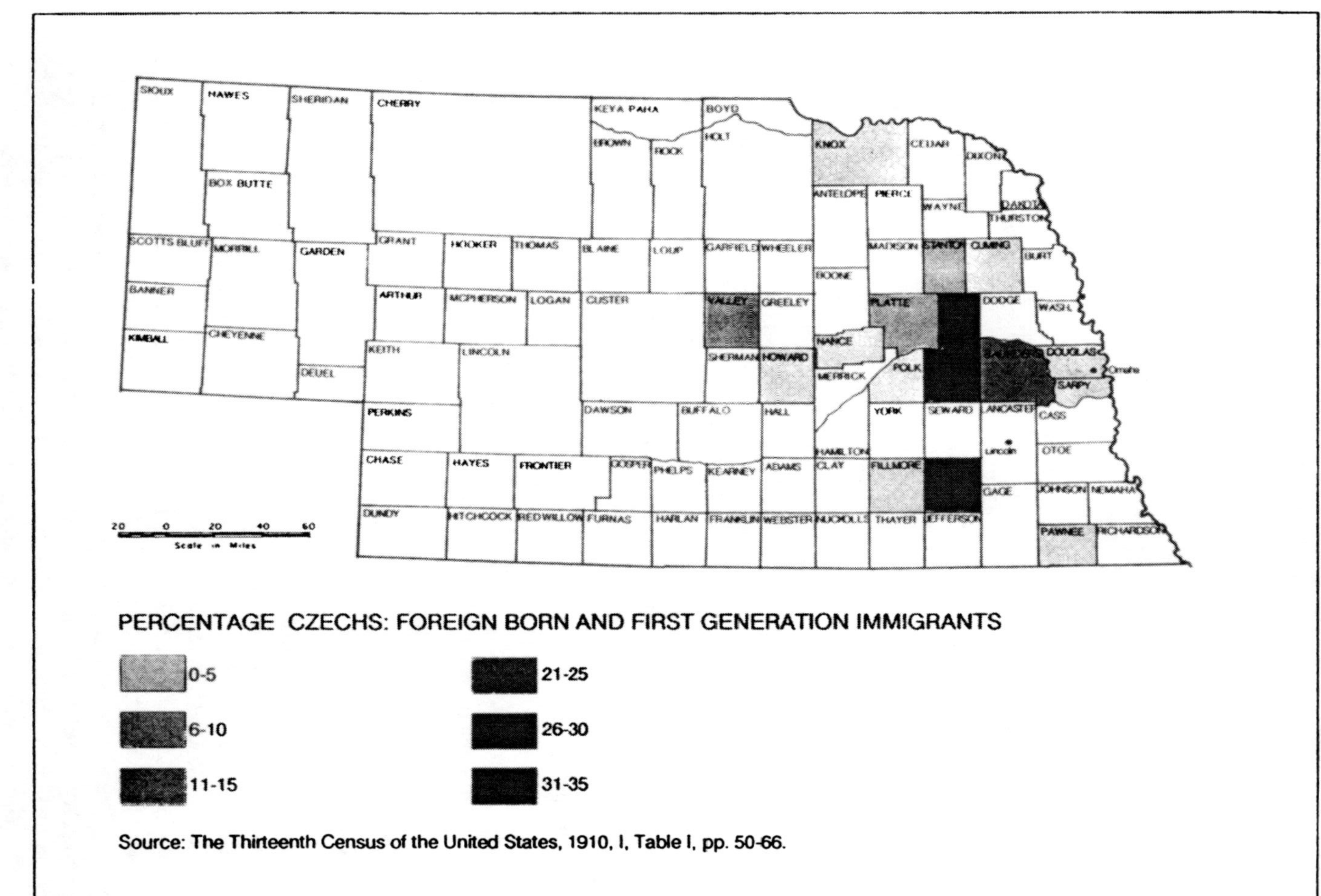

PERCENTAGE CZECHS: FOREIGN BORN AND FIRST GENERATION IMMIGRANTS

Source: The Thirteenth Census of the United States, 1910, I, Table I, pp. 50-66.

Czechs were restricted from burial in the general pioneer cemeteries, most desired burial separate from other immigrant and American groups and, in areas of high Czech settlement, developed exclusive Czech cemeteries. While these may initially have been only individual or family burial plots, they would usually remain the site for later burials. Thus, spread over the countryside, the cemetery became one of the principal forms of early Czech settlement in eastern Nebraska.

In many cases, the impetus for establishment of a cemetery was an unexpected death. Illnesses, accidents and diseases took a heavy toll on the first settlers. The earliest gravesites were often hastily determined, out of necessity. As Mary Jelinek, who arrived with the first Czech settlers in 1865, later reminisced, the first Czech cemetery in Nebraska, the Jindra Cemetery (now called Maple Grove), was established in Saline County south of the town of Crete in 1868 after several deaths demonstrated the need to provide a dignified space for burial:

> The day following the arrival of the first band of settlers, in November 1865, old Mrs. Krajnik died during a snow storm...The men made a coffin out of a wagon box and buried the corpse on the bank of the Big Blue river. A few days later, the three-year-old daughter of my brother-in-law Joseph Jelinek died and was buried the same way, as was the body of a Mr. Aksamit, who met death by drowning. In 1868 my grandfather died and my father-in-law Vaclav Jelinek, who did not want him to be buried thus too, donated ten acres for a cemetery. By 1872 five bodies had been buried there.[11]

The Jindra Cemetery was, at first, the only cemetery in Crete. In 1873, when other non-Czech town residents insisted that it be open to those of any nationality, members of the Czech Reading Society immediately reacted by establishing the first wholly Czech cemetery, called the Big Blue Cemetery.

As the Czechs sought to distinguish themselves from surrounding cultures by developing their own cemeteries, they also highlighted the major division within their own community, between Freethinker and Catholic, by the establishment of separate cemeteries. Towns with significant Czech populations had two Czech cemeteries, one for each group. Bohemian National cemeteries (identified as *Narodni Hrbitov* or *Cecho-Slovanki Hrbitov*) were usually established first by the Freethinkers, while the Catholic cemeteries (with Saints' names in English) were later developed by the Church, which insisted upon a consecrated burial space for its members. By 1920, in Nebraska alone, there were 30 Czech National cemeteries, 22 Czech Catholic cemeteries, and 3 Czech Protestant cemeteries.[12]

The Czech cemetery as it evolved during the pioneer phase and after was distinct more for its association of traits than for any single identifying element. These traits included siting, layout, as well as such specific cemetery elements as entries, enclosures, vegetation and the markers themselves. In addition to its appearance, the Czech cemetery was also defined by the ceremonies and events with which it was associated. Considered separately, some of these traits identified with the Czech cemetery could be observed in other cemeteries, in the area and elsewhere. Within the eastern counties of Nebraska several cultural groups settled—Germans, Swedes, English, Americans. These groups faced similar obstacles and were forced to make similar accommodations to life on the Plains. While many of their burial forms resembled those of the Czechs, the precise combination of these forms varied from one group to the next. A look at the several cemetery traits, beginning with the problem of site, will reveal the extent of the Czechs' commonality with, and distinction from, other cultural groups.

In the old country, the occasions to develop new communities and new cemeteries were few. Czech agricultural settlements were typically circular (*Rundling*) or linear (*Strassendorf*) in arrangement. Towns generally had a church at the center, while the villages featured at most a small central chapel.[13] In one section of northern Nebraska settled prior to Homestead laws, the town layouts loosely adhered to the traditional linear pattern of village settlement along the major transportation corridor—in this case the river—with fields at the periphery.[14] However, the sectioning of land and the attendant requirement that settlers live on their homestead dispersed later settlements on a massive checkerboard and effectively disrupted traditional patterns of settlement. Instead, Czech and other immigrant settlers were required immediately to translate their understanding of community to a foreign and abstract system of settlement.

Several cemetery historians have remarked on the location of cemeteries with respect to cultural and physical features, while only a few cultural geographers have attempted to determine specific siting factors.[15] As an extension of this work, a computer analysis was conducted of the cemeteries in Saline County to determine what, if any, patterns existed in the siting of 25 cemeteries.[16] On the computer, a map of cemetery locations was compared to existing topographical and geographical information to determine several siting factors (see Fig. 4:2).

The computer study indicated that 80 percent of the sites were located on hilltops or rises. Several cemetery scholars have confirmed the predominance elsewhere of elevated cemetery locations, although their explanations for this siting preference differ.[17] The spiritual argument contends that the hilltop is nearer heaven, while there is the practical explanation that rises are better drained, with soil that can be worked earlier in the spring. In the study area, with little vertical relief, the hill location also aided identification of the cemetery from a distance, and afforded a pleasant view of the river valleys. That hilltops were preferred positions is indicated by the fact that while most of the towns are at the lower elevations, near the rivers, nearly every farmhouse is located on the high point of the homestead.

Three-quarters of the cemeteries, like settlements, were located along transportation routes: first the river valleys, then the railroads, then the sectional line roads. The area of original settlement of the county was along the fertile lands drained by the Turkey and Swan Creeks in the central and southern parts of Saline County. Bypassed by the railroad, which followed the edges of the county, the area never developed as a population center. Only the cemeteries

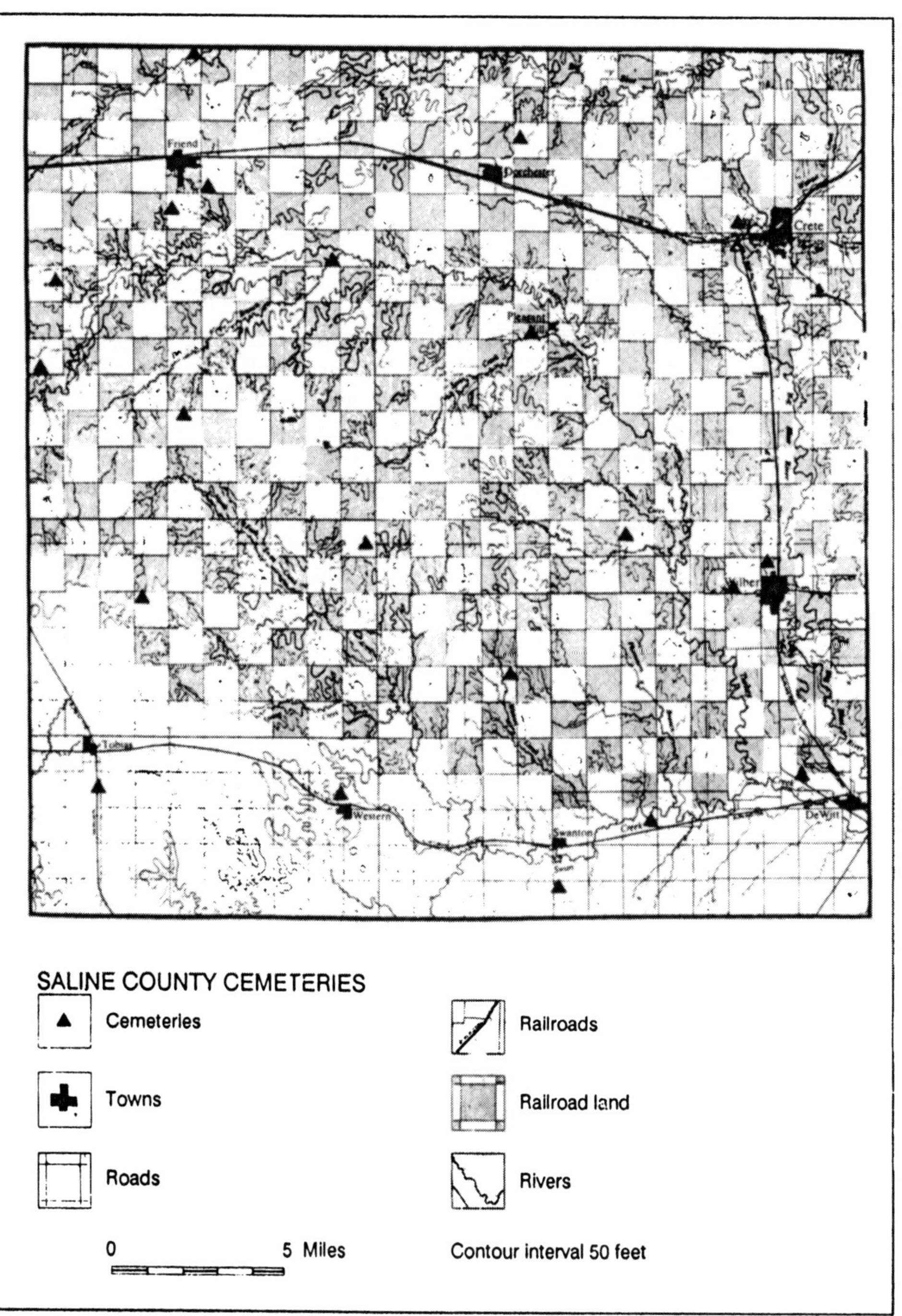

Fig. 4:2. Cemetery locations, Saline County, Nebraska.

remain.

The computer study indicated a surprising relationship between section numbers and cemetery location. Nineteen out of 25 cemeteries are sited on even-number sections. The explanation of this phenomenon, like so many others, can be found in the determinative influence of the railroad. The railroads received odd-numbered sections within their 20-mile right of way. In 1867, the price of railroad lands was three to four times the cost of non-railroad land, which was originally available free for homesteads, or for purchase at $1.25 an acre.[18] Cemeteries were simply located on the less expensive parcels.

Cemeteries were never located in the town center, according to the computer study, but were instead usually at the periphery of settlement, and usually distant from other cultural features, such as churches and schools. While this would at first seem to be due to Freethinker influence, in fact it was true for all cultural groups that settled in the area. Even in areas of greater Catholic settlement, like Saunders County, only a few Catholic cemeteries are adjacent to churches. Instead, cemeteries were located to be within a wagon ride from towns so that they were also accessible to the outlying farm community, dispersed by the homestead pattern of settlement.[19] This resulted in the equal distribution of cemeteries across the county, with no cemetery more than five miles from another, and cemeteries located in every township (six-by-six miles square). Cemeteries effectively marked the geographic radius of towns.

Despite the rigidity of the grid and the speculative nature of American land development practices, settlers were still able to apply many of their traditional notions of settlement and cemetery location. While the grid was based on a two-dimensional geography, settlers recognized hills, views, and valleys as the real landmarks. The section lines and Homestead laws defined a new type of community in the West, by determining transportation networks, property orientation and land values. The cemetery moved to the periphery of this abstracted community, but it remained integral to the settlers' definition of town.

The internal organization of the pioneer cemetery site is not readily apparent. A haphazard scattering of graves rises from an unplowed section of field. On closer inspection, a strong grid underlies the random placement. Unlike contemporary "rural" or "lawn" cemeteries, where the grave layout usually follows a curvilinear road layout or the topographical features of the site, the single most consistent feature of both Czech Freethinker and Catholic cemeteries is their rectilinear layout, with the graves facing east. While this may seem most obviously appropriate in an area where section grid lines dominated the landscape, earlier research by several cultural historians has confirmed this layout in most traditional cemeteries studied in the United States and Europe. Common to Judaeo-Christian tradition, the graves are aligned on an east-west axis, with the feet oriented to the east, so that the dead might face the Maker on Judgment Day.[20] Gordon Riedesel's research in Saunders County indicates that four Czech cemeteries actually deviate from this practice, with the graves facing south. Riedesel conjectures that this is based on the Czechs' differing theological views; however, two of the cemeteries are Freethinker and two are

Catholic. Upon visiting, it appeared that the graves were oriented South to face the road and the view.

In the pioneer phase, there exists little other organization to the cemetery site, except as developed for access. The simple layout, as in the Big Blue Cemetery, is a square or rectangle at the edge of the road. Where the area is fenced, there is a single entrance gate. Sometimes there is an interior road. A row of trees may have been planted later around the perimeter of the cemetery, or at the road's edge.

At first, cemetery improvements were few, and generally restricted to family burial plots. The individual pioneer graves were soon surrounded by the graves of several family members, especially children, following a series of epidemics in the early 1880s.[21] Although they had limited means, the Czech immigrants made very effort to set off and dignify the family burial sites.

Common to all the cemeteries in the area was an attempt to set the cemetery space off from the identical landscape beyond its boundary. In the sea of grass that settlers first found in eastern Nebraska, there would be nothing to distinguish consecrated from unconsecrated land, the cemetery from a farmer's future field. Several of the family plots were raised above the ground within stone or concrete borders and were often further enclosed by wooden, and later iron, fences. The raised plot and the surrounding fence are also common features of other cemeteries in the area.

Extensive plantings, however, distinguish the cemeteries of Czechs from those of other immigrant groups. Particularly in the pioneer cemetery, tree plantings were used to distinguish the low, horizontal graveplots from the surrounding prairie. Old, tall evergreens—Austrian pine, blue spruce, and red cedar—reminiscent of the European forests, mark the center or four corners of family plots, and appear to be as old as the graves (Fig. 4:3). In a landscape where trees were quite rare, their establishment represented the dedication of the families to their buried relatives. Catholic burial plots have fewer trees.

On or behind the grave mound and on the raised family plot relatives planted flowers popular at the time—tigerlilies, spiraea, lilac and yucca. The flowers were an exotic contrast to the prairie. Cemeteries of other culture groups in the area also have graveplot plantings, but none as consistently as the Czechs.[22]

Many pioneer gravestones represent the settlers' improvisations with available materials. There is a very little available stone in eastern Nebraska; the land is overlain by a deep mantle of glacial loess soils. Some of the earliest markers, therefore, were of concrete, wood or metal. Concrete markers are common, with the short epitaph, in Czech, scratched on the surface of the setting cement (Fig. 4:4). A rare wooden cross, undated, graces a grave in the Big Blue Cemetery (Fig. 4:5). Towards areas of greater Catholic concentration, in Saunders County, can be found graveyards that include several metal crosses. These crosses range from old, heavy wrought iron forms, perhaps of unique design, to the more common, purchased zinc ("white bronze") crosses, some with a crucified Christ figure attached (Fig. 4:6).

Commercial stone markers are prevalent, even for the earliest burials,

Fig. 4:3: Cedars mark the four corners of a family plot. Sacred Heart Cedar Hill Cemetery (established 1873), Saunders County, Nebraska.

Fig. 4:4. Concrete markers. Saline County, Nebraska.

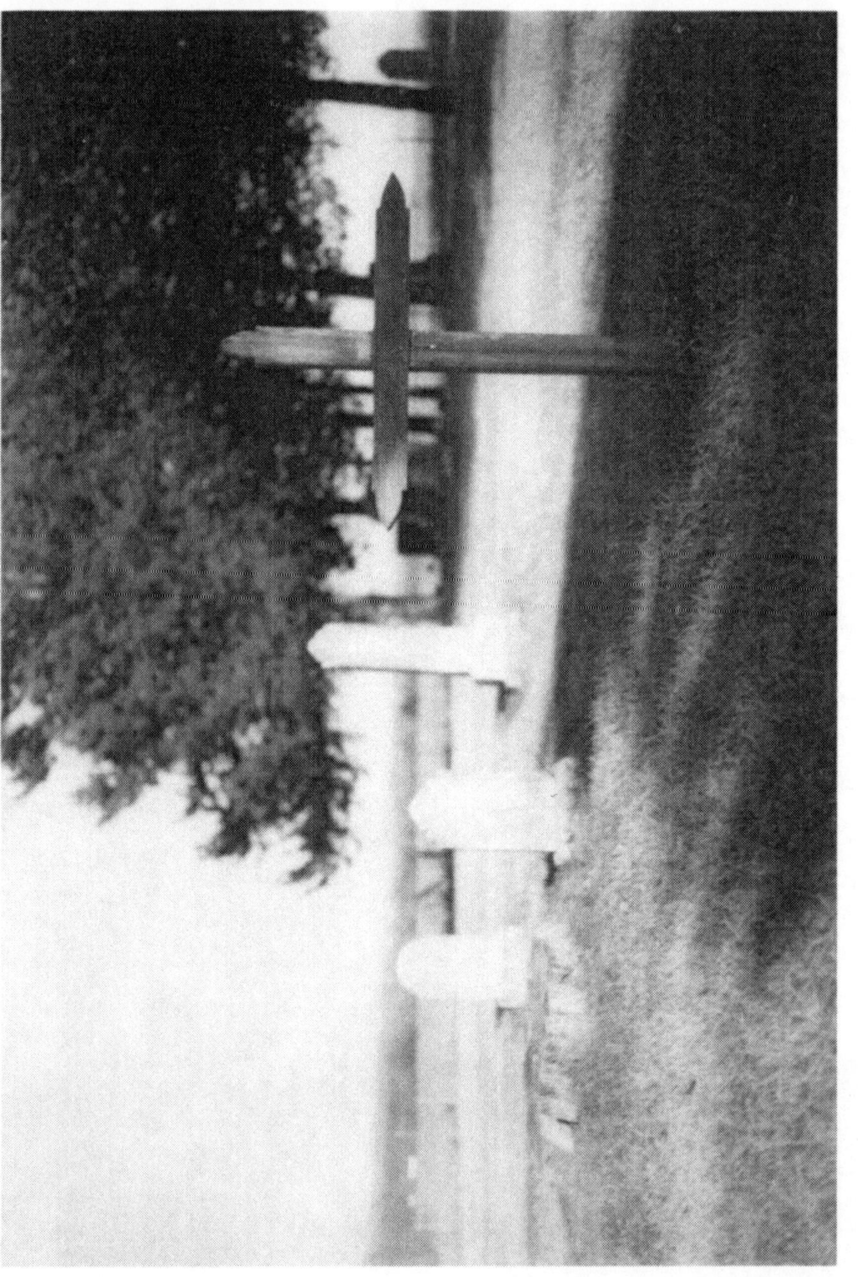

Fig. 4:5. Wooden cross. Big Blue Cemetery (established 1873), Saline County, Nebraska.

Fig. 4:6. Iron crosses. St. Peter and Paul Catholic Cemetery (established 1876), Abie, Butler County, Nebraska.

probably replacing the original pioneer markers. Fashioned from marble, granite and limestone, and following national style trends, in general they are stock items, with one cemetery featuring markers all of the same size and shape, and several different cultural groups purchasing the same type of gravestone. A few markers feature distinctive birds and hearts reminiscent of folk carving (Fig. 4:7). The inscriptions are generally in Czech. According to Riedesel, Czech gravestones are larger and more numerous than those of other cultural groups—Swedish, German, and American—studied in Saunders County.[23] Given their limited assets, the size and shape of the monuments reflected the buyers' concern for position and enduring dignity.

The most elaborate graves, raised, fenced, planted, with substantial markers, presented a dignified resting place for Czech pioneers. Even as they postponed improvements in their own lives, settlers strove to make their family members' place in the afterlife as dignified as possible, and to provide them with a familiar place that stood out from the surrounding, barren landscape.[24]

The pioneer cemeteries grew from one or a few cores, usually the original family plots. The first graves were generally located in the most favorable spot on the site—the high point, the place nearest the road, or the best viewing spot. From these original gravesites the cemetery grew outward, following family and cultural lines. In one cemetery, several American or English names cluster near the east side, later German headstones stand in the middle of the site and, at the western perimeter, several more recent Czech gravesites are placed.

The pioneer cemetery landscape was a quiet space, unvisited except by the birds and rabbits, or a family member. This space was transformed by momentary events. A funeral, with its train of wagons and mourners, briefly defined the sacred space. The earth was opened, the service spoken, the body laid to rest. After the ceremony, the place was quiet again, but the mark—the heap of bare earth—remained, covered with flower bouquets.

As quickly as their homesteads were established, Czech settlers set out to make model communities that would be a source of cultural pride. In Europe, the nationalist movement saw the exploration of traditional folk influences in the outpouring of Czech music, art and literature that is described as the "National Romantic" period.[25] The search for a native architecture led to the revival of the Bohemian Baroque style, celebrated in the construction of the National Theater (*Narodni Divaldo*) in Prague, completed in 1868. In Nebraska, a similar movement was fostered by Czech immigrants and saw expression in the curved Baroque motif of the community halls, or lodges, constructed in every community to house the numerous activities of the fraternal organizations. The town of Wilber even built Nebraska's first Czech theater in 1874, used for dramatic and musical events, including opera.

As a symbol of their pride, the Czech cemetery associations set out to raise funds to acquire more land, to "improve" their hastily developed cemeteries, and in some cases, to develop new ones that would reflect their cultural ideals. While the original pattern of cemetery location was undisturbed, those that were located nearer to developing transportation routes and growing communities were preferred by these associations and saw an increase in size

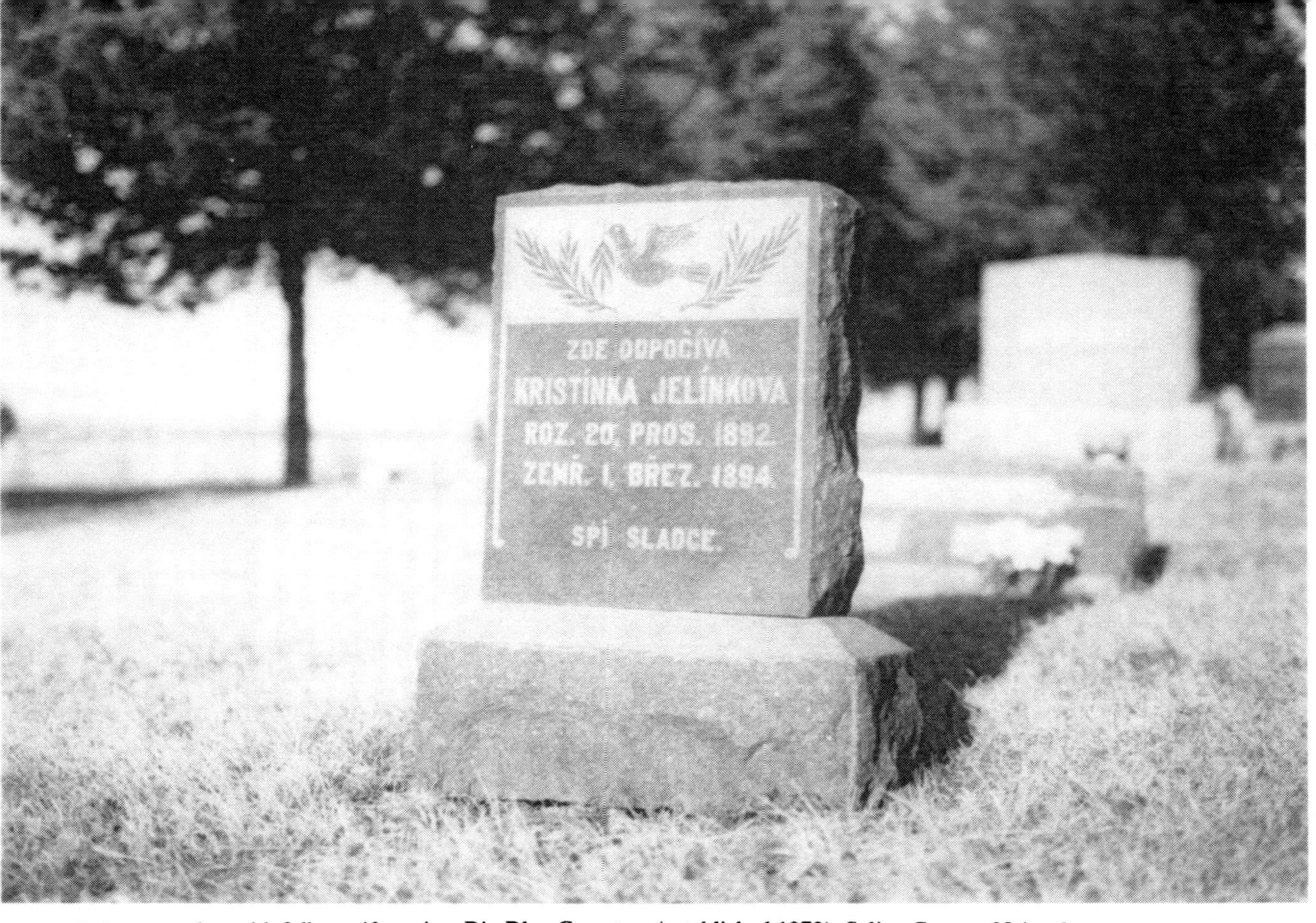

Fig. 4:7. Stone marker with folk motif carving. Big Blue Cemetery (established 1873), Saline County, Nebraska.

and improvements.

During the improvement phase, the same approach that had been taken to dignifying the family plot was extended to the entire cemetery space. As the cemetery was improved, the importance of family plots was necessarily subjugated to the significance of the cemetery as a whole. While family members were still buried in the same area, there was less effort made to distinguish the family plot from the cemetery. Many of the improvements to family plots were removed or restricted.

The most visible improvement to the pioneer cemeteries came in the form of enclosure. The entire cemetery was fenced, first with barbed wire, soon with wooden fencing. Some communities spent more, erecting elaborate cast iron fences, at least on the side of the cemetery facing the road. As cemetery fences were erected, those surrounding family plots were often removed. This corresponded with a general trend in cemetery management nationally, as interior fences were removed to simplify, unify and "modernize" the cemetery space.[26]

At nearly all of these cemeteries, the entry was strongly marked by an iron filigree gate, with the name of the cemetery often written in Czech (*Hrbitov* means cemetery) (Fig. 4:8). These gates were a prominent feature of both Freethinker and Catholic cemeteries, although they were not exclusive to Czech cemeteries, appearing also at a few Danish and Swedish cemeteries. In the vast prairie landscape, the diminutive scale of the arches, their insubstantial frame casting a delicate shadow pattern in the dust, would have instantly focused the funeral assembly as they entered the cemetery. Many of the gates appear to have been a purchased stock item (at least one came from a Cincinnati manufacturer), with the metal lettering added by the community.

As fencing came to define the cemetery space, trees were used to mark the cemetery as a place. Once restricted to the edges of the family plot, red cedars were planted at the perimeter of the cemetery. From a distance, the hilltop Czech cemetery could be easily recognized by the cedars, commonly called "cemetery trees."[27] The neatly aligned trees gave the Czech cemeteries their recognizable formal character. The trees also served to break the prairie wind, providing a calm space atop a windy hilltop (a common notion later applied in the extensive window plantings in the state following the dustbowl years). Freethinkers cemeteries were more heavily planted than Catholic cemeteries, with formal allées and perimeter plantings uncommon north of Saline County.

The Bohemian National Cemetery at Wilber is often reproduced in photographs as the most representative Czech cemetery (Fig. 4:9).[28] While most cemeteries are pioneer cemeteries that were later "improved," the Wilber cemetery was designed from the start as a model Czech cemetery. Property for the cemetery was purchased in 1874, and the cemetery, rectangular in form, was divided by roads into eight equal spaces. There were two entries, which permitted the funeral procession to make a through drive of the cemetery without turning around. A wooden fence was erected in 1886 and replaced by an ornamental iron fence in 1919 at a cost of $2,821.05.[29] The cemetery is best

Fig. 4:8. Entry gate. Bohemian National Cemetery (*Narodni Hrbitov*) (established 1900), Bruno, Butler County, Nebraska.

Fig. 4:9. Entry gate. Bohemian (Czechoslovakian) National Cemetery (*Cecho-Slovansky Hrbitov*) (established 1874), Wilber, Saline

known for its entry gates, cast from zinc ("white Bronze"), and its allées of red cedar, planted in 1898, which define and mark the perimeter of the cemetery. Although the cemetery is not sited on a hill, the allées planting forces the perspective and increases the sense of depth of the space. The trees were annually sheared to accentuate their formal character. The younger allée plantings of cedar in other Czech cemeteries indicate that the Wilber cemetery served as the model for these improvements.

In the prairie landscape, which unlike the urban landscape lacks a clear visual boundary, the interrelationship of the single grave and the cemetery form itself become quite important. In the pioneer phase, the cemetery's apparent form is determined by the outward expansion of individual and family graveplots, and its only order derives from the rectilinear layout of the graves. The common hilltop location helps to give the cemetery further spatial definition. During the second, improvement phase, the formal additions organize the cemetery space from the periphery. The simple, formal design of the Wilber cemetery provides a sense of dignity, of respectability, of permanence against the prairie.

In such an austere, enduring landscape, markers provide one way of distinguishing time, by their change of form, materials , carving and inscriptions over the years. While the original layouts of the cemeteries remain essentially intact, the markers have changed continuously.

In Czech cemeteries, a distinctive gravemarker type developed out of the experiments of the pioneer phase. Beginning in the early twentieth century, the traditional raised, planted plot type evolved into a flat, slab-type marker. Initially, slabs of poured concrete with inlaid pebbles or shells were made by local craftsmen. The idea became so popular that companies started producing precast terrazzo slabs[30] (see Fig. 4:10). The slabs are of regular dimensions, laid close to each other. The name and dates are indicated on an integral marker, referred to as a "pillow," which sits either at the head or the foot of the marker, nearest the access. There are smaller, child-sized slabs, of the same dull-grey color. While upright headstones continued to be installed, the slab marker, setting off the entire gravesite, became the burial form of choice. According to Riedesel, the slab tombstone accounts for about 25 percent of all gravemarkers in Czech cemeteries in Saunders County and nearly all the recent markers.[31]

The development of the slab-type marker has several probable explanations. The slabs are vandal-proof and decay-proof. They are easily, locally produced. However, as likely as such practical reasons, the slab-type marker represents an alternative to the vertical cross, or headstone, with its religious implications. In Saline County, where the Freethinker movement was nearly universal, the use of the slab marker is the most widespread. The slabs emphasize the space of the body, the horizontal resting place, rather than the direction to heaven implied by the upright marker. Similar to other groups with utopian values, the Freethinkers saw death as an opportunity to develop distinctive markers.[32] However, inspired by nationalist, rather than religious, sympathies, they developed a simple, anthropomorphic gravemarker. Freethinkers were not actively trying to promote a new religious cult, only to

Fig. 4:10. Slab markers. Bohemian National Cemetery (*Cecho-Slovansky Hrbitov*) (established 1874), Wilber, Saline County, Nebraska

leave behind the Catholic one.

The effect of the change of markers on the appearance of the cemetery is significant. Across the vast prairie, the original upright markers were the only vertical element in sight, their silhouettes marking the sky. As the preferred hilltop sites were taken, the upright markers appeared less bold. The slabs, however, create a bolder, checkered effect across the hillside.

One of the major cemetery "improvements" of this period was the establishment of separate Catholic cemeteries, or, in some cases, Catholic sections of Freethinker cemeteries. Where a Freethinker cemetery was the first established, Catholics later made efforts to develop consecrated land suitable for church burial. While many towns eventually added a separate Catholic cemetery, several Freethinker cemeteries were later divided between the two groups. The Brainerd Cemetery in Butler County, which spreads along the flank of a hill looking back at the grain elevators of the town, is identified as a Czech national cemetery (Narodni Hrbitov) at its western entry, while the eastern entrance is marked by a large metal cross. For the Catholic church, this was one means of reconciling existing conditions with the need for consecrated ground which no sinner, Freethinker, nor suicide would ever profane.

In Wilber, this separation was averted by the Freethinker leader Frank Sadilek. In 1882, when a Catholic priest wanted to separate the Czech National Cemetery in Wilber between Catholics and non-Catholics, Sadilek refused to break up the cemetery, seeing the unity of the culture as paramount over religious differences. Maintaining a liberal interpretation of religion, he wrote in his reminiscences:

For a long time no priest came to our cemetery, but when they saw that it didn't make any difference in our community and people managed to be born and to die and to be buried without a priest, they got wise and now, when it's necessary, the priest comes when his services are needed and from the point of view of the managers of the cemetery it doesn't make any difference what rites anyone wishes to have. Now we have one of the best managed Czech cemeteries in proportion to the number of inhabitants.[33]

During the period, the cemetery came to have a greater role in the social affairs of the community. For the Freethinkers, funerals provided an opportunity to focus the community around its cultural unity. While there is no mention of special rites associated with Freethinker burials, they were notable events. Sadilek and other Freethinker leaders functioned as circuit priests for the Freethinking community, delivering the final words, and, in doing so, maintaining strong bonds within the culture. Sadilek himself spoke at over 1300 funerals throughout the state. On the strength of his cultural associations, he was elected state senator from Saline County in 1883.

Decoration Day transformed the cemetery into a community park. At the Czech National Cemetery in Wilber, Decoration Day was first observed in 1887, on July 6, the anniversary of the burning of John Hus, the Czech patriot. Two years later, when Memorial Day, May 30, was established as a national day of mourning, the observance of Decoration Day was switched to that date.

In an area were most land was dedicated to agriculture, the cemetery was one of the few outdoor places set aside for gathering. Traditional Decoration Days were major holidays, drawing all of the community from their distant homesteads, reuniting family members and providing an important opportunity for socializing and courting.

The cemetery performed a vital, although unremarkable, function in the progressive Czech community. The cemetery retained the short history of the new community on the prairie, serving as its cultural memory. The cultural associations and events that bound the community together for the present had already been transformed in the few short years since the community had settled. The most permanent record of that growth and change was preserved in the cemeteries, as Jeffrey Hrbek recognized in the following lines from his poem, "The Bohemian Cemetery":

Yonder, the southward hills rise, fair,
And pleasant green fields bask in the sun
The view is broad and lovely there,
Where the dusty road doth upward run.

On the very crown of the highest hill
Where the tallest oaks lift their arms toward God
Above the clatter and din of lathe and mill
White marbles gleam athwart the sod.

'Tis the burial ground of a foreign race,
A race from the heart of Europe sprung,
Men and women of open face
That speak in the strange Bohemian tongue...

Someday these stone-carved tearful rhymes
Shall be a riddle—a puzzle—nay
Folk will doubt that in by-gone times

Many could read each tombstone's lay.
Still, here on the hill in the burial ground
The Chechish dead in their last long sleep
'Neath grass-o'rgrown, forgotten mound
The eternal watch will keep.[34]

Czech cemeteries of eastern Nebraska evoked the cultural heritage of the old country, but responded to the exigencies of the new land. A fifty-year period saw the establishment and improvement of 55 Czech cemeteries in Nebraska. In that period of time, Czechs created a culturally identifiable cemetery type distinguished by formal tree enclosure, gates, slab markers, and special events that reminded settlers that theirs was a progressive, proud community. Much of the impetus came from the Freethinkers, who, with their anti-religious feelings, paradoxically saw cemeteries as a source of cultural strength.

Today there are few outward signs to distinguish the Czech community from any other farming community. The countryside of Nebraska is considered to be the typical American rural landscape. It is only in relatively recent years, though, that rural Czech settlers integrated themselves into the American mainstream. The original insularity of the community was partly due to the difference in language and customs from the surrounding populations; however, it was also self imposed, as indicated by the Czech's desire to maintain separate cemeteries and cultural organizations.

As Czech historian Bruce Garver has shown, this insularity disappeared rapidly.[35] A dual process seems to be at work in accounting for the transformation. First, the reasons for Czech nationalism largely evaporated after World War I. The closing of the country to immigrants in the 1920s ended the influx of newcomers who might fuel nationalist fervor. Also, the aftermath of the war saw the carving up of the Austro-Hungarian Empire and the creation of the democratic Czechoslovak Republic, replete with social and land reforms and a separation of church and state. Much of the impetus for Czech nationalism was thus gone.

Second, the opportunities offered by the American soil made it easy for Czech immigrants to plan their future in accordance with American goals. Second- and third-generation Czechs merged into the American mainstream. Their numerical dominance and economic success in the area undermined their initial radicalism; their energy was redirected toward attaining the American way of life. The wars, in which many immigrants and immigrants' sons served, were instrumental in aligning Czechs with American goals.

While Czech cemeteries in the modern phase retain the original form and the basic elements of earlier periods, the design and labeling of gravemarkers added after the 1920s has reflected national trends more closely than in the past. All inscriptions are in English, and headstones are low to the ground. Slab markers, while unique to the area, are represented by a few commercially produced types.

Memorial Day, however, remains a big homecoming day, and in several cemeteries the Saturday before is the clean-up day for the cemetery. The cemetery is mowed for the first time, the beds are weeded, the trees are pruned, and signs of the season's vandalism are removed. This work is still organized either by local Freethinker fraternal orders such as the Zapadni Cesko Bratrska Jednota (ZCBJ), by the sponsoring Catholic church, or by the American Foreign Legion.[36] But, in this very emphasis, one senses that the cemeteries' function has shifted. Since the wars, the cemeteries have increasingly become the focus for patriotic memorializing of the war dead. War memorabilia decorate the gravesites of veterans. Many sites have flagpoles; some have a separate war memorial within the cemetery. Several towns decorate the perimeter of their cemetery with flags of war dead on Memorial and Veterans Day. The flags transform the cemetery space with their color and movement.[37]

While no official Freethinking movement survives, an amiable distinction remains between the general populace and Catholics, although the increasing number of crosses in Nationalist cemeteries indicates a relaxing of religious barriers. However, an animosity remains toward authoritarian control. Some Catholics elect burial in the Nationalist cemetery, seeing culture as paramount over religion, as the Freethinkers had originally hoped.[38]

Most of the area's residents still choose local interment, although concern for cemetery upkeep has caused community members to favor burial in the better-maintained cemeteries, whether in town or in the countryside. A new memorial park in the capital city of Lincoln, 40 miles away, attracts some with its promise of perpetual care. While the pioneer cemeteries are less active, they are generally still seen as an element of the community. Where burials still occur, even if only at the rate of one or two in the last five years, the cemetery is kept up. It is only those cemeteries which have completely lost their connection to the present, which no longer hold any memories to link the living with the dead, that have been let go.

For the Czech immigrants, particularly the Freethinkers, the cemetery was an important symbol of nationalist pride. These settlers sought to maintain their cultural isolation both through the development of ethnic associations and through the establishment of separate cemeteries. While the basic rectilinear arrangement is common to both Czech and non-Czech cemeteries in Nebraska, as distinct from the contemporaneous rural cemetery movement, the Czech cemeteries are further defined by a formal layout and plantings that reinforce the spatial form of the cemetery and distinguish it from the prairie landscape. The evolution of the slab-type marker reflects the Czech's ability to develop a unique marker form reminiscent of traditional gravestones. Continuing annual cemetery events help to reinforce community ties, even as many of the cultural associations have vanished.

While the plain has grown up around the cemetery, the cemetery is still only a speck in the scale of the countryside. In a landscape where variation is best experienced in a speeding car, the bit of cemetery can only be experienced by stopping the car to walk. The intimacy of these spaces is the key to their strength. In a boundless landscape the visitor is brought to the ultimate unit of scale—the single grave.

Notes

This study was initially funded through a Fall 1987 grant from the Penny White Student Project Fund at the Harvard Graduate School of Design which permitted travel to eastern Nebraska in March 1988. The author would like to thank John Stilgoe, Deborah Ryan, Eric Sandweiss, David Murphy, Norma Knoche and the Marek family for their help with research and with earlier drafts of this essay. All diagrams and photographs in this essay are by Karen S. Kiest.

[1]Willa Carter, *My Antonia* (Boston: Houghton Mifflin Co., 1918), p. 117.

[2]*Ibid.*, pp. 118-119.

[3]"Cemetery" is used here as an all-inclusive term, including park-like cemeteries

(which are also described as "rural," "modern," "garden," "lawn," or "memorial" cemeteries or parks) and traditional cemeteries, which may or may not predate the park-like cemeteries (and may have originally been termed "burial grounds," "burying grounds," or "graveyards"). The term "cemetery," which actually describes a place of sleep, and refers to the more recent conception of death, is used here because the other terminology varies greatly, and because "cemetery" is the word employed in recent analyses by cultural geographers and others.

[4]See D. Gregory Jeane, "The Upland South Folk Cemetery Complex: Some Suggestions of Origin," in *Cemeteries and Gravemarkers: Voices of American Culture*, ed. Richard E. Meyer (Ann Arbor, Michigan: UMI Research P, 1989; rpt. Logan, UT: Utah State UP, 1992), pp. 107-136. Jeane provides a valuable model for examining the history of these cemeteries with his description of the evolutionary models of the folk cemetery of the Upland South—pioneer, transitional and modern. The pioneer model defines the cemetery type itself, which in this case is identified by a scraped ground surface. The transition model indicates the effects of association with the surrounding culture. The modern cemetery, which has appeared since World War II, shows the effects of a larger American influence on regional cultural forms.

[5]See Frederick C. Leubke, "Ethnic Group Settlement on the Great Plains," *The Western Historical Quarterly* 8:4 (1977), pp. 405-30, for a clear essay on the importance of the railroads and foreign-born immigrants to the settlement of the Great Plains.

[6]Czechoslovakia was the county created following World War I from the historic provinces of Bohemia, Moravia, Slovakia and Moravian Silesia or Slovenia. In 1992, the fragile political union came apart—Chechoslovakia is in the process of breaking up into republics composed of the original provinces. "Czechs" are ethnic Slavs who inhabited Bohemia and Moravia, as distinct from Slovaks, who inhabited Slovakia. Immigrants to Nebraska were Czechs. David Murphy, architectural historian, Nebraska State Historical Society, personal communication, January 1990.

[7]Sarka Hrbkova, "Bohemians in Nebraska," *Publications*, 19 (Nebraska State Historical Society), pp. 141-159, interprets the meaning of the catch-all term "Austrians" to include immigrants from Bohemia, Moravia and Slovenia. She estimates Nebraska's "Bohemian" population in 1910 at 100,000, which is reduced by the editor to less than 62,000.

[8]Bruce M. Garver, "Czech-American Freethinkers on the Great Plains, 1871-1914," in *Ethnicity on the Great Plains*, ed. Frederick C. Leubke (Lincoln, Nebraska: U of Nebraska P, 1980), pp. 147-169.

[9]*Ibid.*, p. 148.

[10]David Murphy, from population figures presented in several issues of *Hospodar*, published in the 1890s for the Czech-American farmer.

[11]Quoted in Rose Rosicky, *A History of the Czechs (Bohemians) in Nebraska* (Omaha: Czech Historical Club of Nebraska, 1928), pp. 433-5.

[12]*Ibid.*, pp. 434-442.

[13]Murphy.

[14]*Ibid.*

[15]Fred Kniffen, "Necrogeography in the United States," *Geographical Record* 57 (1967), pp. 426-27, summarizes the limited research on the geography of death. For the most complete treatment of the topic see Larry W. Price, "Some Results and

Implications of a Cemetery Study," *The Professional Geographer* 18 (1966), pp. 201-207. For the single previous paper on the subject to appear in an American geographical journal, see William D. Pattison, "The Cemeteries of Chicago: A Phase of Land Utilization," *Annals of the Association of American Geographers* 45 (1955), pp. 245-257. For much of the source material on Saunders County, see Gordon M. Riedesel, "The Geography of Saunders County Rural Cemeteries from 1859," *Nebraska History* 61:2 (1980), pp. 215-227.

[16]Five additional cemeteries, including three family burial grounds, were identified during the site visit.

[17]Price notes variations in patterns of cemetery and settlement siting by culture groups in 214 cemeteries studied in southern Illinois. English, Irish and Scottish tended to settle hill country and uplands, while Germans settled poorly drained lowlands. Pattison found Chicago cemeteries associated with sandy, well drained, easily excavated ridges. Thomas J. Hannon, "Western Pennsylvania Cemeteries in Transition: a Model for Subregional Analysis," in *Cemeteries and Gravemarkers: Voices of American Culture*, ed. Richard E. Meyer (Ann Arbor, Michigan: UMI Research P, 1989; rpt. Logan, UT: Utah State UP, 1992), pp. 107-136, cited a preferred hilltop location in 41 out of 50 cemeteries, although he dispels the common explanations for their location. John L. Brooke, *Society, Revolution and the Symbolic Uses of the Dead: An Historical Ethnography of the Massachusetts Near Frontier, 1730-1820*, Ph.D. dissertation in History (U of Pennsylvania, 1982), clearly demonstrates the evolving location of the cemetery relative to the town due to changing cultural attitudes. Early Puritan settlements had cemeteries located at distance from the community center, and later, as death came to have greater symbolic meaning, cemeteries were sited in the center of the town. As new towns were located on hills in western Massachusetts, the cemetery was located on the high point of the town. Dissenting Baptists, who had often migrated on the riverways from points south, rebelled against the ideals of "height, earth, and centrality," and buried their dead in low-lying areas.

[18]*Saline County History*, p. 40.

[19]Norma Knoche, Executive Director, Saline County Historical Society, personal communication, March 1988.

[20]John Stilgoe, "Folklore and Graveyard Design," *Landscape* 22:3 (1978), pp. 22-28, points to the existence of this burial orientation as far back as the Iron Age, although the explanations for its use have changed as the pagan practice was appropriated by different cultures.

[21]Riedesel, "The Geography of Saunders County Rural Cemeteries from 1859," p. 220.

[22]*Ibid.*, pp. 226-7.

[23]*Ibid.*, p. 226.

[24]Comparisons with available information on cemeteries in Czechoslovakia indicates that the Nebraskan settlers were attempting to maintain their burial traditions in the orientation of graves and types of gravemarkers. Photographs from a relative's recent visit confirm the rectilinear layout of gravemarkers facing east. Most graveplots are raised and outlined in stone, and planted profusely. Iron crosses predominate in mountain regions of Czechoslovakia, according to Zdanka Pospisil, born in Czechoslovakia and now a professor of architectural history at Connecticut State University, who wrote her

dissertation on iron crosses of the Tyrol. After completing her research, she learned from others who were able to return to Czechoslovakia that iron crosses were found in several lowland communities and were far more common than she had originally anticipated. These isolated examples are only offered to suggest the rich and varied tradition which immigrants recalled as they laid out the grave of a loved one in the new country, and to suggest future directions for research.

[25]See Jaroslav E. Vojan, "Chechoslovak Music, Art and Literature," in *Czechoslovakia*, ed. Robert J. Kerner (Berkeley, California: U of California P, 1945), pp. 327-345, for a description of the celebration of Czech nationalism in music, art and literature. See also David Murphy, "Czechs", in *America's Architectural Roots: Ethnic Groups that Built America*, ed. Dell Upton (Washington D.C.: Preservation P, 1986), pp. 112-17, for an investigation of the development of a "National Romanticism" in Czech-American architecture in Nebraska, as evidenced in 90 lodges established by Czech fraternal organizations in the state.

[26]See *The Cemetery Handbook* (Chicago: Allied Arts Publishing Co., 1921) and Howard Weed, *Modern Park Cemeteries* (Chicago: R.J. Haight, 1912). For an overview of the interior fencing phenomenon, particularly in eastern "Rural" cemeteries See Blanche Linden-Ward, " 'The Fencing Mania': The Rise and Fall of Nineteenth-Century Funerary Enclosures," *Markers* 7 (1990), pp. 34-58.

[27]Norma Knoche, March 1988.

[28]In language reminiscent of the "memento mori" epitaphs once favored on Puritan gravemarkers, the inscription on the left side of the gate translates "what you are, we were," and on the right side "what we are you will be."

[29]See Frank Rejchan, quoted in Rosicky, *A History of the Czechs (Bohemians) in Nebraska*, pp. 433-5, for the best record of the development of a cemetery, the Bohemian-Slovenian cemetery in Wilber, still regarded as the most important Czech cemetery in the area.

[30]Knoche.

[31]Riedesel, "The Geography of Saunders County Rural Cemeteries from 1859," p. 226.

[32]See Margaret M. Coffin, *Death in Early America* (Nashville: Thomas Nelson, Inc., 1976), pp. 123-143, for descriptions of gravestones and places of burial of Moravians, Shakers, Puritans, Amish and other early American settlers.

[33]*My Reminiscences*, trans. Olga Stepanek (N.P.:, 1933), pp. 38-40.

[34]Jeffrey Dolezal Hrbek, "The Bohemian Cemetery," in *The Pulse* (March 1906), quoted in Rosicky, *A History of the Czechs (Bohemians) in Nebraska*, p. 432.

[35]Garver, "Czech-American Freethinkers on the Great Plains, 1871-1914," pp. 163-5.

[36]Knoche.

[37]Knoche.

[38]Paul Marek, Crete, Nebraska, personal communication, March 1988.

Scottish, Irish and Rom Gyspy Funeral Customs and Gravestones in Cincinnati Cemeteries

Paul F. Erwin

In American history and folklore, the wandering Gypsies have carved pathways into the nation's culture while desperately clinging to clannish customs and careers brought from the British Isles and Europe after the Civil War. While most of the estimated 100,000 to 200,000 currently roaming the United States live along the east and west coasts, particularly the Roms of southern European background, Cincinnati cemeteries have become the final resting places for thousands of Scottish, Irish and Rom Gypsies whose North-South annual migrations have passed through the Queen City each spring and fall.[1]

An analysis of the practices for each of the three groups of Gypsies who for more than a century have used Cincinnati funeral homes and cemeteries for their final rites and resting places reveals striking differences and a few similarities. The Scottish clans have erected large red granite gravemarkers in Spring Grove Cemetery, where on Memorial Day expensive floral decorations reflect the deep love of these Travelling People for their deceased relatives. The Irish Travellers, known as "Tinkers" in Ireland, hold funeral masses in St. Patrick's Roman Catholic Church and bury their members in St. Joseph's New Cemetery in Price Hill, where markers carry the names of Gorman, Hamilton, O'Hara, Webb and Wolfe. The Roms, many of English and Hungarian background, have lots in Spring Grove Cemetery, with more modest and traditional gravestones. Whereas cars and trucks have replaced the colorful wagons of these American Gypsies, many of their ethnic and clannish customs remain in evidence and merit historical study and documentation before they too become absorbed by the general American culture.

Nomadic tribes and clans of many ethnic and national backgrounds who make a living as they roam along the roads of the world have long been called "Gipsies" or "Gypsies" in the English-speaking lands. The name originated as a label for the dark-skinned Asian people of Hindustani language out of northwestern India who gradually migrated through Asia Minor and crossed into Europe with the Moslems about 1400 A.D. They claimed or were thought to be from Egypt, hence becoming known as Egyptians, which was eventually shortened to Gypcians and then Gypsies. In Europe and America, these Hindu descendants speak of themselves as Romany people, derived from their word *rom*, which means man or husband. Their Hindu dialect native language, called *Romani chiv*, or Gypsy tongue, has accumulated thousands of words along the way as they moved through Persia, Armenia, Greece, and other Balkan lands. Gypsies of Rom background originally had no distinctive religion of their own but practiced various forms of heathenry, nature worship, tabu and superstition. While retaining their general separateness from peoples in whose lands they have lived or traveled, they have adopted Christianity in the Western world. Baptism and burial rites are scrupulously observed, and, as this essay hopes to demonstrate, Rom as well as other Gypsies in the United States have strong beliefs in the concept of sepulture—the rites of burial within a tomb and the mourning of and proper respect for the dead.

The Roms' ethnic costumes, derived from Southern European cultures, reflect a love for bright colors, bandannas and dresses featuring cross-stitched patterns. Their music and dance for centuries has provided clannish entertainment around campfires and for family ceremonies and has contributed immensely to opera, other classical compositions, and drama of the Western world. Through these and other practices, it was the Roms who would give rise to the common stereotype of Gypsies in continental Europe and America. Their relatively large numbers on the East and later on the West Coasts of the United States have perpetuated the stereotypical image of Gypsies who roam the backwoods in good weather and seek shelter in the larger cities in wintertime.

Although largely of Catholic background, the Roms have also traditionally used Cincinnati's secular Spring Grove Cemetery as a primary burial ground. Most of their graves are found in the old Section 14 on the southern boundary of the landscaped grounds. Rom family names here reflect the years in England of their clans—Boswell, Buckland, Cooper, Gray, Herne, Lee, Lovell, Stanley and Smith. The original Rom tribal names continue to be used by the families and by scholars who study their folkways, but in America the English adopted name invariably appears on the monuments. The gravemarkers of the English Rom Gypsies are relatively modest and blend in inconspicuously with the markers of middle class American families at Spring Grove.

Like their Scottish and Irish counterparts, the British Rom Gypsies migrated from England to America after 1865. In the Queen City, the decades after the Civil War would often find their colorfully decorated barrel wagons (Fig. 5:1) camped along the Ohio River at Riverside and along the Mill Creek at its bends in Cumminsville or Northside, a sight one could find well into the twentieth century. After World War II, fewer numbers of British Roms visited the Cincinnati area and their burials declined. Cars and trucks towing trailer homes had replaced the cheaper horse-drawn Gypsy wagons and added a greater mobility to all travelling clans. Moreover, the Scottish Williamson clans and the Irish Gorman families had taken over the tri-state territory and had come to dominate the Mid-American North-South Gypsy route. Since the turn of the century, Cleveland and the other large steel mill towns near Lake Erie have become the home of many thousands of Hungarians and Balkan peoples, including large numbers of Rom clans, whose families blend into the southern

Fig. 5:1. Traditional Gypsy wagon.

European segments of population clustered in northeastern Ohio.

The origin of the travelling clans of Scottish and Irish background, who use the survival tactics of the Roms and portions of their language, occurred when these Anglo-Saxon peasants were thrown off medieval estates and small farms as part of the process by which landlords in the "enclosure" movement combined vast tracts of farm lands into shepherding ranges to supply the more profitable woolen industry. Thousands went to work in rising factory towns, while others toiled as hired farm laborers for pitifully poor wages. Many wound up in parish poorhouses. Some families took to the road in search of part time work, living in covered wagons, and became known as Travellers. In competition with the roaming Rom families, they too were soon to be called Gypsies, a label they still steadfastly disavow. Travellers and Roms abound to this day in the British Isles, though many of their families crossed the Atlantic in centuries past to ply their trades and seek their fortunes in the New World. Obviously, distant relatives of their clans also came to America with the same surnames: hence in Spring Grove and other Cincinnati cemeteries there are Scottish and Irish gravestones of long established Queen City families such as Williamson, Johnston, Wilson, or McDonald which have no connection to the Travellers of identical surname also buried there.

In Ireland, conditions similar to those prevailing in England historically forced portions of the rural peasant folk into itinerancy through evictions, poverty and famine. Subsequently, as nomads, they developed a secret language or argot called *Shelta*, or *Gammon*. Irish Travellers are synonymously referred to as Irish Tinkers in both Ireland and America. Despite our common modern usage of the word to connote tinkering or bungling—that is, to work unskillfully or without useful results—the true basis of the word centers on tin: *tinekere*, or worker in tin. American Tinkers brought their trade of metal working with them from the "Old Sod,"[2] and as i*tin*erants or Travelling People their adeptness at this tin working often served to distinguish them from their Scottish kinfolk Travellers. George Gmelch, in his recent study, *The Irish Tinkers*, provides an excellent insight into the practices of these itinerant tradesmen in Ireland (which paralleled work by their American cousins):

> The primary trade of most Tinkers was tinsmithing. They practiced this craft both in the countryside and in small towns and villages.
>
> Travellers made a variety of tin articles, including cups, kettles, milk pails, lanterns, buckets, and tubs for both domestic and agricultural use. They also made specialized articles upon request. For the children of families living in coastal areas, they made sand pails; for farmers in the West, they made distilling equipment for bootleg whiskey....
>
> A large portion of the tinsmiths' time was spent "jobbing" or repairing old tinware. They tightened loose handles, replaced worn-out and rusty bottoms, and plugged leaks with solder aided by a "tinker's dam"—a ring of dough or clay placed around the lead to prevent the molten solder from running off before it cooled. They also repaired a variety of other items. Many mended umbrellas; some repaired clocks; others, known as "metal-runners," melted bits of iron and cast metal parts such as a new leg for a kettle.[3]

How many Gypsies are there at present? Accurate head-counts have been difficult to make, and because of the separateness of Gypsies, as well as the itinerancy of their clans, national census figures in Europe and America appear quite unreliable. Professor Ian Hancock of the University of Texas at Austin, who currently is the United States representative to the United Nations and to UNICEF for the International Romani Union, recently estimated that "There are probably between eight and twelve million Gypsies throughout the world, perhaps six million of whom descend from the European Romani populations."[4] Most scholars presenting material at the Gypsy Lore Society conferences suggest far fewer numbers—perhaps two to six million of all people called Gypsies, including the four groups of India homelands: a) the Banjara living in India; 2) the Dom, now in the Middle East; 3) the Lom, living in Turkey and the Caucasus; and 4) the Rom, who migrated to Europe via the Balkans and Hungary and who have moved to many other parts of the world.

Within the United State the Gypsy populations remain elusive. Hancock notes widely disparate conjectures:

> In the United States, for example, estimates of its size range from the U.S. Census Bureau's figure of 1,600 to that of the Illinois Police Department of "over a million"; another police report puts the number at two million. If we take all of the different groups together, there are probably somewhere between 750,000 to 1,000,000 people in America who identify themselves as ethnic Gypsies.[5]

But even Hancock's gross estimate seems largely inflated. Since many Irish and Scottish Travellers would not wish to be claimed as ethnic Gypsies of Rom or Hindustani descent, it might be more reasonable to begin by limiting the count to total Rom numbers in the United States and Canada, perhaps 100,000 to 180,000. So many have been intermarrying with non-Gypsy urban families, particularly among the Hungarians in the Midwest, it is more likely that actual numbers are declining in America. Much the same may be true among the Travellers of Scotch or Irish background, whose total in all of North America I would currently estimate at not higher than 20,000.

These limited figures for Scottish and Irish Gypsy populations in America result from my conviction that the most tangible evidence of Traveller's actual numbers at given times may come from documented study of the number of people of traveller families buried in Cincinnati cemeteries. Using birth and death dates from County records, cemetery records and funeral home journals, a count of the number alive at each decade's census since 1850 should indicate with some reliability the actual number of Gypsies of these clans. Thus far, my Gypsy cemetery "census research" has been devoted to the compilation of the Scottish Travelling clans; in the future I shall be extending this study to encompass the Irish Travellers as well.

Just why the Gypsies traditionally came through Cincinnati and why they chose Queen City cemeteries for their family burial grounds remains to be thoroughly accounted for and historically documented. Some reasonable conjecture seems relevant, however. Obviously, the North-South "flyway" of the clans geographically forced them to stay west of the Appalachians as they wandered from Georgia, and later Florida, via Atlanta towards Detroit, Cleveland and Canada on the Great Lakes. For the Irish Tinkers, whose metal trades included "wipe-tinning" (the repair of thin spots and holes in cooking vessels, kettles and pans of homes and busineses), their most rewarding routes encompassed the string of cities from Atlanta to Lake Erie, and Cincinnati was the largest along that trail in the nineteenth century.

One might argue as well that the opening of Cincinnati's John Roebling Suspension Bridge in 1867—the first bridge below Wheeling, West Virginia across the Ohio River—may have attracted Gypsies and other wagon people to this city. Then too, the extensive wagon roads developed during the Civil War from Cincinnati southward to Nashville, Knoxville, Chattanooga and Atlanta to supply the Union Army divisions over the four years of penetration into the Confederacy may have proved useful in later Gypsy migrations along this route.

One major factor, however, may have been most significant of all in accounting for both Cincinnati's route prominence and for its selection as the primary burial site for the traveling clans. Amongst both the Irish Tinkers and the Scottish Travellers, it had long been customary to hold services for the dead during the week following Easter. By April of each year, their annual northward migrations would have brought them into southern Ohio, and, as most Easters fall in that month, the various divisions of the families could convene in the Queen City for funerals while waiting for the muddy roads of rural Indiana and Ohio to dry before fanning out amongst the farms and towns of the Old Northwest. Moreover, once large family lots had been purchased by the families in the well-established larger "rural" cemeteries bordering Cincinnati, it would make sense that most of their descendants would continue to bury their dead there.

Founded as part of the national movement to create "rural" cemeteries which flourished in the years before the Civil War, Cincinnati's Spring Grove Cemetery was chartered by the State of Ohio on January 21, 1845 as a non-profit and non-sectarian corporation and has grown over the years from an original 166-acre farm to a tract of 733 acres. At present, it is recognized as the nation's largest non-profit cemetery, with more than 188,000 burials. Located on the west side of the Mill Creek, it rises from the flood plain where a series of lakes and ponds now add to its attractive entrance grounds, which ascend nearly two miles toward the crest of College Hill. The historic route of General Wayne's army enroute to the Battle of Fallen Timbers in 1794 had become named Spring Grove Avenue as it paralleled the Mill Creek and was, until the interstate system was created, the major highway into Cincinnati from the north. The Garrard farm, which comprised the original tract of Spring Grove Cemetery, was about four miles from the city's waterfront downtown and just a mile upstream from the bend of Mill Creek where the tents of the circuses and Gypsies were pitched in the Spring of each year.[6]

Spring Grove Cemetery replaced at least 23 church-owned burial grounds in the central city which had become hopelessly overcrowded during the period of rapid population growth when the riverport metropolis was nicknamed "Porkopolis" because of extensive slaughtering houses and packing plants concentrated near the Ohio River. The present Board of Trustees, so declares a current brochure, still subscribes to the founding concept: "Let us then employ some of (the funds...) in rendering the place where our beloved friends repose attractive and consoling at once to the eye and the heart not only for the present but also for the future."[7] A permanent endowment fund has assured the fulfillment of that commitment and Spring Grove ranks as one of the world's most beautiful cemeteries, boasting 14 lakes and a waterfall, 37 miles of roadway, and a protected woodland area. Indeed, it has acquired a national reputation as an urban arboretum over the years, with approximately 1,000 varieties of trees and shrubs to be found in the cemetery, many of which are not indigenous to the region. Much of the credit for the spectacular landscape concept of Spring Grove goes to its early superintendent Adolph Strauch, a Prussian-born landscape gardener with European training and experience.[8]

The grounds are not the only impressive feature of the cemetery, however. Over 40 family-owned mausoleums representing a variety of revival and modern styles stand as memorials of outstanding architectural achievement (Fig. 5:2). First time visitors to Spring Grove marvel at the impressive Norman Gothic gateway buildings and chapel. Monuments within the older section carry names of the city's founding fathers, war heroes, politicians and statesmen, and such captains of industry as Gamble, Baldwin, and Jergens. In style, they represent the entire range of rich and varied forms so characteristic of Victorian mortuary art.

The Roman Catholic churches in mid-nineteenth century Cincinnati likewise found their original downtown graveyard, St. Joseph Cemetery, boxed in between residential city blocks and vastly overcrowded, and, as was the case with Spring Grove, sought to alleviate the situation through establishment of a newer rural cemetery. Since the second and third generations of Germans were multiplying beyond the capacity of the three- to five-story narrow homes in the "Over-the Rhine" district of the city basin, they and their Irish contemporaries took to the western hills across the Mill Creek valley—Price Hill, College Hill, Western Hills, and, more recently, Oak Hills and Delhi Township. In 1854, almost in the center of these parishes, they founded the New St. Joseph Cemetery. Occupying 163 acres bounded by Rapid Run Road on the north and Foley Road to the south, the cemetery was neatly laid out by the lawn plan over rolling hills.[9] Though less famous by far than Spring Grove, it shared many of the amenities of its more renowned secular cousin.

As mentioned earlier, the religious convictions of the Gypsies apparently served as an important reason for the clans to gather in Cincinnati the week after Easter. Generally, until about 1950s, the British Gypsies had all their deceased relatives' bodies embalmed and then shipped in caskets by railroad during the year to be held in the Spring Grove morgue until the post-Easter funeral rites could be held. Among Gypsies, funerals were—and are—especially significant family reunion occasions, with great homage paid to the honored dead.[10]

Fig. 5:2. Classical revival style mausoleum of the Fleischmann family. Spring Grove Cemetery, Cincinnati, Ohio (*Photograph by Richard E. Meyer*).

The week after Easter would find the Travelling People taking over Cincinnati's funeral homes for a series of wakes—all night vigils and gatherings—with each individual given a separate funeral service (and a church mass for the Irish Catholics), and then graveside interment. Food and drink would be brought into the funeral parlors, children would play around the parlors and parking lots, and the Scottish families would expend enormous sums on caskets, vaults and flowers for the deceased. Following the funerals, the clans would often linger in the area around Cincinnati, plying their trades of metal repair, lace and basket selling, fortune telling, and appropriating other goods when necessary, so as to be in a position to return to the cemeteries for Memorial Day. Again, the Scottish in particular would demonstrate their deep reverence for their departed by great floral displays around the family gravestones. For the Irish Catholic Gypsies, especially the Gorman clan, the funeral masses at St. Patrick's Church and the burials in New St. Joseph Cemetery preserved strong ethnic and national Old World traditions.

Two Mill Creek century-old funeral establishments have served the two largest Gypsy families in the Midwest for over a century. In Cumminsville/Northside since 1870, the Charles A. Miller Sons Funeral Home (Fig. 5:3) has embalmed and buried most of the Irish Travellers. The majority of the Irish Gypsies buried in Cincinnati stem from descendants of the James Gorman family, whose burials date back to the 1870s. The Busse and Borgmann Funeral Home, originally located on Freeman Avenue in the old West End of Cincinnati and since 1933 on Central Parkway above the Hopple Street Viaduct over the Mill Creek, traditionally served the Scottish Travelling People, who as Protestants have purchased cemetery lots in Spring Grove Cemetery, where red granite gravemarkers flanked by two stone urns mark the related families of Williamson, McMillan, O'Conner, Stewart, Keith, Johnston, McDonald, Wilson, Murphy, Reid, Gregg and many others. Ironically, the Catholic Busse and Borgmann funeral directors buried the Protestant Scottish Gypsies and the Protestant Scottish descended Charles A. Miller family provided the needs of the Irish Catholic Tinkers of the Gorman clans. Today, the Miller firm, owned by Will Book, owns and operates both funeral homes and serves both British Gypsy Groups.

Nelson (Pete), Miller until his death in 1983 the last surviving member of the family associated with the Northside funeral home, recalled how an accident led to the long association of his firm with the Gormans. Colonel James Gorman, a veteran of the Civil War like Charles A. Miller, often had bought horses from the livery stable which Miller operated on Hamilton Avenue after the war.[11] One day in the Fall of the year as the Gorman clan was driving south through Cincinnati, one of his children was killed, run over by a wagon on Spring Grove Avenue, the major road in and out of the city that follows the Mill Creek. Short of money, Col. Gorman asked Miller if he would bury the child and trust him for the expense until the next spring when he promised he would pay all costs. "Grampa," recalled Pete Miller, "understood the ways of the Gypsies and made a casket, bought a lot and provided the funeral."[12] From that day forward, the Gormans utilized the services of Miller's Northside funeral

Fig. 5:3. Etching of Charles A. Miller Sons Funeral Home, Cincinnati, Ohio (*Courtesy Charles A. Miller Sons Funeral Home*).

home for family burial purposes.

Four major families of Irish Travellers account for most of the gravemarkers in New St. Joseph Cemetery. The Gorman family, comprising the largest number, also go back the farthest in burial dates, with the Hamilton, O'Hara, and Corrigan clans constituting the remainder. In recent years, new divisions of these families have erected gravemarkers at New St. Joseph Cemetery next to the older Gorman and Hamilton lines; lots and headstones carry the names of Webb and Wolfe. In the Gorman lots, the two most important first names of the male lines are James and Patrick: many of them were buried here before World War I. However, cemetery staff report that few of the Irish Gypsies buried here actually died in Cincinnati. Today, many are reported to have died in Indiana, indicating the clans now are headquartering in that area of the Midwest.[13]

Numerous recent burials of members of these Irish Gypsy families demonstrate that many of the Irish clans, like their Scottish counterparts, still utilize the Cincinnati cemeteries as their permanent home. The Gorman and Hamilton lots are numerous within New Joseph Cemetery, and the large number of children is readily marked by name stones surrounding the family monument. But the Tinkers' gravemarkers lack the significant identification signs and symbols so prominent on the Scottish Gypsies' stones. No extensive use of red granite, no extra tall pillars or matching urns (except in one or two cases), and no excessive floral pieces at Easter or on Memorial Day. Neither angels nor crosses top the gravestones as in some Roman Catholic cemeteries, although a slanted cross often is carved at the top of the family monument. One conspicuous exception to this general simplicity stands just inside the cemetery's north gate—a massive (six feet in diameter) Gorman family marker in the shape of a wheel, perhaps a permanent reference to the wandering tradition of that clan in both Ireland and America (Fig. 5:4). Yet on the whole, the Tinkers' gravemarkers reflect a more modest and less expensive demonstration of affection for the dead than that of the Scottish Travellers found in Spring Grove Cemetery.

Earlier, I suggested that the existence of Cincinnati's major cemeteries may have been a significant factor in the selection of this city as a Gypsy burial site. For the Scottish clans in particular, this may have offered an additional attraction. Living apart from conventional Americans, the Gypsies probably quickly learned that their funeral customs would be less noticeable if located within cemeteries already clustered with tall markers of the more affluent urban dwellers.

In Spring Grove Cemetery the Scottish Travelling clans found a near-perfect location for their burial grounds. There they preserved their national love for Scotland by erecting relatively large red granite (Scottish marble) family monuments of special designs, usually flanked by two stone urns on the base foundation (Figs. 5:5, 5:6, 5:7). Standing five to ten feet high, these dark red (sometimes grey) memorials have the family surname carved boldly on the front, with scroll-like engravings near the edges showing either thistles (the national flower of Scotland) or twigs of acacia (an element in Masonic

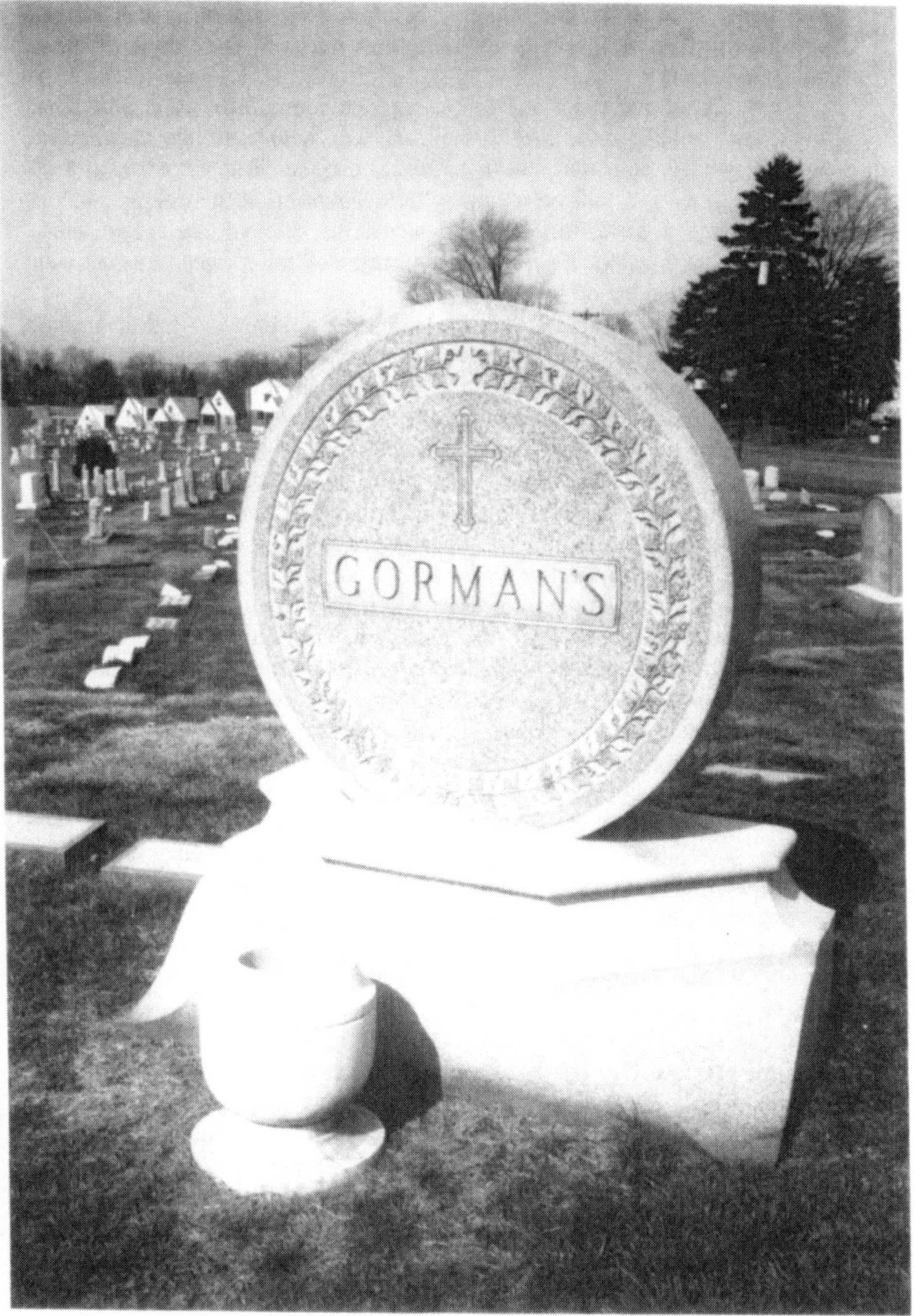

Fig. 5:4. Wheel-shaped monument for Irish Gorman family. New St. Joseph Cemetery. Cincinnati, Ohio.

symbolism). Frequently, the Masonic Scottish Rite symbol is still ordered implanted on top of the cement vault lowered over the casket of these Travelling people.[14]

Each lot has one major marker carrying the family name only; individual graves have smaller ground-level name markers with birth and death years engraved on each. Sometimes these individual markers also bear a design such as a thistle or a cross, and occasionally the relationship of the person, such as father, mother, or child, further distinguishes the beloved one buried there. Many individual markers describe as well as the military service of a man who fought in one or another of America's wars.

For many decades, the Scottish clans have demonstrated a marked preference for their dark red granite monuments because the material was the native stone of their ancestral homeland. Such stones were originally imported from Scotland until shipping costs became prohibitive. Presently, the bulk of this red granite comes from quarries in Minnesota, Wisconsin, Missouri and Arkansas, and carries descriptive trade names such as Wisconsin Ruby Red, Wausau Red and Mahogany.[15] While most markers are found with carved letters cut into the stone face, it is traditional amongst the various Williamson families to order the more expensive form of markers where the name stands out from the flat surface of the face of the stone, a practice which requires that all the stone face be ground off except for the extending letters (Fig. 5:8).

Many American cemeteries have red granite markers scattered amongst the more common blue-grey variety, which since the 1830s have been shipped from quarries near Barre, Vermont. Often these are chosen because of their warm red color and placed in family lots by persons who have no knowledge of the special significance these red markers have for the Travellers. Within Spring Grove Cemetery, not far removed from the lots of the Scottish Gypsies, are clusters of graves for Greek families using a very similar mahogany stone. The difference between the ethnic groups shows most graphically on Memorial Day, however, when the Travellers traditionally decorate their lots with highly elaborate floral displays, all provided by one trusted florist of greater Cincinnati.[16] Some Scottish graves will have twelve to twenty baskets or heart-shaped displays filled with fresh-cut flowers. Recently, one grave was graced by two large matching hearts composed entirely of blue orchids; the displays were approximately four feet tall and mounted on special tripods. A number of Cincinnati area informants have recalled for me how elaborate and expensive were the floral displays around these gravemarkers in the 1950s. One year, so I am told, a local florist in Northside was paid $35,000 for Memorial Day flowers which completely covered a number of chicken-wire designs of symbolic meaning to the Travellers—an empty rocking chair, a grandfather clock, an oxen and split-tongue wagon, a broken wagon wheel and a Masonic emblem. The tradition continues: in February, 1990, I was fortunate enough to witness a similar collection of these elaborate floral arrangements which had first been placed around the casket at the funeral home and were then taken to the gravesite and re-erected around it (Fig. 5:9).

All of the cemetery lots utilized by the Scottish Travellers were purchased

Fig. 5:5. Red granite monument for Scottish Keith family with urns and other decorative motifs. Spring Grove Cemetery, Cincinnati, Ohio.

Fig. 5:6. Monument for Scottish Gregg family with urns and decorative scrollwork. Spring Grove Cemetery, Cincinnati, Ohio.

Fig. 5:7. Monument for Scottish Gregg family with Masonic (Shrine) emblem and Scottish thistles. Spring Grove Cemetery, Cincinnati, Ohio.

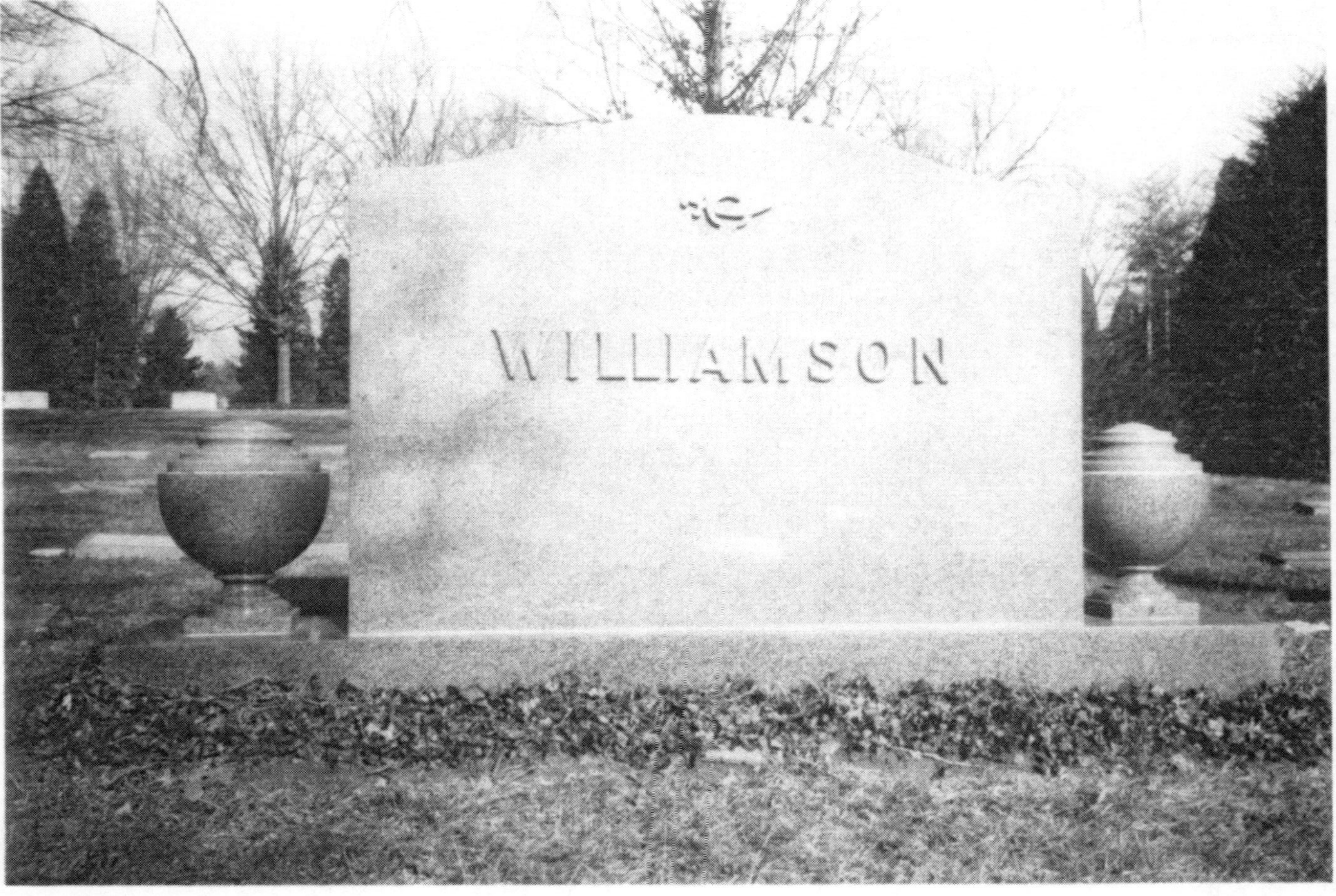

Fig. 5:8. Red granite monument for Scottish Williamson family with Masonic (Shrine) emblem and raised lettering. Spring Grove Cemetery, Cincinnati, Ohio

after the Civil War and therefore were selected in the upper half of Spring Grove Cemetery. Many of them border the woodland area where tall trees offer a sheltered and shaded site very appropriate for a folk long accustomed to campsites in wooded glens. While there are a few expensive lots down near the lakes belonging to the Johnston clan and featuring tall gravestones of grey granite post and lintel format (Fig. 5:10), the hilltop Sections 114, 117 and 118 hold lots bearing the names of Stewart and McDonald descendants, with most of the others resting in Sections 124, 125, 126, 127 and 128. Virtually every lot was deliberately purchased along the roadways: none were within the interior of the sections. Perhaps, one might speculate, this fact reflects yet another manifestation of the clans' traditional love for the road.

The funeral rites of the Protestant Scottish Travellers often add non-conventional elements to contemporary customs. One funeral director related the intriguing story of an aged woman of the McMillan clan, who, nearing death, was quickly taken by family members aboard a jet liner and flown to Phoenix, Arizona, where a special glass-topped golden casket was available. She died within hours of her arrival there, was embalmed and placed in the casket the same day and then, accompanied by one member of her family, was flown to Cincinnati for interment in Spring Grove Cemetery. At the Miller funeral home, where her casket remained until the clan could gather for proper ceremonies, instructions were given that a light must be turned on all night where her casket was located. On the day of the funeral, an extraordinarily large crowd of family members attended. The florist who delivered the myriad of floral arrangements was instructed to come each day and replace any wilted flowers. At another woman's funeral, following a rather traditional Protestant service with readings of Scriptural selections from the Old and New Testaments, the family requested that the casket be sealed with red sealing wax and all participants remained to watch as the funeral directors carefully lowered the lid and squeezed the red wax from the tube containers.[17] One wonders what the motivation was—to keep her body and spirit safe within or to keep evil spirits out?[18]

Several Cincinnatians have told me stories of their recollections of Gypsies in the city. One, a native of Northside, related how, as a child before World War I, she had often seen the Gorman wagons come into the neighborhood and camp along the Mill Creek. She also remembered "a gorgeous man's funeral" in 1940 that brought a large number of people to the Miller Funeral Home. "They drove big cars, wore diamonds, and were well-to-do," she said. A businessman recalled that in one day an auto agency sold the Gypsies 35 new Cadillacs, and they paid cash. Another told how the Gypsy family of a leader, who had a leg amputated in Christ Hospital and died there, took over an entire wing of the hospital, put their children in the sunroom, and cooked their own food in their rooms during his confinement.[19]

All told, the funerary traditions of the Scottish Travelling clans present a distinctive and highly complex set of ethnically based traits. Ultimately, the question must be raised: why do these practices—in some cases extraordinarily expensive and elaborate ones—exist, and, perhaps even more importantly, why

Fig. 5:9. A portion of elaborate floral arrangements at Scottish Stewart family gravesite. Spring Grove Cemetery, Cincinnati, Ohio.

Fig. 5:10. Grey granite monument in post and lintel style for Scottish family Johnston. Spring Grove Cemetery, Cincinnati, Ohio.

do they persist within this group's experience?

To begin with, my years of observation and research into the Traveller's traditions have thoroughly convinced me that the special religious rituals and cemetery customs of the Scottish clans are a direct reflection of their version of the Christian belief in the immortality of the human soul. This is immediately evident in the extremely widespread use on their gravemarkers of both the engraved symbols of the Christian cross and of the Masonic twigs of acacia as an emblem of faith and of the immortality of the soul. Both the beliefs themselves and the physical symbols of these beliefs were brought over from Scotland as part of their "cultural baggage" when the clans migrated to the United States. From the Calvinist doctrine of "double predestination," meaning that both reprobation (not among the elect or saved) and election (chosen by God for salvation) were within the active will of God, came the Calvinists' earthly sense of uneasiness about one's own election, and they were constantly looking for outward signs of it. Placing these symbols on their gravemarkers were one manifestation of this search for reassurance of heavenly reward. Moreover, for these Scottish clans, the extravagant and highly visible expenditures of monies for large family monuments would signal not only how God had rewarded their earthly endeavors but permanently tell the Cincinnati community by such outward signs of their economic achievements within America.

A second, and perhaps even more compelling motivational force for these traditions is reflected in the elements of strong Scottish nationalism which have been carved into the massive red and grey tombstones of these extended Traveller families found in Spring Grove Cemetery. Scotland was an independent nation from the eleventh century until brought into the United Kingdom in 1717 and was ethnically and geographically composed of numerous divisions ever since ancient Scots moved from Ireland into the Northern portion of the British isles. Though decimated by wars with England and by migration outward to Northern Ireland (the Scotch-Irish) and more recently to the New World and other British colonial outposts, the Scottish—at home and abroad—have maintained a deep love for their native land and customs. In folklore, what St. Patrick and the shamrock have meant to Irish Catholics around the world has been paralleled by the lore of St. Andrew as patron saint of Scotland and by the symbol of the Scottish thistle for its dispersed emigrants everywhere.

As its national flower, the Scottish thistle (a weedy species of *Cirsium* of the plant genera of the family *Asteraceae*) was a prickly-leafed durable plant which had dense heads of small pink or purple flowers on ruddy stalks that grew three to six feet tall and could spread rapidly across pasturelands. In the New World, where dispersed Scotsmen founded New Caladonias (Caladonia was the original name of Scotland), often in mountainous and hilly locales reminiscent of the native highlands, these thistles soon became a part of the natural—and symbolic—landscape. The fierce desire to cling to Caladonian symbols in order to sustain the honor and tradition of the homeland within the hodge-podge of ethnic immigrants in America extended far beyond conventional national garb of tartan plaids or musical instruments such as the Scottish bagpipe, and it was this same impetus which impelled these Scottish Travellers to proclaim their love of old Caladonia by carving Scottish thistles upon their various clans' monuments and gravemarkers (Fig. 5:7).

In a similar vein, this heightened sense of nationalism also caused them to import and erect large monuments of Scottish red granite for most of their family lots. Geographical descriptions of Scotland all detail the deep glens and valleys between mountains and lochs wherein vast granite mountains protrude. Stonequarrying gave employment to thousands, and stonemasons were in abundance. In America, it is evident that the Scottish Travellers deliberately selected native red granite for their monuments out of pride and nostalgia for their ancestral rock-ribbed homeland, and by so doing they colorfully tied together their kinfolk and family burial lots within a strange new land. It is interesting as well to note that the lots which the clans purchased within Spring Grove were virtually all located among the higher hilltops of the wooded sections, seemingly yet another effort to provide for the deceased a final resting place in resonance with the geography of the ancestral homeland.

A final factor which underlies these funerary practices—and one which is common not only to the Scottish Travellers but to all the Gypsy groups—is potentially the most important of all, and this involves the rich collage of Gypsy ethnic and folkloristic elements which permeate the clans' gravestones and funeral rites. And yet, it is precisely this area where great caution must be exercised in interpreting what is outwardly observable but not easily understood. Contemporary historians and interpreters of cemeteries, taking a theme from modern students of architecture, are prone to dwell—and quite legitimately so—upon the concepts of space and the environment in relation to the multitude of motives and motifs related to cemetery design and to burial practices. As all historians writing so-called "intellectual history," we who try to draw new conclusions about ethnic and nationalistic dimensions of gravemarkers must walk softly, for we are surely on grounds "where angels fear to tread" (even though stone images of them abound there). To state categorically why Gypsies, from whatever clan, tribe, or national origin, observe and make such extraordinary efforts in relation to the funeral and burial customs of their families is a very difficult, and potentially dangerous, task. For one thing, Gypsies are prone not to tell *gaeje* (non-Gypsies) anything about their own folkways, and, as some have concluded, it might be misinformation if any were given by them. Furthermore, cemetery administrators have learned to be quiet about the very existence, not to speak of the number and location, of Gypsy gravesites in order both to protect their rights of privacy and to avoid anything which might jeopardize their continued patronage of that particular cemetery. Finally, until more recent times American Gypsies seldom attended school and few learned to write: hence very little in written form has been left by members of the clans themselves.

Given these limitations, there are at least two ethnically based considerations peculiar to Gypsy worldview which seem quite evidently at work in influencing their burial practices. One stems from a trait common to all

Gypsy lifestyles: Gypsies intentionally distance themselves from the rest of the population and live, outside of their necessary contacts brought on by trading, selling, reading fortunes, and part time labor, largely unto themselves. The clan and family comprise their world: to them, all other ways appear less worthwhile. Many still declare with conviction that travelling the roads is in their blood. Furthermore, possession of material property, perhaps long impossible for poorer clans, never stood as a major goal for traditional Gypsy groups, in contrast to the capitalistic dreams of most Americans. While bank checking accounts and even credit cards are being used by ever-increasing numbers of contemporary Scottish Travellers (a fact documented by funeral directors who assist in arranging their funeral services), most of traditional Gypsy business has been conducted with solid cash. While living in tents along the road or in small trailers has in recent times given way to stopping in motels or renting empty storefront buildings for longer stays, the essentially mobile lifestyle of Gypsies remains an important element in their character and serves to keep them apart from the mainstream of American life. Intermarriage amongst Gypsy families further preserves this separateness, and the avoidance of permanent employment by any one plant or company eliminates being tied down with ordinary American workers. The commandment of brotherhood amongst Gypsies remains largely to brethren related by blood, and it is this sense of distinctiveness, of separateness, which translates itself in numerous subtle ways to cemetery and other funerary practices of Scottish Traveller and other American Gypsy groups.

A second ethnic factor—at least within the Scottish and Irish clan traditions—seems to be a potent motivating force behind funerary practices, and that is the intense sense of competition in demonstrating, often quite ostentatiously, an aura of success while venerating the passing of a family member, particularly a beloved father figure. Each large family in the more numerous clans, such as the Irish Gorman or Hamilton clans or the Williamson, Stewart, or Gregg families of Scottish travellers, looks to a single leader as a sort of "Godfather" who settles disputes, bails out the arrested, doles out money to relatives in need, arranges territories for those wandering the countryside and calls the clan to attend all funerals. Financial dues are given to him during his years as leader. Upon his death, and annually thereafter, great reverence is shown by the family around his gravestone on Easter or Memorial Day, and it is on these occasions—as well as upon the erecting of the original monument—that the non-hostile but costly demonstrations of economic clout are flaunted before the other families. This trait is particularly apparent in Cincinnati cemeteries, and while the historical and psychological explanations for its perpetuation remain to be fully explained, its continuing physical manifestations are one of the most identifiable elements of Gypsy deathways.

For more than a century the Springtime funeral customs and burial rites as well as the special gravemarkers of the Scottish Travelling people, and of their cousins, the Irish Tinkers, have added a colorful dimension to the Cumminsville/Northside section of Cincinnati. The poorer Roms, with their wonderful music and blazing campfires, now leave fewer impressions and gravestones in the Queen City than in years past, though they still spark bright recollections of their annual appearance at the bend of the Mill Creek. They Gypsy folklore of these three wandering groups has richly contributed to the impressive and diverse European culture in Cincinnati and throughout the American Midwest. When the clans annually arrive in Cincinnati to decorate their family gravesites, they are honoring the permanent resting places of family members at the end of the long road. Long known as readers of others' fortunes, their gravestones tell eloquently of their own.

Notes

I owe a vast amount of appreciation to the entire staff of the Charles A. Miller Sons Funeral Home and to its president, Will Book. They have toured the cemeteries with me, allowed me to participate in the services of Scottish Travelling clans, and generously provided detailed information for the writing of my various papers on Gypsies in America. Also, a word of deep thanks must be extended to the leaders of the Gypsy Lore Society of North America, who invited me to read my first Gypsy paper at the Eighth Annual Meeting and Conference on Gypsy Studies, held in New York City in 1986. And to the editor of this volume, Professor Richard E. Meyer, who has graciously invited me to present papers in his sections of the American Culture Association Annual Meetings in Montreal (1987), New Orleans (1988), St. Louis (1989), and Toronto (1990), and who has offered so many scholarly editorial suggestions for all my papers, I extend as well my sincere thanks. All photographs in this essay, unless otherwise indicated, are by Paul F. Erwin.

[1]This essay concentrates largely on the American funeral customs and burials of families of people who call themselves (Scottish) Travellers and (Irish) Travellers. Cincinnatians commonly refer to these folk as Gypsies and confuse them with the Rom families from southern European background who also have passed through this city and camped on its outskirts for a century or more. Published literature on American Gypsies, beyond the standard encyclopedia articles, which describe the southern European Rom Gypsies largely, remains extremely limited. The old and new *Journals of the Gypsy Lore Society* in England and the publications of the Society's North American chapter have been the major source of studies about Gypsies worldwide. However, very little has been published about the British-descent Irish or Scottish Travelling People in the American Midwest. The most helpful introduction to the literature on American Gypsies is the bibliography in Rena C. Gropper, *Gypsies in the City* (Princeton, NJ: Darwin P, 1975), pp. 215-227. Quite enlightening and seldom quoted is H.L. Mencken, *The American Language: An Inquiry into the Development of English in the United States*, 4th ed. (New York: Alfred A. Knopf, 1963), which has a section entitled "Cant and Argot" (pp. 709-714) that presents the English origins of and scholarship about beggars, vagabonds, and Gypsies. For my introductory essay on Scottish Travellers see "Scottish Gypsies and their Burial Customs: Facts and Folklore," *Urban Resources* 4:3 (1987), pp. C1-C4. A number of articles, quite derogatory and repetitive, based upon material released by Better Business Bureaus, have appeared in popular national periodicals about some of the families of Scottish Travelling people, particularly the Williamsons, whose families

are buried in Cincinnati cemeteries. For examples see: "Family Pride," *Newsweek* (16 July 1956), p. 26; John Kobler, "The Terrible Williamsons," *Saturday Evening Post* (27 October 1956), pp. 25; 62 (later condensed in *Reader's Digest* issue of January 1957); Fred Dickenson, "Beware the Terrible Williamsons," *Reader's Digest* (September 1966), pp. 175-179; Jay Robert Nash, "Tidal Wave Con Clan," in his *Hustlers and Con Men* (New York: M. Evans and Co., 1976), pp. 225-227; Ford N. Burkart, "The Terrible Williamsons," *Free Enterprise* (February 1978), pp. 23-24.

[2]Prior to World War I, virtually all poor Travelling People depended upon horses, mules or donkeys to pull their wagons, and all Gypsies became famous for horse trading and metal work. Because the extreme poverty of rural Ireland limited the income possible from metal working, Tinkers also performed seasonal farm labor, while women told fortunes and begged to support their families.

[3](Prospect Heights, Illinois: Waveland P, 1985), pp. 14-15. This work contains a highly useful 13-page bibliography of books and articles on the Irish Travellers. The pioneering bibliography about Irish Gypsies remains that by George and Sharon Bohn Gmelch, "Ireland's Travelling People," *Journal of the Gypsy Lore Society*, 4th Series, 1:3 (1977), pp.159-169. See also Sharon Bohn Gmelch, *Tinkers and Travellers* (Dublin: The O'Brien P, 1975); and Farnham Rehfisch, ed., *Gypsies, Tinkers and Other Travellers* (London: Academic P, 1975).

[4]"Gypsies: Their Origins and Diaspora," in *The World and I* (Washington, D.C.: *The Washington Times* Corporation, 1989), p. 613. Hancock's articles draw upon material from his book, *The Pariah Syndrome: An Account of Gypsy Slavery and Persecution* (Ann Arbor, Michigan: Karoma Publishers, 1987).

[5]*Ibid.*

[6]Spring Grove Cemetery has been the subject of considerable interest almost since its inception. Two nineteenth century works which still merit attention are Officers of the Corporation of Spring Grove, *The Cincinnati Cemetery of Spring Grove* (Cincinnati: Bradley & Webb, Printers, 1862); and (Adolph Strauch), *Spring Grove Cemetery: Its History and Improvements with Observations on the Ancient and Modern Places of Sepulture* (Cincinnati: Robert Clarke, 1869). In more recent times there has been an outpouring of shorter scholarly articles on many aspects of this spectacularly landscaped cemetery, but still lacking is a truly comprehensive study along the lines of Blanche Linden-Ward's *Silent City on a Hill: Landscapes of Memory and Boston's Mount Auburn Cemetery* (Columbus, Ohio: Ohio State UP, 1989). Nonetheless, the following sources are highly recommended: Blanche Linden-Ward and David C. Sloane, "Spring Grove: The Founding of Cincinnati's Rural Cemetery, 1845-1855," *Queen City Heritage* 43:1 (1985), pp. 17-32; Blanche Linden-Ward, "Putting the Past Under Grass: History as Death and Cemetery Commemoration," *Prospects: An Annual of American Cultural Studies* 10 (1985), pp. 279-314; Blanche Linden-Ward, "Nature by Design: The Art and Landscape of Cincinnati's Spring Grove" [Documentary Video] (Cincinnati: Center for Neighborhood and Community Studies, 1987); Blanche Linden-Ward, "Strange But Genteel Pleasure Grounds: Tourist and Leisure Uses of Nineteenth Century Rural Cemeteries," in *Cemeteries and Gravemarkers: Voices of American Culture*, ed. Richard E. Meyer (Ann Arbor, Michigan: UMI Research P, 1989; rpt. Logon, UT: Utah State UP, 1992), pp. 293-328; David C. Sloane, *The Last Great Necessity: Cemeteries in American History* (Baltimore: The Johns Hopkins UP, 1991).

[7]*A Visitor's Guide to the Beauty and History of Spring Grove* (Cincinnati: Spring Grove Cemetery and Arboretum, 1990).

[8]Strauch and his contributions to Spring Grove and the American rural cemetery movement have been well documented, most recently by David C. Sloane, *The Last Great Necessity, passim*.

[9]Information from current brochure published by New St. Joseph Cemetery. Old St. Joseph's Cemetery, on West Eighth Street and Enright Avenue, remains about halfway between the new one and downtown Cincinnati and occupies about 100 acres. No Gypsies were buried there.

[10]Interview with Wilber Book, president of the historic Charles A. Miller Sons Funeral Home, in Northside, Cincinnati, March 15, 1983. Under Book's leadership, Charles A. Miller Sons, Inc. has purchased and remodeled the Busse & Borgmann Funeral Home on Central Parkway, which was founded in 1895 by Edward J. Busse. Book joined the Miller firm in 1957 when it was still owned and operated by Charles A. Miller and Nelson (Pete) Miller, grandsons of the firm's founder.

[11]*William's Cincinnati Directory*, editions of 1873 and 1874, list the Charles A. Miller Livery Stable on Railroad Street, Cumminsville. The 1874 and 1875 volumes cite Miller as an undertaker also. Sergeant Miller had enlisted at the age of 19 in the Fifth Ohio Volunteer Cavalry in 1861. He was wounded at Shiloh and returned home, only to re-enter the Civil War in Company I of the Thirty-Third Regiment, Ohio Volunteer Infantry, which fought across North Carolina in a series of battles just prior to General Robert E. Lee's surrender. Miller returned home after being mustered out in October, 1865.

[12]Interview with Nelson (Pete) Miller, Cincinnati, Ohio, April 26,1983.

[13]Interview with staff members of the New St. Joseph Cemetery, March 30, 1989. The Irish Travellers' burial lots are scattered widely about the cemetery grounds, but most of the Gorman and Hamilton family lots are located near the north gate on Rapid Run Pike in Sections 10 and 17. While the cemetery managers now want to remove them, many of the Irish Travellers' gravemarkers are bordered closely by a pair of cedar trees, some of which are tall and scraggly. Whether these were planted as small shrubs to serve as symbolic urns cannot be determined, but they are not found around many of the Roman Catholic gravemarkers of non-Traveller families. While taking photographs in another section, I once watched a woman drive up before one of the Gorman lots below me, get out of her Cadillac, and tie a dozen artificial red roses into the branches of the twin cedar trees that stood about 15 feet high on each side of the family marker.

[14]The connection of the American Travellers of Scottish descent with Masonic orders has yet to be adequately determined. Many of the men of the Hoffner Street First United Church of Christ in Cincinnati are members of the Masonic orders, and on a night in which I presented a slide show of these red Scottish Gypsy gravemarkers, many of which have a carved Masonic symbol upon the face of the marker and above the name of the family, these men confessed they could not explain how such clans could claim membership in American lodges or orders. One suggested that ancestral natives in Scotland might have belonged to local unit there, and the clans migrating to America might have continued to use the symbols or even organized their own renegade body and included the male members of their families in it. The freemason's symbol of the compass and square intertwined about the letter G (i.e., God) frequently appears on

gravestones of the Williamson, Stewart, E.W. Wilson, Johnston, and McMillan clans. Some Williamson and Gregg stones have the symbol of the curved short sword through a crescent above the family name (See Fig. 5:7, 5:8). Just how the Scottish Rite order and these Scottish Travelling families are connected historically needs further explanation and study.

[15]Information supplied by contemporary Philadelphia area stonecarver and monument dealer Harvard C. Wood III at Annual Meeting of the Cemeteries and Gravemarkers section of the American Culture Association, Montreal, Canada, March, 1987.

[16]In recent years, Travellers—both Scottish and Irish—have begun to embalm their dead and fly with them to Cincinnati for funeral services and burials as soon as the families can gather for their relatives' funerals. But, while air travel has outmoded the old practices of after-Easter week wakes, the traditions associated with Memorial Day carry on.

[17]Interview with Gary Liles, funeral director, Charles A. Miller Sons Funeral Home, Feb. 15, 1990.

[18]In the normal course of observing and analyzing traditional customs, the fieldworker might be expected to pose questions such as these directly to those performing the rituals. Gypsies present a somewhat difficult problem here: their intense desire for privacy has led this researcher at least to respect that desire. Thus, a number of the questions raised by my observations remain unanswered other than by speculation.

[19]From an interview with Ellen Sewell of Cincinnati, Sept. 14, 1987. Her father was a stonecutter for a monument firm near Spring Grove Cemetery all of his life.

American Jewish Cemeteries: A Mirror of History

Roberta Halporn

Only Yesterday We Drained the Cup of Sorrow[1]

There is an old Jewish saying that if you bring two Jews together, you get an argument. Bring three Jews together and you end up with three newspapers. The implications of this morsel of comic self-analysis frame the difficulties in trying to explain Jewish memorial customs and cemeteries.

It implies that Jews are very stubborn, believe the pen is mighter than the sword, and disagree with each other about almost everything except monotheism. While these traits account for the survival of this people when all of its ancient enemies have perished, it also accounts for continual group infighting, reflected in every part of the Jew's life cycle.

One must also be cognizant of the fact that Jewish thought has, since biblical times, diverged on two basic paths—Orthodox (or what we might call "strict constructionists"), and adaptive Jews who believe in assimilation with their host culture and the times in which they live.

It is thus impossible to interpret an American Jewish cemetery without some awareness of 5,000 years of world history. After all, the last time the Jews could be identified as a national group was in 72 C.E., the year the classical Romans destroyed the Second Temple, drove the Jews from their original home, and carted them off to slave camps in Spain. The creation of the modern state of Israel does not modify this fact; it only makes for more difficulty in defining the answer to the age-old question, what is a Jew?

From that fateful moment in the first century, the Jews fled from country to country, and culture to culture, always seeking an unattainable sanctuary from persecution. As Arthur Koestler has noted: "The dreary tale always starts with a honeymoon and ends in divorce and bloodshed. In the beginning, Jews are welcome because they alone have the secret of how to keep the economy turning...But with the growth of a native mercantile class, they become gradually excluded."[2]

As soon as they settled in one place, another state-sanctioned wave of terror was unleashed and they had to flee again, often salvaging only those possessions they could carry on their backs, and significantly, in their heads. On these travels, they picked up local customs like barnacles, influencing their cuisine, their clothing styles, and of course, their memorial customs.

Most American Jews come from three very different European groups, in three distinct time periods, each putting its own individual stamp on its cemeteries. So to this day, one cannot interpret a Jewish burial ground without knowing 1) when its founders arrived here, 2) from what country they came, and further, 3) whether they were Orthodox or adaptive.

In the beginning, following *Genesis* 3:19—"Dust thou art and to dust returneth"—the Jews interred their dead in family caves, in niches cut out of the rock. Unlike the Egyptians, they did not believe in embalming. Unlike their Greek and Roman neighbors, they did not believe in cremation. They interpreted the Biblical injunction as a requirement to allow natural disintegration, a return to the earth from which we came. The first recorded evidence of this custom is found in *Genesis* 23, which recounts Abraham's purchase of the Cave of Machpelah for his wife, Sarah. Contemporary archaeologists even think they have determined where it is.[3]

Jews retained this custom for many centuries. The Gospels (*Matthew* 27:59, *Mark* 15:46 and *Acts* 5:6) indicate that this custom was still being followed at the time of Christ. The cave was sealed with a massive rock, called a "golel," which could be rolled away when the cave was needed again. Many Christian readers of the Bible do not realize that it is this "golel" that is referred to as part of the evidence of the resurrection.

Time and dispersion gradually erased the memory of cave burial, so that by the twelfth century we find Jews being interred in the earth in community graveyards. Because the talmudic ordinance was not linguistically precise, the noun "golel" (when the *stone* is set in place), signifying the beginning of the mourning period, was interpreted by the medieval rabbis as the moment when the last bit of earth was dropped onto the grave.

The Sephardim—The Spanish/Portugese Jews

Prior to 1492, the Jews participated openly in Spain's Golden Era. Prominent philosophers, doctors of medicine, counselors to Kings, they were part and parcel of the country's richest period of history. But a proselytizing Christian mania would sweep Spain, leading to the dictatorial power of the Inquisition. At first only aiming its efforts at witches and infidels, it soon extended its reach to any non-Catholic group.

By the year Columbus discovered America, there were only two ways Jews could avoid being burned at the stake. Either they became "New Christians," or Marranos, practicing their true faith in secret, or they had to leave the country. Many of those who could get away were welcomed in the Netherlands. Gradually the Jewish community there developed into a multi-lingual group—speaking and writing both Dutch and Spanish or Portugese in their daily lives, and Hebrew for worship. They melded their Iberian customs with those of their Protestant neighbors, but did not lose all of them.

The Dutch East Indies Company had staked out a large portion of Brazil and offered the Dutch Jews the opportunity to handle their commercial interests there because they could understand both modern languages in which business was conducted. This time leaving voluntarily, they settled in Brazil, representing what they now considered their homeland, or Holland. They spread out over the Caribbean on islands such as Nevis and Curaçao, openly resuming their ancient faith.

This "honeymoon" lasted only 30 years, until their enemy returned in the train of the Portuguese capture of Brazil accompanied by their fanatical priests. The first mission of these standard bearers of Catholicism was to cleanse the area of "heathen" belief. The Jews were given three months to sell all they owned and leave or again submit to the Inquisition. This historical imperative was responsible for the entry of the first Jews into *Nieuw Amsterdam*, or what would become America. There were more Jews in Brazil than space in the Dutch flotilla sent to pick them up, so Portuguese ships were made available for the rest. Most reached Holland, but one vessel, the Ste. Catherine, was lost or captured by Spanish pirates, which then deposited its passengers in New York, in 1654.

The best preserved colonial Jewish cemetery in the Americas may be found in Curaçao, a Dutch island floating off the coast of Venezuela. Somewhat unique among cities, the capitol actually lists its ancient Jewish graveyard as one of its premier tourist attractions. Even after the intervening centuries, members of the synagogue here display their Castilian genetic heritage, with olive skin, dark hair and eyes, as well as their startling linguistic abilities. They still speak Spanish and Dutch, and to this has been added perfectly idiomatic English and a local language called *Papiamento*, in addition to the Hebrew in which their services are conducted.

The graveyard itself, founded in 1659, is located on an arid, windy plain, still redolent of the Shell Oil Refineries nearby which used to contribute a substantial amount to the island's income. All the stones are elevated horizontally on above-ground tombs because of the high water table. They are cut from the same local rock used to construct most of the public buildings—an ugly, concrete gray, but shot through with tiny sea shells and marine fossils. For some reason, the local historians insist the markers were carved in Holland and shipped back, but to this writer it seems unreasonably costly to transport such an inferior grade of material *both* ways for such a purpose.

The design motifs on these markers are often so Christian that the Jewish viewer is almost astonished to find Hebrew epitaphs. To be sure, many stones display common Jewish motifs, such as the crown of learning, and broken flowers. But the death's head, so dear to Puritan and Spanish Catholic eyes, appears with astonishing frequency as an artistic element (Fig. 6:1). Violating the prohibition against "graven images," or representations of people, we find scenes from the deceased's life, such as one striking monument to a sea captain (Fig. 6:2). All contain the Portuguese blessing, *Sua alma goze de gloria* (May his soul enjoy the glory).

In contrast to the florid work found in Curaçao, the extant Sephardic cemeteries in the United States are models of restraint. Because the original group settled in New Amsterdam (over Peter Stuyvesant's vigorous protest), three of the oldest are located in Manhattan. A fourth can be found in Newport,

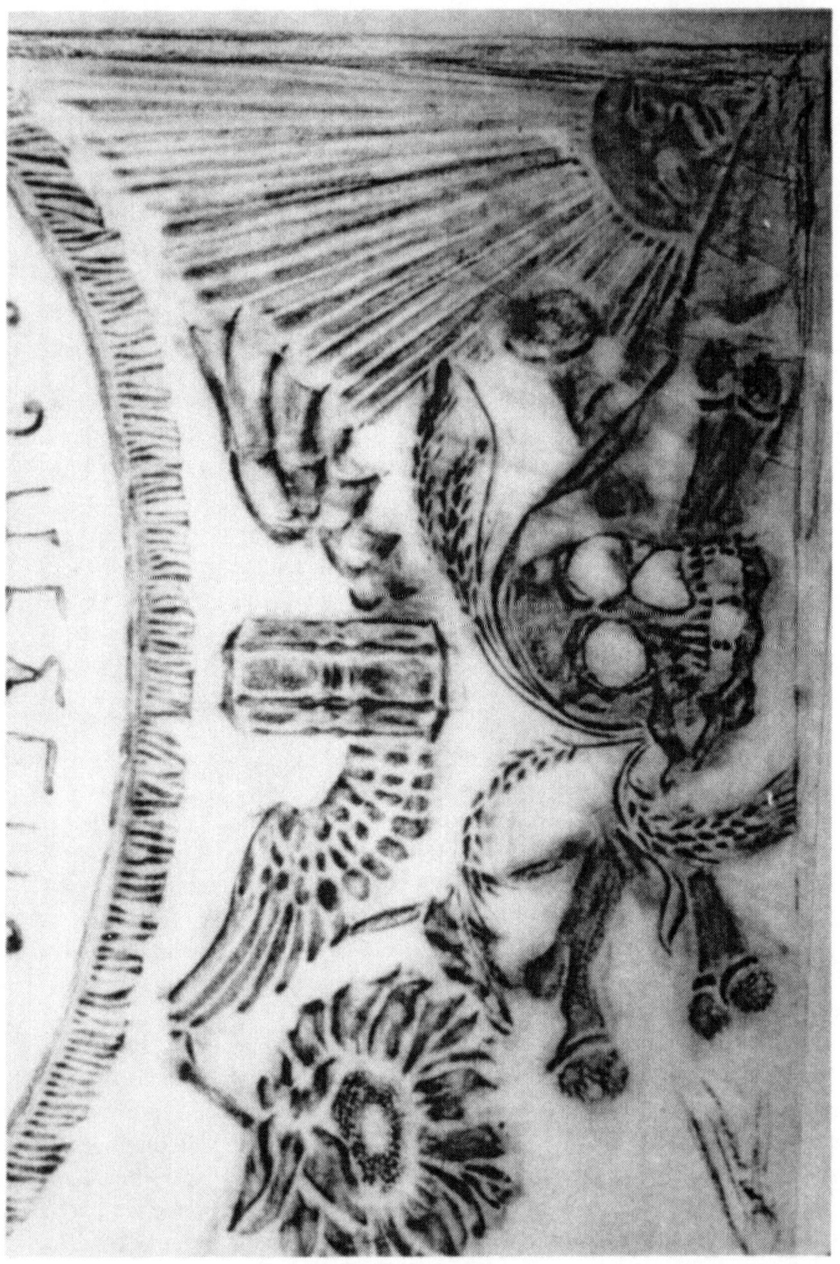

Fig. 6:1. Rubbing of the sepulchre of Mordecai Hisquiau Naimas de Crasto, died 5750 (1715), with skull and winged hour glass motifs. The Jews Graveyards, Curaçao, N.W.I.

Fig. 6:2. Rubbing of "The sepulchre of the... Abraham, son of Daniel Moreno Henriques who died on the 16th of Adar... the year of 5480[6?]. May his soul enjoy the glory." Note depiction of ship. The Jews Graveyard, Curaçao, N.W.I.

Rhode Island near the most venerable existing synagogue, Touro. Two more remnants of this early community lie in Philadelphia, their markers so eroded they are unreadable, and in South Carolina.

Newport's cemetery, established in 1677, is the oldest extant, since the original "hook of land"[4] granted to the first congregation in New York has disappeared, a victim of landfill. By another quirk of discrimination, Newport's Touro synagogue and cemetery is owned by the congregation in New York.

What is now called New York's Shearith Israel I, founded in 1682, is located at what was once a good distance away from the Dutch town at the base of Manhattan. Presently it is surrounded by Chinese restaurants and an Italian funeral home on Chatham Square. Raised high above the street, the stones are nevertheless visible through the spiked fence which surmounts the wall. A group of its original markers was moved in 1859 and 1860 to Shearith Israel III, a cemetery on 21st Street established in the nineteenth century. Neglected for many years, restoration funds have only recently become available and may help to preserve this historic cemetery for some time.

The Shearith Israel markers are of two basic types: rectangular above-ground tombs at least seven feet in length and built up with red brick sidewalls and horizontal tops in imitation of those in the Caribbean islands, and vertical tombstones. Most are sedate rectangles, containing little more than the name of the deceased, a descriptive legend in English or Spanish and in Hebrew or archaic Ladino (which uses Hebrew letters), plus, of course, the birth and death dates. On almost every stone appear the mysterious initials *SBADG*, inexplicable without reference to the full sentence (see above) cut into the stones in the Caribbean. The layout of the lettering often constitutes the only design element, as illustrated by the stone of Sarah Rodriguez de Rivera (Fig. 6:3). The simplicity of the New York stones is even more remarkable because there was constant travel between the two Jewish communities, and the Americans must surely have known what the southern markers looked like.[5]

Language obviously presented difficulties as well. As David De Sola Pool has pointed out:

> We know that often and perhaps usually the mason was a Gentile, assumedly unfamiliar with the Hebrew or Iberian language he was copying....Whoever seems to have been the stonecutter in 1740 (and one hand seems to be responsible for all the lapidary lettering from that period), he has left abundant...evidence of his fallibility....The same mason carefully copied his mistakes from one stone to another—with impossible Hebrew forms and meaningless misspellings in the Spanish epitaph[s].[6]

This same problem occurs in Newport. Though located in the home base of some of the master gravestone carvers of colonial America, the Touro cemetery exhibits a mixture of styles—stern, undecorated pieces such as the marker of the Rev. Moses Seixas, and standard designs such as that for Rebecca Polock, an unsigned stone which appears to be the work of John Stevens II (Fig. 6:4). One does not need a knowledge of the language to be aware of this carver's clumsiness with the Hebrew letters he cut by rote, as contrasted to his normally

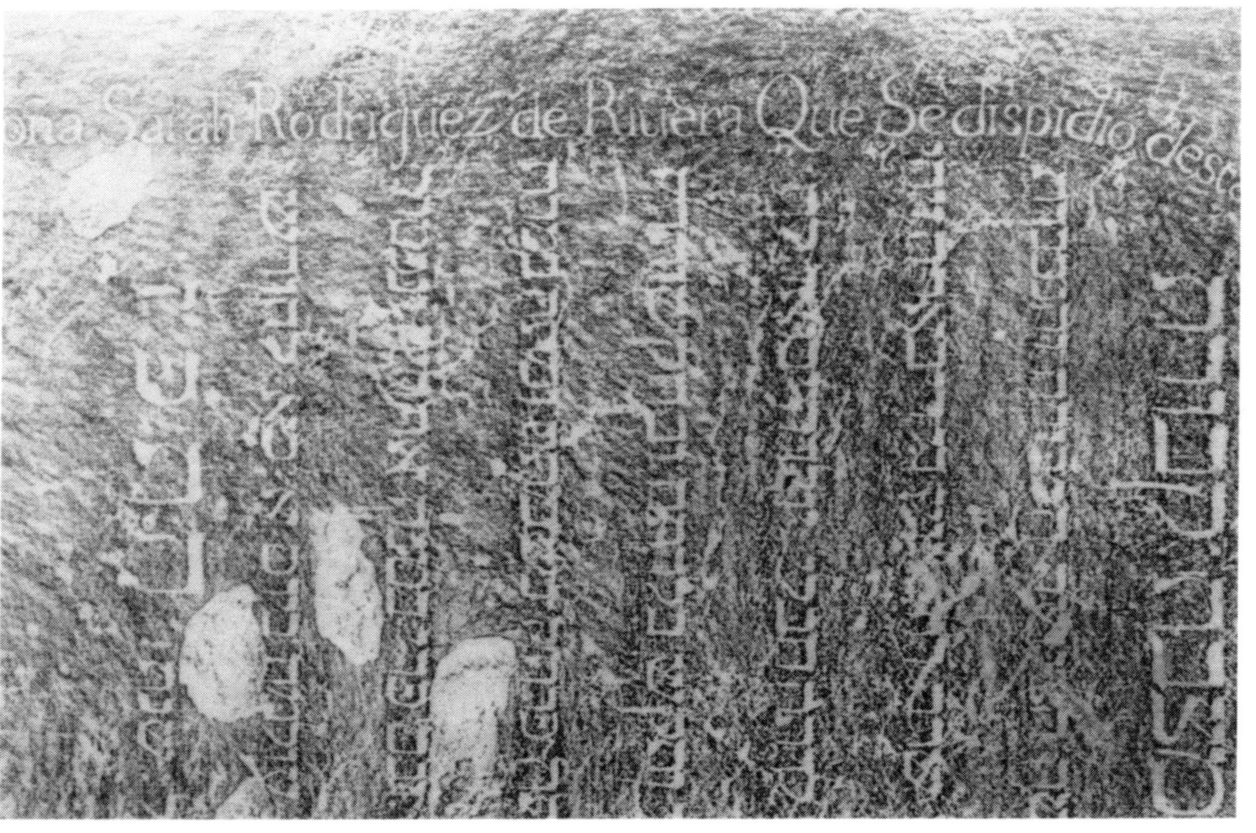

Fig. 6:3. Rubbing of gravestone or tomb cover of Sarah Rodriguez de Rivera. Shearith Israel III, New York City.

Fig. 6:4. Rubbing of gravestone of Rebecca Polok, died 1764, with awkward carving of Hebrew lettering. Touro Cemetery, Newport, Rhode Island. (*Rubbing by Jerry Trauber*).

graceful English inscriptions.

One very handsome sculpture does stand in Chatham Square's Shearith Israel I: the grave of Walter Judah, a young medical student at Kings College (now Columbia University) who died "in that dreadful contagion" that visited New York, probably yellow fever (Fig. 6:5). In the well-sculpted oval, one can see the hands of heavenly angels chopping down the Tree of Life (*Etz Chaim*), and in the center, a panorama of old New York—the East River, breasted by the charming Dutch houses (the architectural style of these early structures can still be viewed today in Curaçao), and sailing vessels of the period.

As of the time of the first census in 1790, the entire Jewish population of North America amounted to little more than 1,500 to 2,000 souls. Yet even as tiny a group as this was perceived as an important and integral part of the republic. All colonists were steeped in the Bible and perceived their few Jewish compatriots as bearers of a rich moral and ethical heritage that formed the values of the new nation. For the Jews, "long an object of persecution, this new government had special promise."[7] Freely allowed to follow any trade for the

Fig. 6:5. Rubbing of richly illustrated tomb cover for Walter Judah, died 1798. Shearith Israel I, Chatham Square, New York City.

first time in 700 years, they assimilated easily, becoming successful and civic-minded merchants and professionals.

They had not, however, completely left all prejudice behind. In the activities of daily life, black and oriental targets of discrimination can easily be located since their race is visible to the eye. By conforming to local dress customs, the Jew, on the other hand, blends into the dominant culture without difficulty. But in the cemetery, the situation is, in effect, reversed. By the time of the emancipation of the slaves, when cemetery markers for blacks had become widespread, you generally could not tell their graves from any other Christian's. But the minute the Jew was buried, the Hebrew lettering on the neighboring tombstones immediately gave his status away, and cemeteries were considered fair game for hoodlums. The following sorry notice appeared in the Pennsylvania *Gazette* in 1751:

> Whereas, many unthinking people have been in the habit of...firing several shots against the fence of the Jews' burying ground, which not only destroyed said fence, but also a tombstone; there being a brick wall now erected, I must desire the sportsmen to forbear...firing against said wall. Nathan Levy, President of the Congregation.[8]

The story was repeated in New York and New Jersey. In 1751, the New York congregation advertised in the New York *Gazette*:

> Whereas several evil minded People have at Sundry Times broken down the wall of the Jewish burying Ground, and very much damaged the Tomb Stones belonging thereto; the Elders of the congregation...do humbly desire and request all Peoples to desist from committing such violent outrages for the future...[9]

The German Jews

Despite the outbreaks of vandalism directed against Jewish cemeteries, the fact remains that in the Republic, unlike any other country in which the Jews had sojourned, such actions were condoned neither by the law or the local authorities. News of the potential liberties that were to be found spread throughout the Jewish communities of Europe. Nowhere did it have a greater impact than in Germany. Worsening prejudice and economic conditions in that country were responsible for the voluntary migrations that followed. In the twenty years from 1839 to 1850, the Jewish population in America increased from 2,000 to 150,000, almost all from German-speaking nations. And instead of continuing to concentrate almost solely on the East Coast, they settled throughout the Midwest and South as well. By 1870, there were 80,000 Jews in New York City alone.[10]

Most of these immigrants arrived penniless but in possession of the skills necessary to flourish in a mercantile economy. They needed unskilled jobs until they could learn English, so many started by peddling on foot. At first carrying small items the rural housewife could not easily purchase, they built up their businesses, penny by penny, into some of the most successful department stores in the country. Many saw the wisdom of investing excess capital and developed brokerage houses that still influence Wall Street. Other investment money was sunk into the newspaper industry, producing, among others, the *New York Times*. And by patiently depriving themselves, they earned the funds to bring one relative after another over to the "Golden Land."

The German Jews quickly learned to dress, speak, and act like the successful Christian models around them, copying their mansions, their opera endowments, and favorite charities. Though they did not discard their ancient faith, religious practice was severely curtailed to the highest holy days. Others, such as the fabulous millionaire, Auguste Belmont, changed both their names and the church to which they paid lip service. Though the first arrivals joined the Spanish synagogues already in existence, within 30 years religious houses were built whose rites more nearly conformed to Jewish practice in their homeland.

It is no wonder that their gravemarkers and cemeteries became almost indistinguishable from their Christian neighbors. Imitating the "classical" style that replaced the wonderfully handwrought colonial markers, both in Germany and in the United States, they commissioned Victorian urns, Greek columns and Roman catafalques to create pagan-inspired marble wonderlands (Fig. 6:6), incongruously lettered in their own biblical tongue, as well as English and German. Since Judaism has rarely placed much emphasis on the hereafter, this touching sentiment found on the marker of young Cora Meyers in the Atlanta (Georgia) cemetery personifies the agnostic sentiment of the successful and adaptive German-Americans:

> If there's another world she lives in bliss
> If there is none, she made the best of this.

The Rest of Us—The "Russian" Jews

The majority of Jews in the United States today are descendants of those who arrived here from countries dominated by Russia—the so-called "Russian" Jews. This actually means that they originated in countries as varied as Poland, Yugoslavia, Czechoslovakia, Ukraine, Bohemia, Bulgaria, Armenia, Roumania and Turkey, as well as Russia itself.

Having been constantly pressured tighter and tighter into ghettos, isolated from their Christian peers, their Jewish culture was pervasive. They spoke a common language—Yiddish (a mixture of Hebrew, German and the language of their host country). The dominant flavor of their faith was Chasidic—a form of Orthodoxy which fixed their religious practice in the eighteenth century, but gave them the strength to survive heartbreaking poverty and state-sanctioned violence.

Starting in 1871, possibly inspired by an effort to distract the Christian peasants from their own privation in a corrupt monarchy, tacit approval was given to use the Jews as scapegoats, spearheaded by the Czar's own Cossaks. From isolated incidents, the pogroms increasingly expanded—villages burnt to the ground, synagogues destroyed, random murder encouraged. Another reason for the persecution was the desperate attempts of Jewish workers to organize

Fig. 6:6. Classical column style monument for Admiral levy. Shearith Israel IV, Cypress Hill, New York.

labor strikes against the 18-hour work day through their *Algemainer Iddisher Arbeiter Bund*. The assassination of Czar Alexander II (the "good" Czar), however, erased all hope for relief from these conditions. As poor as they already were, the Jews realized that escape from the continent was their only hope of life.

At that time America was seeking workers to support its unprecedented economic growth, and American capitalists "invited workers to man the mines, build the railroads, fill the assembly lines, and make clothing for and distribute food to the rapidly growing worker class....The American Jewish community multiplied more than five hundred fold—to more than a million."[11]

"The new arrivals," as Stephen Birmingham points out, "were ragged, dirt poor, culturally energetic, toughened by years of torment, idealistic, and socialistic."[12] The previously established—and largely acculturated—German Jews were often horrified by what they perceived as the vulgarity of this new crowd, not to say nervous about their own hard-won security.

For their part, the "Russian" Jews seem to have despised their German patrons equally, largely for their sins of what the Yiddish Jews considered apostasy. But in spite of the German and Spanish rejections of orthodox practice, the deeply ingrained feeling for family remained. Influential educators and philanthropists banded together to aid their Yiddish cousins' assimilation by establishing settlement houses, health clinics, and night classes for adult learners. Their sympathy is fully expressed on the bronze plaque at the gravesite of Sephardic Jew, Emma Lazarus, also engraved on the Statue of Liberty (see Fig. 6:7).

Another great adult university was the Yiddish theatre. It interpreted the new world in the language of the old, reinforced lessons that the children brought home to the cold water flats from their American classrooms, and acted as an escape valve from the stress of the work week (see Fig. 6:8).

Most of the immigrants were pressed into unskilled jobs in clothing factories or home piece work assignments where entire families were needed to place even the most minimal amount of food on the table. Drawing on their socialist labor experience, the Jewish workers fought back against the inhuman 80-hour work weeks and the miserable conditions of the workplace. It took a major disaster to draw public attention to their plight. Though the memorial to the unidentified victims of the Triangle Factory Shirtwaist fire which stands in an empty field in Evergeen Cemetery, Brooklyn, is not lettered in Hebrew (and does not, for that matter, in any other fashion indicate the ethnicity of those it commemorates), it remains as a monument to the early twentieth century Jewish experience in America (Fig. 6:9).[13]

Of course, being crammed into poorly ventilated factories by day and returning home to the filthy streets and crowded conditions of the Lower East Side of New York by night, the mortality rate among the Russian Jews was high, and the immigrants' sheer numbers required a huge expansion of cemetery property. To those making only starvation wages, purchasing a plot for future use was a real hardship. The plots were therefore laid out as tiny and as close together as possible to cut the cost, a spatial practice quite visible and often

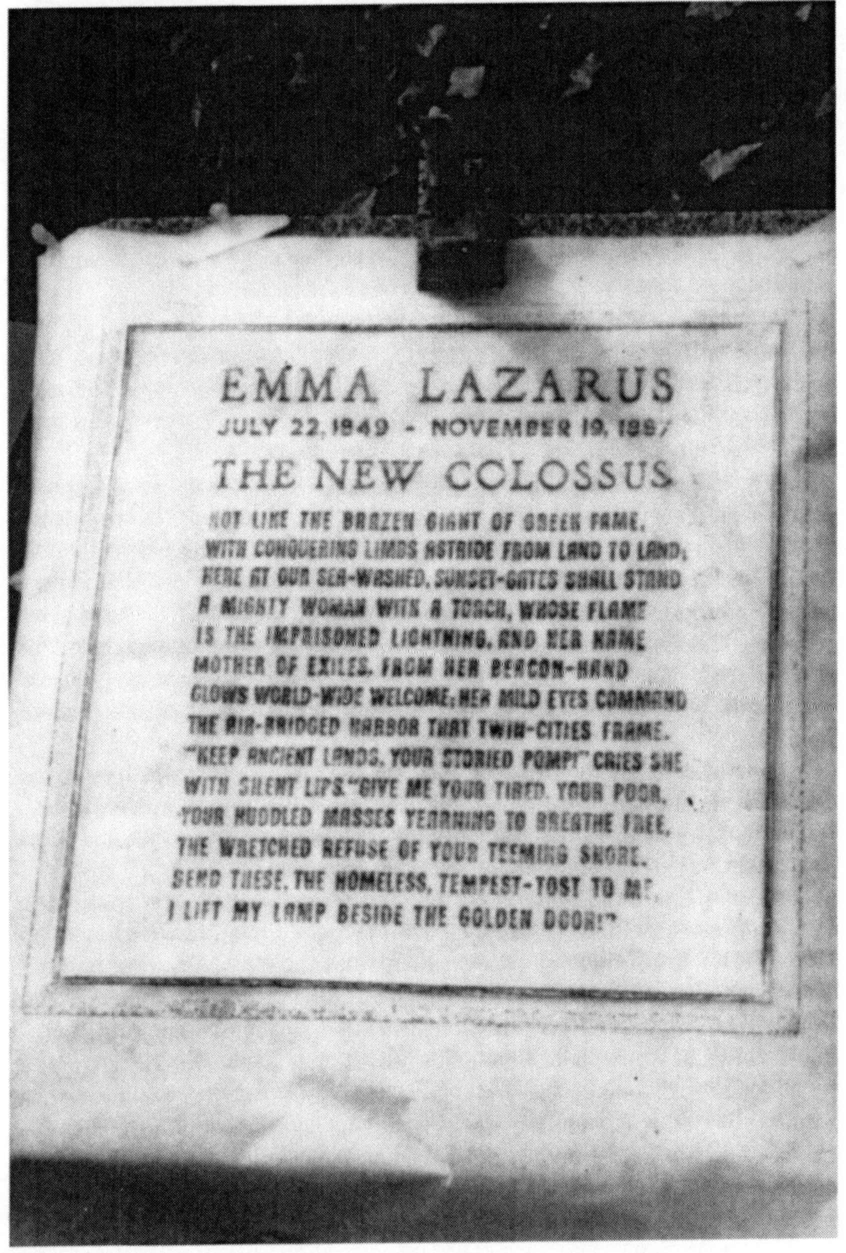

Fig. 6:7. Rubbing of bronze plaque in front of Lazarus family plot. Shearith Israel IV, Cypress Hills, New York.

Fig. 6:8. Marker of Maurice Schwartz, died 1939, one of the founders and actors of the Yiddish Theatre. Yiddish Theatre Alliance Plot, Mt. Hebron Cemetery, Flushing, New York.

Fig. 6:9. Monument to the unidentified victims of the Triangle Fire of 1911. Evergreen Cemetery, Brooklyn, New York.

puzzling to contemporary cemetery visitors. This closeness did not surprise the Jews who had been forced to live in the Russian ghettos. From the Middle Ages on, even cemetery land was restricted by the governments of the nations in which they lived. So they had already developed the practice of burying six and seven deep in the same plot, while observing strict customs about how to do it and about how many feet of earth between the buried would constitute sanctity.[14]

These recent immigrants remembered a fine monument tradition from Europe. A photograph taken from Monica Krajewska's *Time of Stones* shows quite clearly the consumate skill of the European stonecutters (Fig. 6:10).[15] But in America, handwork had become a luxury only for the very rich, and the machine age had also by this time profoundly affected the monument industry. Though the gravestones still bore the same Jewish symbols, they were not works of art like their predecessors. Machine processing had wiped out good design and skillful craft work. A few odd looking images did present themselves as heirs to new technology—the presence of actual photographs of the deceased attached to the stone under glass or celluloid.

In many respects the most charming aspect of the early twentieth century Jewish cemeteries is the manner in which they testify to the communalism brought from home. If Europe had taught the Russian Jews anything, it had taught them that "in union there is strength." And like every other problem the Russian Jews faced, they solved the cost of burial by forming a committee. Benevolent Associations were organized to purchase cemetery plots and sell individual spaces for a few pennies at a time to those who would eventually need them. Plots such as that of the Philadelphios Benevolent Society in Flushing, New York's Mt. Hebron Cemetery (Fig. 6:11) are typical of the many small units still to be seen in every Jewish cemetery over 50 years of age.

In one generation, the offspring of this wave of desperate refugees jumped into the educated middle class of America. The more assimilated they became, the less ornament their monuments exhibited, until in more contemporary Jewish cemeteries one can now view acres of stones, bearing little more design than the name of the deceased and the death date. A few maverick sculptors do survive and follow the ancient attention to the beautiful calligraphic potential of the Hebrew letter (Fig. 6:12), but such are now decidedly the exception and not the rule.

And yet the evolving story is not over. Suddenly Russia has unbarred its exit door to its Jewish citizens and they are coming to New York in the thousands. With them they have brought a decided preference for one of the newest techniques in contemporary monumentation—laser photoengraving on stone (Fig. 6:13). On this author's most recent visit to Washington Cemetery in Brooklyn, these highly polished artifacts were seen everywhere—easily spotted between the more sedate and dignified Victorian and twentieth century gravestones.

As we near the end of the twentieth century, it may seem hard to imagine that we will ever again witness waves of anti-semitism like those which drove the Jews of all countries to our shores. And yet, regretfully, even more recent

Fig. 6:10. Example of traditional European stonecarving art. Unidentified graveyard Poland. *(Photograph by Monica Krajewska).*

Fig. 6:11. Gate to the Philadelphios Benevolent Society plot. Mt. Hebron Cemetery, Flushing, New York.

Fig. 6:12. New Jersey gravemarker by contemporary Brooklyn designer, Jerry Trauber. *(Photograph by Jerry Trauber).*

Fig. 6:13. Laser photoengraving on black granite marker, with inscriptions in Hebrew, English, and Russian. Washington Cemetery, Brooklyn, New York.

history reminds us that it is still possible. Standing in one of the most attractive association plots in Queens, New York, the Workman's Circle, one finds the tragic cenotaph to Arthur Zygelboim, a member of the Polish Parliament in Exile in London, who took his life in despair less than half a century ago because of the psychotic destruction of the Polish ghetto by the Nazis (Fig. 6:14). Perhaps the long journey is still not over.

Postscript on Jewish Mortuary Imagery

The reader may have been surprised to notice that there is not a single Jewish star, the familiar six-pointed *Mogen David*, featured in any of the photographs which illustrate this essay. Now the emblem of Judaism to the world, this symbol does not appear, except as a minor ornament, until the late 1800s when, according to Israel Shanks, it was adopted by the European Zionist movement to identify its cause.[16] Instead, from biblical times onward, the most universal symbol of a Jewish grave has actually been the *Menorah*, the seven-branched candlestick on three legs. It is possible that Hitler actually placed the star on the "map" of world consciousness by making the Jews wear this symbol on their arms. When the new State of Israel chose the Zionist emblem for their flag, the adoption was complete. Now even most Jews believe it is their oldest traditional icon.

Besides the *Menorah*, several other symbols are generally widespread on Jewish gravemarkers:

-The pitcher and ewer, standing for a Levite (or servant of the priests);

-The hands of blessing, which signify a Cohen, descendant of the ancient priests of Israel (Fig. 6:10);

-The *Lulav and Etrog*, a palm branch and citrus fruit, associated with the harvest festival of Sukkot;

-The *Etz Chaim*, the Tree of Life (see Fig. 6:5), which is also another name for the *Torah*, the first five books of the Bible.

Another ancient symbol frequently employed is a representation of the door of the Ark which contained the *Torah*. Originally copying its panelled doors, the symbol was often abstracted into an interesting image of shadow and light. Its use always depicted a pious man. The symbol of learning and religiosity was also represented by a bookcase (see Fig. 6:10) full of scholarly tomes. Since women were not supposed to take an active part in religious study, they could not attain to such an exalted adjective; they could, however, be described as holy women by the placing of a *Menorah* over their graves.

In the middle European Jewish cemeteries, the custom developed of creating images which were representations of the meaning of a person's name. Thus, a man named Jonah might be symbolized by the dove on his monument, Judah or Leo by a roaring lion, Adler by an eagle, Hahn by a rooster, and Hirsch by a stag. Other representations are less literal (and in some instances not solely restricted to Judaic symbolism), such as broken lilies for a small child, a serpent swallowing its tail as an emblem of infinity, or the crown, a symbol of both

Fig. 6:14. Rubbing of four-sided cenotaph to Arthur Zygelboim. Workman's Circle, Interborough Parkway, Queens, New York.

learning and piety. And, from the eighteenth century on, many Jews could proudly display on their gravemarkers their membership in the Mason's fraternal organization by the familiar symbols of that order.

Yet another distinctive element to be noticed on Jewish gravemarkers is the dating of the death by the Jewish calendar. Since the Jews reckon their calculations from the sixth day of Creation, the year 1989-90, for example, is translated as 5,750 and often is given in Arabic characters (see Fig. 6:2 for an example of this style of dating). Subtraction using the current year from that on the inscription will enable the reader to determine the secular year of death.

Finally, the non-Jewish visitor will perhaps be surprised by the number of loose pebbles to be found lying on the top or foot of gravemarkers in Jewish cemeteries. This results from the fact that Jewish visitors to a gravesite have been taught to leave the pebbles there as a sign of a visit, and of respect. Though deeply embedded in Jewish mortuary ritual, the origins of this traditional practice remain obscure.

Notes

Unless otherwise indicated, all photographs in this essay are by Constance H. Halporn. All rubbings, unless otherwise indicated, were done by Roberta Halporn.

[1]From *The Gates of Repentance: The New Union Prayerbook for the Days of Awe* (New York: Central Conference of American Rabbis, 1978), p. 158. (*The Gates of Repentance* is the Reform Prayerbook for the Days of Atonement before *Yom Kippur.*).

[2]Arthur Koestler, *The Thirteenth Tribe: The Khazar Empire and Its Heritage* (New York: Random House, 1976), p. 161.

[3]Archaeological studies suggest this cave rests upon the West Bank of the Jordan River. See Benzion C. Kagonoff, "From Machpelah to Beth She'arim: A History of Burial Customs Among the Jewish People," *American Cemetery* 46:9 (1973), p. 4.

[4]David De Sola Pool, *Portraits Etched in Stone: Early Jewish Settlers, 1682-1831* (New York: Columbia UP, 1952), p. 67.

[5]For an excellent example of this frequent intercourse, see the case of Isaac Pinheiro discussed in Malcolm H. Stern, "A Successful Caribbean Restoration: The Nevis Story," *American Jewish Historical Quarterly* 61:1 (1971), p. 22.

[6]De Sola Pool, *Portraits Etched in Stone*, pp. 164-65.

[7]Abraham J. Karp, *Haven and Home: A History of the Jews in America* (New York: Schocken Books, 1985), p. 18.

[8]De Sola Pool, *Portraits Etched in Stone*, p. 58.

[9]*Ibid.*

[10]Karp, *Haven and Home*, p. 52.

[11]*Ibid.* p.185.

[12]Stephen Birmingham, *Our Crowd: The German-American Jews* (Philadelphia: Little, Brown & Co., 1980), p. 344.

[13]The Triangle Shirtwaist Factory Fire in 1911, which led to the formation of the International Ladies Garment Workers's Union, possibly started in some oily rags used to clean the sewing machines. The laborers were locked into the workrooms to keep

them from unauthorized rest breaks. There were no fire escapes. More than 150 women, men and small children were killed in the stampede attending the attempts to break the door down, or when they tried to jump from the windows.

[14]"Tomb and Tombstones," in *The Jewish Encyclopedia* (Jerusalem: Keter Publishing House, 1971), p. 271.

[15]Monica Krajewska, *Time of Stones* (Warsaw: Interpress, 1973).

[16]Israel Shanks, *Judaism in Stone: The Archaeology of Ancient Synagogues* (New York: Harper and Row, 1979), p. 68.

The Agua Mansa Cemetery: An Indicator of Ethnic Identification in A Mexican-American Community

Russell J. Barber

On a small knoll overlooking the Santa Ana River of inland southern California lies a small and largely forgotten *camposanto*, a sanctified burying ground in the Spanish-Mexican tradition. In the century and a half since the occupants of this cemetery entered southern California, time has taken a heavy toll on it. Many of the early wooden markers have been lost to wildfires or termites, and some of the later markers of wood, concrete, and stone have been vandalized or removed by unknown agencies. But despite any limitations in its preservation, this cemetery—along with a few vague indications of land sculpted by agriculture—constitutes the only surviving above ground traces of the early Californian Mexican communities of Agua Mansa and La Placita, known collectively as San Salvador. The cemetery also serves as a slate on which the Salvadoreños wrote the history of their transition from a community of distinctive newcomers to a community that merged more effectively with their neighbors. The writing on the slate is smudged and partly erased, but the message remains clear.

Agua Mansa Cemetery (Figs. 7:1, 7:2) was the community burying ground for the settlers of San Salvador; it was used and continues to be used by a few of their descendants and a few others living in the area. The site lies in present-day Colton, California, about 70 miles inland from Los Angeles, along fertile agricultural land watered by the Santa Ana River, the major waterway in the series of inland valleys known as "the Inland Empire." Parish records show that about 600 persons have been buried at the Agua Mansa Cemetery, but only a few over 200 gravemarkers remain visible and substantially intact. Alas, the greatest losses have been from the period where information would be most welcome: the earliest period, when wooden gravemarkers were nearly universal (Fig. 7:3).

Although a few Euro-Americans were living in the Inland Empire from about 1810 onward, the establishment of *ranchos* in the late 1830s signaled the beginning of serious Euro-American settlement.[1] These ranchos immediately began suffering stock losses, attributed primarily (and probably correctly) to marauding Indians. To combat this problem, the rancheros sought aid from experienced Indian fighters. Since no Indian fighters were available locally,

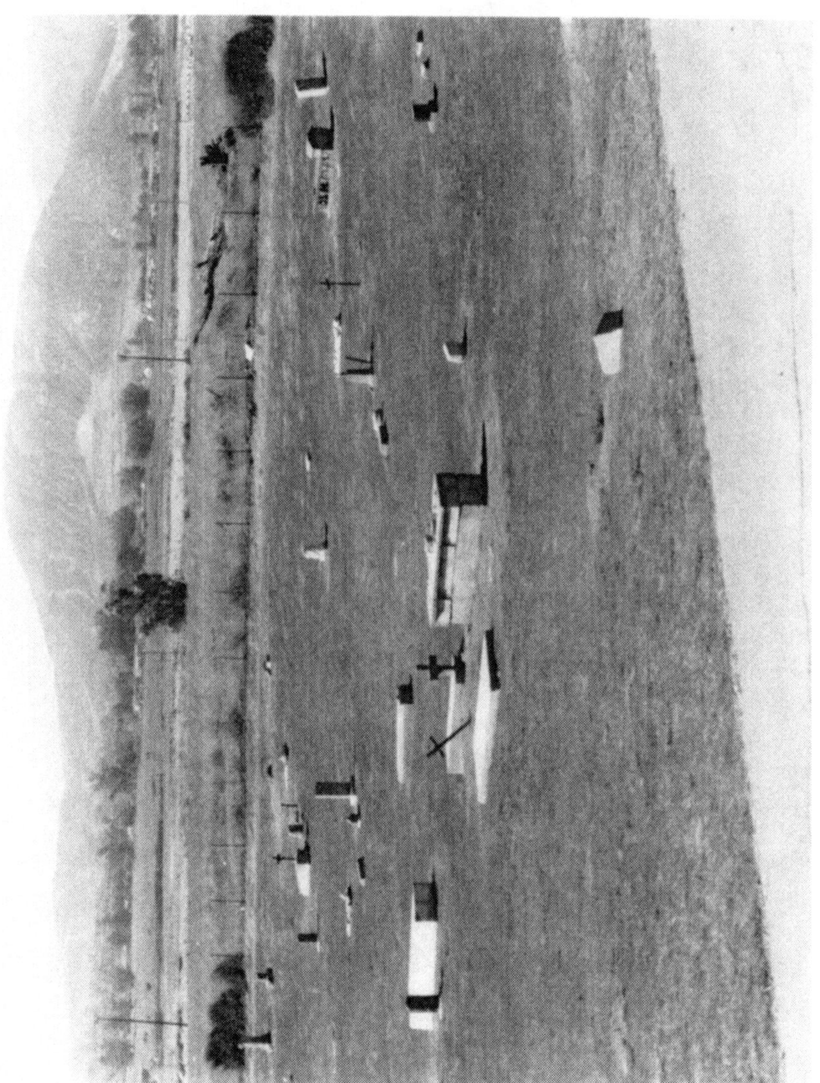

Fig. 7:1. Overview of the Agua Mansa Cemetery, Colton, California.

Fig. 7:2. Molded concrete marker (1888) at Agua Mansa Cemetery with crudely incised inscription. The misspellings, grammatical looseness, and idiosyncrasies of script are common.

Fig. 7:3. Wooden cross, probably from the 1920s. Such wooden crosses dominated the Agua Mansa Cemetery before fires and neglect destroyed most of them.

they tried to entice New Mexicans, familiar with Indians raids and defending against them, to emigrate to the San Bernardino Valley. The New Mexicans they attracted became the core of San Salvador.

Since around 1830, trading parties had passed overland from New Mexico to California via the Old Spanish Trail. The eastern trailhead was at Abíquiu, a small community near Santa Fe. As a trailhead, Abíquiu had been especially subject to Indian raids, since goods had been amassed there preparatory to departure for the west. This unpleasant circumstance made the inhabitants of the village good candidates as Indian fighters, and many of them had seen California as members of parties carrying goods along the trail. They were approached by the local rancheros, and in 1841 the first group of New Mexican immigrants arrived in the San Bernardino Valley. Their initial agreement was with the Lugo family, one of the two prominent ranching groups in the area, but that quickly soured, and the party accepted a new agreement with Juan Bandini from the other prominent rancho. By 1843, the group resettled and a New Mexican colony was established at San Salvador.

The establishment of San Salvador was important for several reasons, but of especial interest here is the ethnicity of its inhabitants. Other Euro-American inhabitants of the area were also Mexican, but they mostly came directly from Mexico and partook of the mainstream culture of central Mexico. Even Juan Bandini, who was born in Peru and was of Italian extraction, had lived in Mexico and considered himself Mexican. In contrast, the Salvadoreños were Mexicans who had passed through the filter of New Mexico. That filter had left them significantly different from their compatriots in Mexico and California, especially in three respects.

First, the New Mexicans had a strong infusion of Southwestern Indian culture. In their native Abíquiu, they were known as *Genizaros*, Hispanicized Pueblo Indians or individuals of mixed parentage who were welcome in neither the Indian nor the Spanish-Mexican world.[2] The Pueblo Revolt of 1680, arguably the most successful of all Native American resistance movements against Euro-American intrusions, was a strong force in maintaining Pueblo Indian culture as a vibrant and vital entity in the Southwest, even among those who did not affiliate themselves directly with Pueblo culture.[3]

Second, the Catholicism of New Mexico was profoundly different from that of the rest of Mexico. After the Mexican Revolution and independence from Spain in 1821, various political and religious factors came together in such a way that Catholic priests were recalled from New Mexico, leaving the deeply Catholic New Mexicans without clergy. As a result, between 1821 and 1848—when the region became territory of the United States—religion was handled predominantly by lay societies. These lay societies, subsumed under the blanket term of *cofradía de Nuestro Padre Jesus Nazareño* ("the fraternity of Our Father Jesus of Nazareth") or more simply the *Penitentes*, gave a unique flavor to New Mexican Catholicism, a flavor that persists in many villages today, despite over a century of attempts to eradicate it.[4] Such differences would be expected to manifest themselves strongly in such a religious activity as burying and commemorating the dead.

Third, New Mexico and California differed in their basic approaches to settling the land. California was settled primarily as a few large towns, sometimes built around missions, and many large, rural ranchos. These ranchos were large tracts of land, granted by the king or his delegate to a single individual or family, that operated as a large corporate body. While stock raising was the main occupation, support operations (leather tanning, vintnering, coopering, and the like) would be carried on at the rancho; these and all other operations were under the direct management of the owner or his manager. This economic organization led to a settlement pattern characterized by a moderately dense central cluster where most activities took place, coupled with a thin scatter of activities and settlement over the rest of the rancho. The ranchos were largely self-sufficient entities, organized around the recognition that one family was the owner and the other families were their employees. Often the owners preferred to spend much of their time in the sophisticated surroundings of San Diego or similar communities, leaving the rancho in the care of a hired manager. In contrast, the basic unit of New Mexican settlement was the village, inhabited at all times by more-or-less equal partners in the community. San Salvador was the first village of this sort in interior southern California.

These factors made the Salvadoreños truly different from the Mexicans around them when they first came to California, and historical analyses provide hints—but little more—that they saw themselves as distinct from their neighbors.

A major change came to the San Bernardino Valley in 1851: Anglos settled the area in force. San Salvador had always included a few Anglos; indeed, there were a few French and Danes as well.[5] But the 1851 entrada consisted of several hundred Anglos, Mormons from Salt Lake City who founded the city of San Bernardino. San Bernardino, located about 5 miles northeast of San Salvador, reflected the Midwestern roots of its Mormon founders and was laid out on a grid oriented to cardinal points. Like San Salvador, it was a community founded on the principle of partnership of equals, but it differed in that the Mormon Church took a very strong role in planning and developing the city. The stockade that originally surrounded the city, the first school, and other public works were centrally planned and were built under central organization. While the Mormons were recalled to Utah in 1857 when it was feared that the United States would declare war on Utah, many of the original settlers stayed on, forming the core of the city that would dominate the area through today. By 1860 the population of San Bernardino had grown to over 6000 inhabitants, nearly all of whom were Anglos.[6] From this time forward, the Salvadoreños would have had to adjust to political and economic domination coming from the Anglo world.

San Salvador's history makes it a unique settlement in California, and it also makes the community an excellent laboratory for examining the question of ethnic identity. When in contact with other cultures, a community must make a series of decisions. It can maintain itself as a distinct entity, surrounded by communities that are alien to a greater or lesser degree, or it can abandon portions of its own culture and adopt the culture of its neighbors; put in the jargon of social science, it can maintain itself as an ethnic enclave or it can acculturate. Either way, it must display its decision in overt symbols, usually termed ethnic markers. Ethnic markers can manifest themselves in dress, food preparation, or myriad other aspects of culture, but the aspect of immediate concern is cemetery behavior.

So long as the Salvadoreños viewed themselves as ethnically distinct from their Mexican neighbors, we would expect the Agua Mansa cemetery to display mortuary art unique to that group; alternatively, if the Salvadoreños saw themselves as basically the same as their neighbors, we would expect shared mortuary art. Further, if the Salvadoreños opted to maintain their distinct ethnicity, we would expect that the ethnic markers they would choose would be drawn largely from those they brought with them as cultural baggage from New Mexico.

Christian burial in eighteenth-century New Mexico typically was beneath the floor of the church, following a long-standing European tradition. The numbers of Christians were small, and the church itself served as the memorial to the deceased, both marking the grave and protecting it from desecration. By the early nineteenth century, however, Christians had become markedly more populous, and a century or more of burial beneath the churches had filled these areas to capacity, sometimes jeopardizing the structural integrity of the buildings above them. At this time, churchyards or another adjacent areas became the burying grounds, the *camposantos*. Only then did a distinctive cemetery tradition begin in New Mexico.

There is little detail known about the cemetery art of this early period, but it is clear that wooden crosses were the dominant form of marker. While apparently none survive today, the prominence of a small cross surmounting a large one in late nineteenth-century and twentieth-century crosses in village New Mexico (especially as related to Penitente crosses) suggests that this form might have been in existence earlier. Some authors believe that *cerquitas* (low fences around graves) followed shortly after the development of outdoor burial, perhaps as a protection from wild animals, but there is much room for disagreement here, in terms of both the chronology and the function of *cerquitas*. Carved stones and other more-or-less permanent markers were an innovation of the later nineteenth century.[7]

The Salvadoreños, then, brought with them a set of ideas about cemeteries that was only about a generation old. That they embraced the new tradition is clear, since their earliest dead were buried in the *camposanto*, not under either of the chapels that they built in their early years at Agua Mansa. (The first chapel collapsed in 1852, shortly before it was completed, and was replaced on a different site in 1853.) But did they maintain their distinctive mortuary tradition as an ethnic marker of a New Mexican enclave, or did they adopt the mortuary tradition of the Mexicans around them as an indicator of their perceived sameness?

To examine this question, I compared the surviving grave markers at Agua Mansa cemetery to contemporary markers at several Mexican cemeteries (or Mexican sections of cemeteries) in nearby southern California, focusing on traits that are distinctive to the mainstream Mexican folk tradition in that region. In addition, I compared the Agua Mansa traits to those believed to have characterized village New Mexico at the time the soon-to-be Salvadoreños left there. The scarcity of hard data on early nineteenth-century New Mexico forced me to base that comparison largely on motifs linked to the Penitentes. Tracing this analysis over time offers a view of San Salvador's changing ethnic self-perception.

The Mexican folk cemetery tradition in southern California is characterized by a variety of motifs and traits that are shared in part with Mexican folk cemetery traditions elsewhere in the southwestern United States.[8] The distinctive traits on which I have focused are:

concrete cross: a molded cross of concrete, typically about 3 feet high and reinforced with a metal rod, often with an incised inscription on its arms (Figs. 7:4,7:5);

cerquita: a low wood, metal or occasionally concrete enclosure surrounding an individual grave or (rarely) the graves of closely related individuals (Fig. 7:6);

relicarito: a deep recess built into a grave marker to receive an item connected to the deceased or a holy object;

nicho: a shallow relicarito, often to receive a picture, usually a photograph of the deceased but sometimes a holy picture (Fig. 7:7);

grave curb: a low enclosure around a grave, typically nearly flush with the ground and made of concrete; and

potholders: cylindrical recesses, usually cast into a concrete footing to hold floral bouquets and the like.

While most of these traits can be found in non-Mexican cemeteries, all but the grave curb are uncommon in non-Mexican cemeteries in southern California. Since the analysis was quantitative, it was not necessary that a trait be unique to the Mexican cemetery tradition, only that it occur in distinctive frequencies. With the possible exception of the *relicarito* (which can require a considerable amount of concrete, as well as a substantial investment of labor), none of these traits is particularly more expensive than another for homemade markers, so economic status of the survivors should not be a major confounding factor.

Comparisons were drawn with the San Gabriel Mission Cemetery (San Gabriel), the Mexican section at Hillside Cemetery (Redlands), the Mexican section at Pioneer Memorial Cemetery (San Bernardino),[9] the Mexican section at Lompoc Evergreen Cemetery (Lompoc), and the Mexican section at Old Sunnyslope Cemetery (Banning). With six traits, five cemeteries, and 14 decades, the data matrix is quite sizable and cannot be presented in its entirety

Fig. 7:4. Concrete cross, probably from the 1910s. These crosses are common in Mexican traditional cemeteries in southern California, often with pictures or statues in the niches.

Fig. 7:5. Intricately molded concrete cross (1936).

Fig. 7:6. Granite commercial marker customized with a concrete *cerquita* (1932).

Fig. 7:7. Homemade concrete false tomb with *nicho* for flowers or a holy statue (1923).

here. Instead, I will trace each trait individually, using the technique of percentages per decade.

This technique is based on some of the assumptions that underlie seriation and related techniques. The basic model is that innovations often follow a general temporal pattern consisting of its introduction, an increasing of popularity to a peak, then a waning of popularity to a point of disappearance. If two communities are in direct contact with one another and acting as one in terms of accepting or rejecting a particular trait or style, we would expect them to show similar patterns of popularity of that trait; this would be reflected in terms of what percentage of the population accepted that particular trait at a particular date. In essence, then, the percentage of a trait per decade becomes an index by which cultural similarity can be compared between communities.

The concrete across first occurs at Agua Mansa around 1892 and maintains a percentage per decade that varies from 11.5 to 22.2 through the 1940s, at which point it falls into disuse. Concrete crosses first appear at the other cemeteries between 1894 and 1911 and maintain slightly lower percentages, ranging from 6.4 to 14.3. There, too, concrete crosses either cease to be used or are used only very rarely after World War II.

The earliest extant *cerquita* at Agua Mansa dates to 1884, and the form occurs sporadically after that. Unfortunately, the wood of a *cerquita* is susceptible to all manner of destruction and scavenging, and many (perhaps most) that once existed are now marked by no trace. Further, some of the cemeteries in the comparison sample—notably Pioneer Memorial Cemetery—apparently enforced restrictions on the building of certain folk markers, including *cerquitas*. Though it might have been an important ethnic marker, it is unusable in this analysis.

Relicaritos appear rarely at all of the cemeteries, possibly because of the large investment in labor and materials they require. At Agua Mansa they appear only in the 1920s and 1930s, never exceeding 3.3% per decade. At other cemeteries they follow the same general pattern of greatest prominence in the years between the two world wars, although they persist into the 1950s and perhaps beyond at Old Sunnyslope Cemetery.

The *nicho* appears at Agua Mansa in 1909 but attains its first numeral significance in the 1920s and 1930s (over 20%), then trails off in the 1940s. At other cemeteries similar patterns obtain, though *nichos* have maintained their popularity at Old Sunnyslope Cemetery through the 1980s.

Grave curbs at Agua Mansa begin replacing *cerquitas* as a means of demarcating graves around 1900, although the *cerquitas* makes an apparent comeback around the 1930s. The same pattern generally follows at the other cemeteries, with the exceptions that the replacement of *cerquitas* with curbs begins about five years earlier at San Gabriel and never occurs at Old Sunnyslope. I suspect that the more multi-ethnic cemeteries might have encouraged the use of less obtrusive curbs in preference to *cerquitas*.

Potholders may provide the best evidence for similar trajectories in the development and acceptance of a trait in all of the cemeteries studied. They appear first in Agua Mansa in 1923, exactly the same year as in Hillside

Cemetery; at San Gabriel they appear in 1921, in Lompoc in 1924, at Pioneer Memorial in 1924, and at Old Sunnyslope at an undated grave probably from the 1920s. After their appearance at Agua Mansa, they occur 34.5% of the time through the 1980s, with little variation over time. Much the same patterns obtain at the other cemeteries.

This analysis shows that the Salvadoreños buried at Agua Mansa Cemetery shared a substantial number of grave traits with the Mexican-Americans of other nearby communities from the 1890s onward. Unless the traits selected for study were especially inappropriate, it is difficult to escape the conclusion that San Salvador had opted for acculturation to the broader Mexican pattern by the late nineteenth century. Many of the distinctive Mexican folk elements begin dropping out of both Agua Mansa and the other cemeteries shortly after World War II, and the cemeteries begin taking on more of the appearance of Anglo cemeteries, probably the result of a further acculturation hastened by the experiences of wartime soldiers and the general post-war development of southern California. (The persistence of typical Mexican traits longer at Old Sunnyslope Cemetery suggests that the patrons there have chosen not to acculturate to the same degree as others and have retained more traditional ethnic markers.) Happily for the student of cemeteries, there has been a resurgence of distinctiveness beginning in the 1960s at some of the cemeteries, and this may mark a reinvigorated sense of ethnic pride.

This general pattern of distinctiveness of Mexican-American cemeteries before World War II and greater similarity to Anglo cemeteries after probably finds its roots in several factors. First, by the 1940s, language barriers were beginning to fall. Before this period, many older Mexican-Americans (those most likely to be making grave marker decisions) were not fluent or at least comfortable with English. Discrimination in the workplace and differential access to education maintained low levels of interaction between Mexican-Americans and Anglos, and Spanish-language services in the Catholic Church helped to diminish the need for English. As education began stressing English and opportunities to use it increased, contact with Anglos increased and acculturation increased. Further, World War II experiences helped many Mexican-Americans (and others) become more aware of the world outside their own ethnic community, and the postwar ethnic of the melting pot, urging ethnic groups to submerge themselves in a greater composite American culture, had its effects, at least until a counterethic of cultural pluralism arose in the 1960s. With the rise of that counterethic, Mexican-American cemeteries began a conscious return to their ethnic distinctiveness, suggesting that the "acculturation period" might best be seen as a temporary divergence from the historic pattern, perhaps even as an experiment in acculturation.

But what of the earlier period, when the Salvadoreños were still newcomers to the region? Unfortunately, this is the period where the greatest losses of markers have occurred at Agua Mansa. Further, comparisons are difficult, since the earliest Mexican grave at the other cemeteries is from 1882; earlier markers, probably of wood, have simply disappeared over the years. The assessment here will have to be based on the degree of similarity to the cemetery marker tradition believed to have characterized New Mexico at the time of the emigration.

In modern times, the Penitentes have been as concerned with politics as with religion, but in the early nineteenth century, spiritual issues were paramount. In particular, they were responsible for holding religious rituals, especially those associated with Lent and Easter and those associated with the death and burial of members of the community. The Penitente mindset was acutely attuned to suffering in atonement for sin. Penance, self-flagellation, and even mock crucifixion held major places in Penitente ritual. This concern was reflected in their folk art, focusing heavily on the Passion of Christ, saints (especially martyrs), and death angels.[10]

Given that the Penitentes had a near-obsessive concern with atonement and suffering as well as a responsibility to organize death and burial rituals, it is reasonable to assume that early Salvadoreños might have brought with them ideas that would translate into grave art that emphasized gory crucifixions, Christ's crown of thorns, the bloody Sacred Heart, the scourging of Christ, and similar images. They also might have brought the double cross described earlier as a form that occurs on recent Penitente graves. But we see none of these on the Agua Mansa graves. Instead, the surviving gravemarkers from 1859 to the 1870s are adorned primarily with simple crosses and unassuming stars or rosettes, motifs that occur on contemporary Mexican-American graves at other cemeteries; a couple of markers even bear ivy leaves and a placid lamb, clear borrowings from Anglo grave art. In short, there is no evidence of distinctive New Mexican grave decoration, but, of course, there are no surviving gravemarkers that antedate the Mormon entry into the area.

The analysis of the Agua Mansa Cemetery reveals the community of San Salvador to have been quite different from the insular community that one might have imagined. While it may or may not have reflected its New Mexican roots strongly in its earliest years, by 1859 contact with other communities is clear. From this date onward, the gravemarker styles at the Agua Mansa Cemetery are part of a larger, regional cemetery tradition that encompasses the Mexican-American cemeteries of much of southern California; marker types, motifs, and styles are adopted, become popular, and fall into disfavor on a broad front and in close synchronization. This can occur only if there is significant and persistent contact between the participants in this tradition, and only if they feel enough ethnic affiliation to wish to share ethnic markers. Between 1859 and World War II, the vast majority of elements link Agua Mansa with other Mexican-American cemeteries, but even during this period there are a few cases where clearly Anglo symbols are adopted. After World War II, however, the patrons of Agua Mansa look more to the Anglo world for their models, apparently an indication of the weakening of their strong sense of ethnic identity. A resurgence of the positive evaluation of ethnic pride in the 1960s and since is reflected in a renaissance of old-fashioned, traditional marker styles, such as *relicaritos*, and a return to the frequent use of Spanish for inscriptions. The analysis suggests that the inhabitants of San Salvador have generally opted for limited acculturation: a willingness to enter the melting pot, so long as the melting is not complete.

This pattern probably is a common one. So long as there are contacts between the larger society and the ethnic group in question, it is likely that certain characteristics of the larger society will "rub off" on the other; indeed, this is the thinking behind some of the more mechanical versions of diffusion theory. The major exceptions probably occur when the ethnic group finds itself in direct conflict with the larger society, the society with political and economic power that can affect that ethnic group's success. In that case, it probably is necessary (or at least highly adaptive) for the ethnic group to maintain its distinctiveness in all symbolic ways possible, in order to present a united front against the hostile world. If one is willing to accept this generalization, acculturation might be seen as one index of the degree of acceptance or hostility that an ethnic group perceives in its treatment from the larger society. And, as has been the case with Agua Mansa, the ethnic cemetery emerges as a major focal point wherein to test these hypotheses.

Notes

All Photographs in this essay are by Russell J. Barber.

[1]The facts of the history of San Salvador come primarily from Joyce Carter Vickery, *Defending Eden: New Mexican Pioneers in Southern California, 1830-1890* (Riverside, California: The Department of History, U of California, Riverside and The Riverside Museum P, 1977). Responsibility for the interpretation of those facts, of course, remains mine.

[2]The Genizaros are discussed well by Frances Leon Swadesh, *Los Primeros Pobladores: Hispanic Americans of the Ute Frontier* (South Bend, Indiana: U of Notre Dame P, 1974).

[3]Edward H. Spicer, *Cycles of Conquest* (Tucson: U of Arizona P, 1962).

[4]The Penitentes are discussed particularly well in Marta Weigle, *Brothers of Light, Brothers of Blood: The Penitentes of the Southwest* (Albuquerque, New Mexico: U of New Mexico P, 1976). A more brief but equally authoritative account is Marta Weigle, *The Penitentes of the Southwest* (Santa Fe, New Mexico: Ancient City P, 1970). A somewhat different account is provided by Lorayne Ann Horka-Follick, *Los Hermanos Penitentes* (Los Angeles: Westernlore P, 1969).

[5]Vickery, *Defending Eden*, p. 69

[6]This figure comes from Leo Lyman, personal communication, 11 December, 1989, reflecting as-yet unpublished research on the demographic history of San Bernardino.

[7]Several authors present summaries of early nineteenth-century burial practices in village New Mexico, but none presents a level of documentation that supports much detail. These summaries are found in Nancy Hunter Warren, *Villages of Hispanic New Mexico* (Santa Fe, New Mexico: School of American Research P, 1987); Nancy Hunter Warren, "New Mexico Village Camposantos," *Markers* 4 (1987), pp. 115-129; and Roland F. Dickey, *New Mexico Village Arts* (Albuquerque: U of New Mexico P, 1970).

[8]Mexican folk cemeteries in Texas and the Southwest are discussed in John R. Stilgoe, "Folklore and Graveyard Design," *Landscape* 22 (3) (1978), pp. 22-28; Terry G. Jordan, *Texas Graveyards: A Cultural Legacy* (Austin: U of Texas P, 1982); Warren, "New Mexico Village Camposantos."; and John O. West, *Mexican-American Folklore* (Little Rock, Arkansas: August House, 1988).

[9]I have retained the data from Pioneer Memorial Cemetery, even though I have doubts about its proper use. Since collecting the data I have learned that some members of San Salvador elected to be buried there for unclear reasons: see Maria C. Gamboa, *The Legacy of Pioneer Mexican-Americans in South Colton, California* (M.A. thesis, California State U, San Bernardino, 1989). R. Bruce Harley, Historian for the Diocese of San Bernardino, believes these were the economically better-off members of the community (personal communication, March 16, 1989). In a sense, this cemetery and Agua Mansa together represent the burial tradition of the Salvadoreños. The Pioneer Memorial Cemetery data is muddled, however, because most of the graves are not those of Salvadoreños.

[10]New Mexican folk art is described and discussed variously by Dickey, *New Mexico Village Arts*; Robert L. Shalkop, *The Folk Art of a New Mexican Village* (Colorado Springs, Colorado: The Taylor Museum, 1969); and Robert L. Shalkop, *Wooden Saints: The Santos of New Mexico* (Colorado Springs, Colorado: The Taylor Museum, 1967). These sources all touch on the relationship between the Penitentes and folk art.

The People of Rimrock Bury Alfred K. Lorenzo: Tri-Cultural Funerary Practice

Keith Cunningham

Transitions from one culturally determined role and relationship to another culturally determined relationship and role are folklife foci, and the greatest of these is death. Of such import and finality is death's separation that those who remain find themselves assaulted by all-embracing, potentially devastating mutability as their relationships with others, the realities of their lives, and even their senses of themselves change. Nothing, furthermore, recalls death so much as death; the death of one individual eloquently declaims the mortality of all. The mutability and the sense of mortality engendered by death call into play cultures' cosmologies and eschatologies as cultures answer anguish with and through funerary practice. From the complex, culturally specific process of notifying relatives and friends of a death through the preparation of the body for burial and the traditional funeral and graveside services to public and private funerary meals, gatherings and markers, cultural values and beliefs are dramatized and enacted as rites of passage insuring that cultures survive the death of individuals.[1] Because of who he was and who they are, this complex of customary folklife was particularly important and evident when the people of Rimrock buried Alfred K. Lorenzo.

Alfred K. Lorenzo's funerary practices had all of the important functions of any other burial to fulfill, but their task was greater than that of most because Alfred was a citizen of Rimrock. Rimrock, New Mexico, is one of the few, select areas in America, like Middletown, which research has fixed in time and space and caused to become a part of American culture's view of itself.

Rimrock is an area of the "Land of Enchantment," New Mexico's motto, located in the west central portion of the state south of the town of Gallup and east of the Arizona state line. The area is the home of several cultures: Zuni, Ramah Navajo, Mormon, Texan and Spanish-America.

The prehistoric Mogollon and Anasazi cultures fused to create Zuni, a pueblo people whose prehistory ended abruptly in 1539 when the Spaniard Friar Marcos de Niza took possession of their villages for his God and King. Zuni culture is one of the most frequently observed and described in the world. The varied literature dealing with Zuni affirms that the Zuni have a strong sense of their place in the world; they have long been reported to, by and large, be pleased to be Zuni and to take pleasure in their historical and mythological past and present. A frequently noted feature of Zuni culture, rooted in their acceptance of themselves and their place in the universe, is their attitude toward other cultures, other technologies. The idea that people should "be courteous not only to your people, but to the people that come your way,"[2] is common at Zuni. The vast majority of the Zuni today live within the village of Zuni, New Mexico, which is surrounded by their tribal lands.

Today most Navajos live within the Navajo Nation, located north and east of Flagstaff, Arizona, and including portions of northeast Arizona, southwest Utah, and northwest New Mexico, but approximately one percent of the total Navajo population live in a much smaller area located around the community of Ramah, New Mexico, 40 to 70 miles from the main reservation where 99 percent of the tribe resides. The Navajo in general, and the Ramah Navajo living in this west central area of New Mexico in particular, have been described by cultural studies as a living laboratory illustrating and emphasizing the paradox of acculturation that a culture can borrow extensively from other cultures and yet retain its essence and not become progressively like the culture from which it borrows. Evon Z. Vogt, for example, described Navajo borrowing as "incorporative acculturation" and quoted Clyde Kluckhohn's description of the process:

> Elements from other cultures are incorporated into Navajo culture in such a way that the structural framework of the institutional core...is maintained, and the borrowed elements are fitted into place and elaborated in terms of pre-existing patterns.[3]

Classic studies have described Navajo incorporative acculturation of silversmithing and jewelry making,[4] weaving,[5] architecture,[6] domestic animals and animal husbandry patterns[7] and religion and ritual.[8]

The Ramah Mormons occupy the town of Ramah, New Mexico, and the valley surrounding it following a settlement pattern, landscaping tradition and vernacular architecture "typical of that of other Mormon settlements throughout the American Great Basin region."[9] The Mormons of Rimrock are, of course, defined by their membership in the Church of Jesus Christ of Latter Day Saints (LDS), which flourishes all across this folk-cultural region of the American West. There are a number of ways believed by Mormons in rural Arizona, New Mexico, and Utah through which non-Mormons may achieve the blessings of the Mormon afterlife. I have often heard expressed in these areas a belief that the nature of God is such that all people shall receive His salvation and be reunited at some point after death.

The Rimrock community and the Spanish-American, Texan, Zuni, Ramah Navajo and Mormon cultures which existed side by side in the area were the subject of a six-year Harvard intercultural study, the books *The People of Rimrock*[10] and *Variations in Value-Orientations: A Theory Tested in Five Cultures*,[11] and numerous scholarly articles.[12] The cultures studied 30 years ago at Rimrock are today largely comprised of the descendants of the people who were the subject of the earlier research.

There have been changes in the Rimrock area and cultures in the years since the Harvard study of values. The Texan community has lost many members as individuals and families have returned to Texas, moved to other areas, or established businesses in nearby communities such as Gallup. The Texans return every other summer to Fence Lake for a reunion, but only a few still live in the area. Likewise, the population of the Spanish-American community has diminished through outward migration. Zuni, the Ramah Navajo, and the Ramah Mormons, on the other hand, have increased in population and prospered. The present day Rimrock is very much aware of its place in the history of cultural research.

Alfred K. Lorenzo (Fig. 8:1) was born and lived his entire life on the borders between cultures. He was a Ramah Navajo raised in a traditional Ramah Navajo home (see Fig. 8:2) and family well acquainted with the Zuni and Mormon cultures of his own land and with other cultures of other areas. He lived in Los Angeles while he attended a watch repair school, was employed as an extra and stunt man in Texas during the filming of the movie *Arrowhead*, and traveled all across the Western United States working on the railroad. His wife was one-half Pima-Maricopa and one-half Zuni. He lived at Zuni for several years, both when he was a child attending a mission school and later as an adult living with his wife in her traditional Zuni family home (Fig. 8:3). Circumstances surrounded him with cultural diversity; he welcomed it and sought to experience it to the fullest possible extent. He left home as a young boy to work on the railroad, he secured employment in the film industry, and he attended services at a Native American Church as a participant-observer to see what it was like. Alfred spoke Navajo as it is spoken in the Ramah area, knew the country and many of the families who lived in the isolated "outfits," observed his mother translate for Clyde Kluckhohn and Dorothea Leighton (her assistance as co-researcher is described at some length in *Children of the People*,)[13] and had a great interest and ability in interacting with people cross culturally. His many and varied experiences, and his curiosity and sense of wonder, which caused him to have the experiences in the first place, made him an indefatigable cross-cultural fieldworker, and that is why and how I knew him.

My wife and I met Alfred when we were concluding a series of interviews at Zuni as a part of a United States Department of Education grant to study Native American concepts of disability and rehabilitation. We told our co-researchers at Zuni we were going to conduct similar research with the Ramah Navajo and were looking for a co-researcher in that community. Based upon their personal knowledge of the skills and interests which are necessary for succeeding at and enjoying cross-cultural research, our Zuni friends, who knew Alfred and his family because he was married to a Zuni woman and had children and grandchildren living at Zuni, suggested him. We discussed our project with Alfred, his wife Rita, and their daughter Kim, and all later assisted us with our research. Kim served as our co-researcher helping us interview a group of English speaking Navajos. Alfred served as co-researcher and

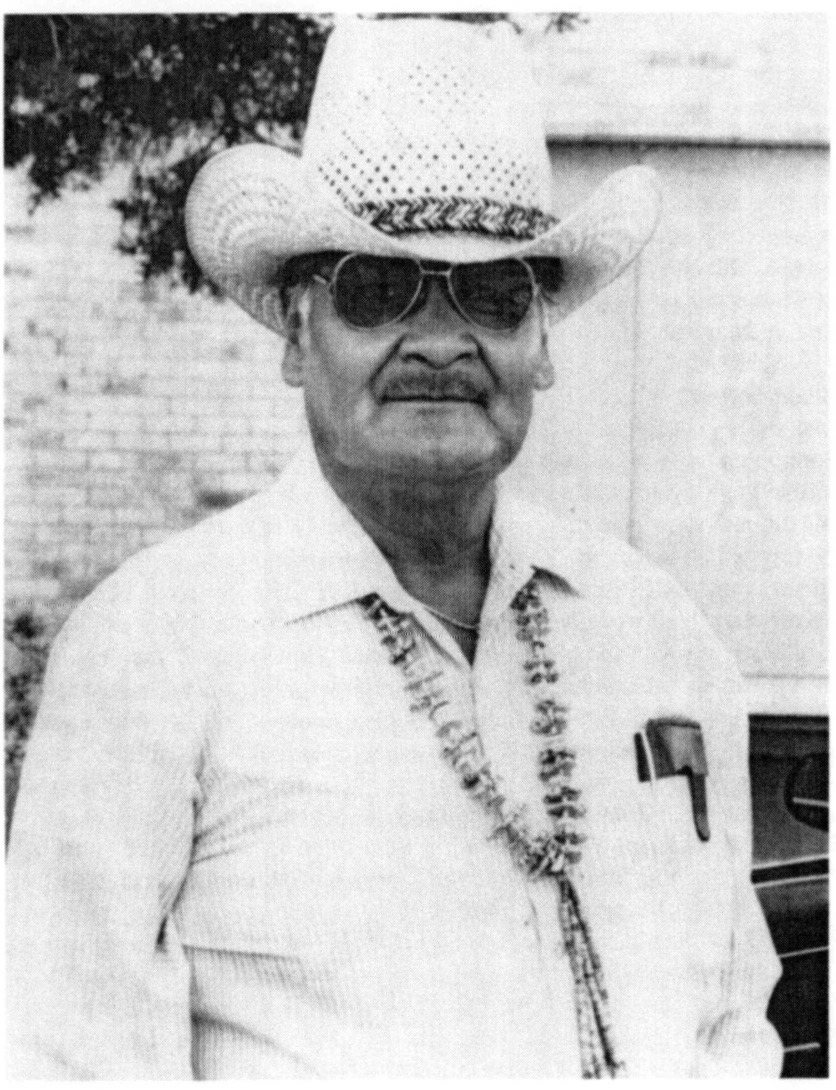

Fig. 8:1. Alfred K. Lorenzo. (Photograph furnishrf by the Lorenzo Family).

Fig. 8:2. Bertha Lorenzo's home southeast of Ramah, New Mexico.

Fig. 8:3. Rita Lorenzo's home, located in the vilage of Zuni, New Mexico.

translator when we interviewed his father and assisted us in contacting and interviewing a group of non-English speaking Navajos. Rita served as co-researcher and was invaluable in the preparation of this essay.

During the year Alfred translated for us, he told family stories about his grandparents and great-grandfather, stories about his boyhood adventures and misadventures, and stories about the landmarks we passed as he guided us through the Ramah area. He told us that he was the great-grandson of Many Beads, one of the seven headmen who with their outfits had settled in the Ramah, New Mexico, area south of Gallup and east of Zuni when the Navajo confinement at Fort Sumner ended in 1868. By stories, comments, and example he led us to know and appreciate the Navajo culture at Ramah. He was a natural fieldworker with great patience and quick humor and was skilled at listening carefully and responding appropriately. There are relationships in fieldwork, as in life in general, which are characterized by quickly achieved mutual understanding, acceptance, concern, and enjoyment; Alfred and I shared such a relationship. We had "visited hogan to hogan" [*hootaaghá* in Navajo], each of us had rescued the other from unexpected fieldwork pitfalls, and we had discussed field observations and ideas with great openness and concern for each other's ideas and opinions. We did not undergo a blood brother ceremony like that featured in a cowboy and Indian movie I enjoyed as a child and in which he had acted as a young adult, but in a sense we were brother researchers. We worked together on the Department of Education project and on another project, and we were planning to work together on others in the future.

Kim called me late in the evening March 8, 1988, to tell me that Alfred had died. One of the first funerary customs called into play by a death is the notification of family and friends. Alfred's mother Bertha and his sister found his body that day on the bed in his apartment near the University of New Mexico branch campus at Gallup. He was lying comfortably on his stomach with his head propped up on his hands, his face towards his television, which was still running. Because of his serious health problems including diabetes and high blood pressure, and the peaceful setting, his death was attributed to natural causes. Alfred had moved into the apartment when he enrolled in the University of New Mexico, majoring in social studies, and had been living alone there.

Alfred's body was prepared for burial by Rollie Mortuary of Gallup. Bodies were prepared for burial in their homes in the not very distant past by Zuni, Navajo and Mormon families, but today all three utilize the services of funeral homes. After she was notified of Alfred's death, Rita had a special bolo tie made by a Zuni jewelry maker who is a friend of the family. The bolo tie had three spider web turquoise stones on it, and each tip also contained a piece of turquoise. Alfred owned a traditional Navajo jacia necklace which was his favorite piece of Indian jewelry; he wore his necklace when his family took his picture (see Figs. 8:1) and for other dress occasions. He also had a gold wristwatch with a matching gold expansion band. After his death, his mother Bertha purchased a new Pendleton Indian blanket. The new blanket, the old watch, the old necklace and the new bolo tie were sealed in the casket with Alfred and buried with him.

Alfred's funeral service was held in the Church of Jesus Christ of Latter-day Saints Ward Building in Ramah and was planned by Alfred's daughters and the Mormon leaders who officiated. Alfred's casket was placed at the front of the room in which the funeral service was held. It was covered by a new Pendleton blanket Rita had purchased and had a framed photograph of him sitting on it. There were several floral arrangements decorating the front of the room.

A mimeographed bulletin was distributed by the ushers standing at the entrances to the room where the service was held. It listed the place and time of the service, the interment at Ramah Cemetery, the pallbearers, the honorary pallbearers and the schedule of service (see Fig. 8:4). Necessitated by someone being unable to attend and by requests and suggestions made after the bulletin was prepared, there were changes in the actual service announced by those presiding. The funeral was basically a Mormon funeral and began with an "Opening Prayer" given by one of the members of the local congregation. Next, the Relief Society Sisters sang "I know That My Redeemer Lives." The "Eulogy" was given by Marvin Lewis, who is thanked in the Preface of *The People of Rimrock* for his assistance to the Harvard Study:[14]

> Alfred Kirk Lorenzo was born May 19, 1934, in Ramah, New Mexico. He was the third child born to Thomas and Bertha Lorenzo. He passed on on March 8, 1988, in Gallup, New Mexico. Alfred is remembered by his family as an adventurous and energetic young boy. He constantly was seen riding his roan pony, performing tricks in front of his siblings. Alfred had a unique sense of humor which never failed to cheer up the family and people around him.
>
> He attended school at Rehoboth, New Mexico, and later at Albuquerque Indian School. He received his diploma through Ramah Navajo School Board Adult Education Program in June 1973. Prior to receiving his diploma, he attended a watch repair school in South Gate, California.
>
> Alfred's first job in the community was as an instructional aid at Ramah Dormitory. In 1976 he transferred to working for the Ramah School Board as an illustrator. He worked there until early 1985. When he resigned he had already completed several bilingual books which are now in libraries across the country.
>
> Alfred was a gifted artist receiving various awards for his art work. He always had a sketch book wherever he was. Some of his paintings are displayed at the Philbrook Art Museum in Oklahoma and at the Smithsonian Institute in Washington D.C.
>
> He married Idella Rita Enote on November 5, 1957. They had five children, two of whom passed on before him: Adrian Kirk in December 1973 and Alfreda Kaylene in December 1979. He is survived by Audrey Kim, Annette Marie, and Fedrick Thomas.
>
> Alfred was attending the UNM-Gallup Branch as a full-time student working toward his Associate of Arts Degree in Social Science at the time of his passing on. His children will deeply miss that special man they called "Daddie." The family will miss the special light he shed upon life.[15]

The "Message," next in the order of service, was given by Mormon High Counselor Leon Lambson, whose father is featured in Clyde Kluckhohn's *To*

IN LOVING MEMORY OF

ALFRED K. LORENZO
May 19, 1934 - March 8, 1988

PLACE AND TIME OF SERVICES
Church of Jesus Christ of Latter-Day Saints
Ramah, New Mexico
Saturday - March 12, 1988 - 2:00 P.M.

INTERMENT
Ramah Community Cemetery

PALLBEARERS

Art Begay	Eugene Pablano
Freddie Lee	Timothy Maria
Michael Begay	Dodge Chatto

HONORARY PALLBEARERS

Fred Enote, Jr.	Thomas Lorenzo
Louis Lorenzo	Ronald Lorenzo
Keith Cunningham	Ernest Begay
Alexander Phillips	Loy Lewis

Hugo Sanchez

SCHEDULE OF SERVICE

Conducting............Bishop Steve Davis

Opening Prayer.............Richard Evans

Song......"I Know That My Redeemer Lives"
by Relief Society Sisters

Eulogy......................Marvin Lewis

Song......................"Oh My Father"
by Relief Society Sisters

Message.....................Leon Lampson

Songs................."One Day At a Time"
"Same Ole Me"
by Leon Lambson

Closing Prayer.............Felix Martine

****

ARRANGEMENTS BY
ROLLIE MORTUARY
Gallup, N.M.

the Foot of the Rainbow.[16] To illustrate his talk, Mr. Lambson made use of a set of narratives recounting personal experiences he had shared with Alfred and his family; he told a number of stories about Alfred and Alfred's mother Bertha:

> I remember we was kids, you know, Vance and I—Vance's dad had a trading post on one side of the road and my dad had one on the other side right across the highway—and those people didn't have any transportation in those days. It was either a wagon or horseback, and Bertha was just a young woman, and she'd come in there, and Vance and I got to teasing her dog, and boy, she just reached up on one of them trees and grabbed a switch, and she just whaled the daylights out of both of us, (laughter) and we was a'taking off down the street, you know, and it was the best thing in the world to a couple of onry little kids, you know. I've been grateful for that, you know.

The Mormon, Zuni, and Navajo audience laughed appreciatively at the image of the High Counselor as an "onry little kid" being whipped by the respected, elderly Navajo matron as a young mother. Then he concluded his story:

> Kids need discipline, and they need it when somebody sees what they're doing. Then you discipline, you know, not to go home and tell their mom and dad, you know. They don't know, and they don't get the same feeling. I've been pretty grateful for that all my life that she had courage enough to say, 'Hey, here's a couple of kids out of line. I'll just put them in.'[17]

After the "Message" Mr. Lambson and his daughter sang "Beyond the Sunset," a song which describes reunion in heaven. Their second song was "It's Still the Same Old Me," a song about the continuity of personality and love. Mr. Lambson also explained to me that he had learned the song the evening before the service because Alfred's daughters had specifically requested it be sung at their father's funeral.

Next in the order of service, although it did not appear on the mimeographed program which was distributed, Alfred's niece read a poem about him she had written especially for the service:

> There once was a man strong and bold,
> There once was a man lonely and sad,
> He was torn and tattered from life
> Yet he refused to be sad and lonely,
> He rose from the ground and soared to
> The skies.
> He is strong and bold once again.

The final elements of the service were a "Closing Prayer" and the announcement "This concludes our service." After the "Closing Prayer" and the announcement, the congregation walked slowly by Alfred's casket.

While walking by the closed casket, the congregation directed their attention to his family, starting with his mother and father and ending with his youngest grandchild. The family remained seated in the front rows of pews, shaking hands with the people who went by and accepting their condolences.

After everyone but the family had left the church, the casket was loaded into the hearse. Then there was a procession of automobiles following the hearse to the cemetery. Alfred's children considered burying him at the Zuni cemetery where their brother and sister who had preceded him in death were interred, but in Navajo tradition it is the Navajo mother's decision where her son is to be buried, and the children honored their grandmother's decision that her son be buried in the Ramah Community Cemetery on the knoll south of Ramah.

The grave had been dug on the east slope of the cemetery. Folding metal chairs had been set up on the north side of the grave a few feet from its edge. Alfred's mother and father, his wife, his children and their mates and their children were seated on the chairs. The other members of his family stood behind the chairs, and the rest of the people who were attending the graveside service stood facing the grave on the other three sides.

After the casket was unloaded from the hearse and placed on the braces across the open grave, the new Pendleton Indian blanket which Rita had purchased was again placed on top of it. Then one of the Mormon elders consecrated the grave. The guidelines for the consecration of graves given in a church handbook for elders direct:

> Address our Heavenly Father in prayer, dedicate and consecrate the burial plot as the resting place for the body of the deceased by the authority of the Priesthood, appropriately if desired pray to the Lord that this spot of earth may be a hallowed and protected place until the time appointed for the body to be resurrected and united with the spirit, request the Lord to comfort the family, express such other thoughts as the Spirit dictates in the name of Jesus Christ.[18]

The prayer to consecrate Alfred's grave contained each of these parts. The words used in the request were "to protect this place from the elements." After the consecration Alfred's casket was lowered into the grave.

Alfred's Zuni family and friends walked by the grave in a circular pattern starting at the north side of the grave, and one by one took a pinch of white cornmeal from one of two small bowls placed by the head of the grave following the Mormon consecration. Alfred's Zuni family held the cornmeal between their left thumbs and forefingers, made a circle over their heads, and then sprinkled the cornmeal on the casket. As they performed the ritual, they said prayers in Zuni asking the dead person to pass on and not linger with the living. Then each of the Zuni took a pinch of white cornmeal between the right thumb and forefinger and sprinkled it in a long line indicating the path the spirit was to follow while they offered prayers asking for long life for the people remaining. The cornmeal that was left in the bowls when each of the Zunis present at the grave had passed by was emptied into a cotton cloth which was placed in the grave with the casket.

After the Zuni ceremony was concluded, members of the Mormon congregation shoveled dirt onto the casket until its top was completely covered. Then one of the group used a front-end loader to fill and mound the grave.

When the Mormon men had smoothed the mound, Alfred's Navajo friends and family placed plastic flowers on it. The younger children each placed an individual flower in the mound. The older children and young adults laid arrangements in the forms of a cross and a wreath of plastic flowers attached to Styrofoam bases.

Funerary meals are customary in many cultures; the funerary practices which marked Alfred's burial included four funerary meals. After the graveside services were concluded, people left the cemetery, returned to their cars, and drove to their homes or to the Ward Building where the Relief Society served a meal consisting of chili beans prepared several different ways, home baked and commercial breads, jello salads, several kinds of sheet cakes, and water and punch. Many of the people who attended the dinner stopped by the tables where Alfred's mother and father and his wife were seated to visit and express sympathy.

After the public meal at the ward building, there was another gathering at Zuni at the home of Alfred's wife and another meal which was brought by Zuni family and friends and then yet another gathering at his mother's home southeast of Ramah and another meal which was brought by Navajo family and friends.

It is customary at Zuni to have a more directly culturally specific funerary meal four days after a death. This meal is for both the family who remain and for the one who is going on and includes the Zuni ritual of feeding the dead. Because Alfred's Zuni family knew that he had attended and observed such meals and rituals during the time he lived in the village and "knew the Zuni ways," they felt that this ritual and meal should be held for him, and so it was. The ritual meal was held four days after Alfred's funeral because no one knew exactly when he had died. At dawn the doors of the family home and car were opened so that Alfred's spirit would have free egress. Rita butchered three sheep from her flock; her family brought in four 25-pound bags of Bluebird flour; they helped her bake Zuni bread in her outdoor oven, make mutton stew, and prepare all the accouterments of a Zuni ritual meal. All who attended the ceremony ate; portions of stew, servings of Zuni bread, helpings of all of the salads, and pieces of apples and oranges were place upon a fire built outside her home; special Zuni prayers were offered by one of Alfred's male Navajo relatives; and Alfred's spirit was fed.

Alfred's grave runs east to west, and the head of the grave and the end of the casket containing his head are placed so that his head points toward the west, and he would be facing east if he sat or stood up. The mortuary placed a small metal plaque and holder with his name, date of birth, and date of death incised on it at the head of the grave. Kim and Rita went to an Albuquerque monument company and selected a gray granite tombstone for Alfred's grave. The people at the monument company showed them a book of designs and letter types and styles they incise on their stones, and Rita and Kim designed a marker using options shown in the book. They chose a cross and praying hands as petroglyphic elements, the words "in loving memory of," Alfred's full name, and his date of birth and death to be included on the stone (see Fig. 8:5). Kim and her husband transplanted iris plants from his family cemetery at Zuni and outlined the high mound of Alfred's grave by placing them around its edges.

The tri-cultural funerary practices with which the people of Rimrock buried Alfred K. Lorenzo included the notification of relatives and friends of his death, the preparation of his body for burial, the traditional funeral and graveside services, and the public and private funerary meals, gatherings, rituals, marker selection and gravesite decoration. Together, these practices evince the cultures which created them and a cross-cultural configuration of acceptance and consideration toward those whom we know and with whom we live which has been accepted by this generation of the people of Rimrock.

Zuni, Mormon and Navajo traditions functioned together to notify family and friends of the death of Alfred K. Lorenzo. Within the Mormon community there is a traditional, informal three-tiered notification system activated whenever a funeral is to be held at the ward building. The immediate family of the deceased notifies other family members, close friends and the church leadership. The leader of the church who is contacted by the family notifies other church leaders and organizations that are to be involved in the funeral service, the graveside service, or the meal which is customarily held at the ward building after the graveside service. These people in turn notify others whom they feel would want to know about the death and the services. Formal notification of the community at large is provided by an announcement published in the local newspaper.

Word of a death was spread rapidly by word of mouth within traditional Navajo culture in the past. Today Navajos announce someone has died by having members of the family notify others by telephone when possible or in person in the case of isolated outfits not having telephone service. As Leighton and Kluckhohn indicated, the reason for notification in the past was to help people avoid accidentally being in the presence of a body rather than to insure that people attended its burial.[19]

Matilda Coxe Stevenson described the traditional method of notification of a death which was practiced by the Zuni at the time she did her research: "A death is usually announced as soon as it occurs by a woman of the immediate family to a member of the clan of the deceased and to one of the clan of the spouse, and they in turn spread the news among the clans and intimates of the family."[20]

The objects which were buried with or alongside Alfred are culturally significant. Bolo ties are of Anglo-American origin; the one buried with Alfred was made by a Zuni craftsperson and was buried with him as was his wristwatch, a typical Anglo-American artifact, and his jacia necklace, a traditional Navajo necklace which may well have been made by a Navajo craftsperson, although such pieces are also made and worn by the Zuni. Both his wife and mother buried with him an Indian blanket woven by the Pendleton Woolen Mill in Oregon and of a type and design used by Zunis, Navajos, and

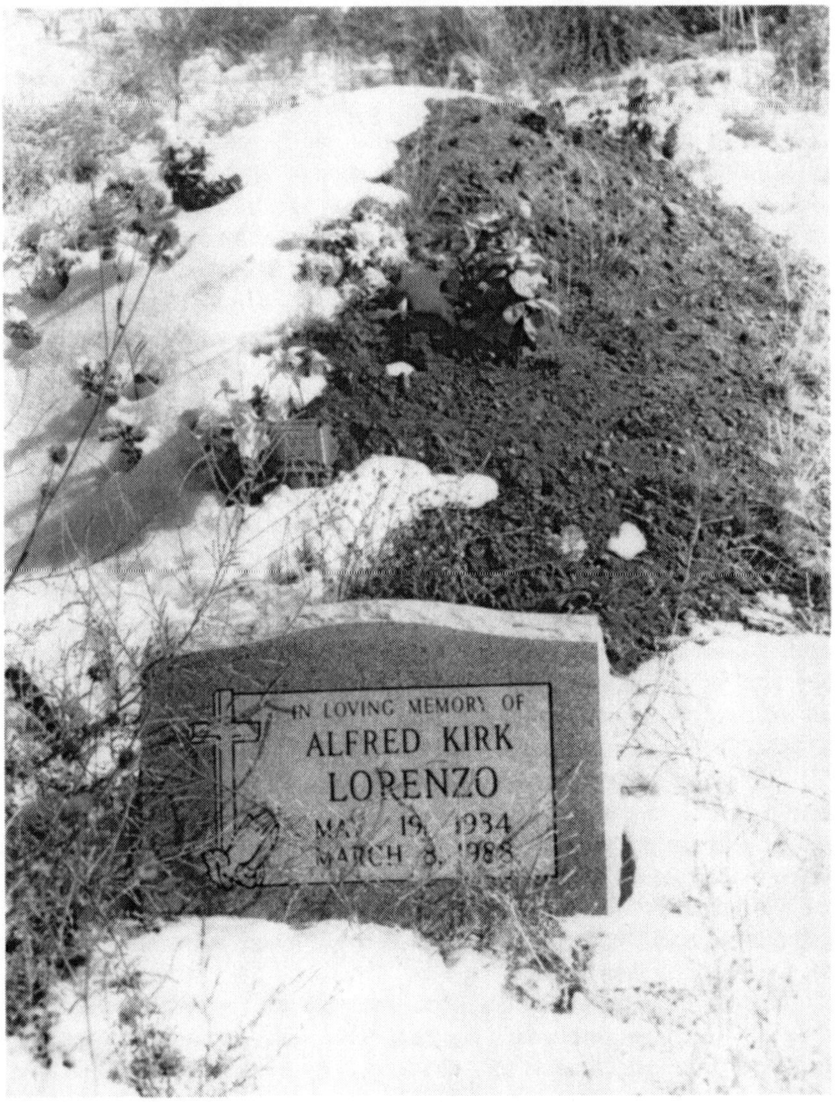

Fig. 8:5. Alfred K. Lorenzo's grave in the Ramah Community Cemetery, Ramah, New Mexico.

many other Native American groups. The only object buried with Alfred which was culturally specific was the Zuni cornmeal wrapped in a plain cotton cloth.

The burial objects themselves derived their meanings primarily from Zuni and Ramah Navajo cultures. In Zuni tradition, objects are buried for living and for the dead. Personal objects which are closely associated with an individual serve as reminders of loss; therefore, Zunis traditionally buried individuals' personal objects as a part of funerary practices. Rita said that the mortuary returned Alfred's personal effects, including his watch, to her, and she "gave them back to him." For the Zuni, another purpose of burial objects is to provide the spirit of the deceased with things needed or desired. Thus a Zuni dancer, and all Zuni men have the opportunity to become Zuni dancers at some point in their lives, has his sacred dance paraphernalia buried so that he may participate in ceremonial dances; and Alfred, not being Zuni and thus having no Zuni dance paraphernalia, was buried with a new Pendleton blanket and a new bolo tie so that he could be a well-dressed spectator at ceremonial dances.

Objects are also buried for both the living and the dead in Navajo tradition. Alfred's jacia necklace most closely matched the Zuni concept of personal goods for the Navajo, and it was buried with him primarily because of the idea that it was so closely identified with him that he would want to have it with him. Kluckhohn analyzed concepts of death among the Navajo and concluded:

> Death is evil, and the dead are feared. Every item in the funeral ritual is intended to prevent or cajole the deceased from returning to plague his relatives. The corpse's property is deposited with him, but this is no spontaneous gesture of affection nor a disinterested desire to promote well-being in the afterworld. Navaho lore teaches that any stinginess on the part of the living will bring swift and terrible retaliation.[21]

Ramah Navajo eschatology and cosmology have certainly not remained static since Kluckhohn's observations in the late 1950s, but Alfred's body may well have been buried with the traditional jacia necklace and Pendleton blanket at least partially for traditional Navajo reasons.

The funeral service held for Alfred was influenced primarily by Mormon funerals and to a lesser extent by Navajo tradition. The obituary, the narratives included in the message, and the song "It's Still the Same Old Me" were all typical of the Mormon funeral tradition which emphasizes the life of body and spirit after death. Mr. Lambson's story he told about Bertha established a close inter-relatedness between him and the Lorenzo family; Bertha functioned as mother in his narrative, and Alfred was therefore presented as brother. Mr. Lambson explained to me in a later interview, "First, you want them to laugh and feel good, and then you communicate with them." Mormon humorous narratives at Rimrock exist primarily to teach Mormon polity, practice, and perception. Story became exemplum; the message used the death of a brother to teach brotherhood.

The poem written by Alfred's niece was a distinctly Navajo element in the funeral service. Although written in English, the poem's reliance upon syntactical parallelism as its major structural device rather than rhyme is more closely related to Navajo ethnopoetics than to traditional Anglo-American versification.[22]

The graveside services called forth Mormon, Navajo and Zuni customs and belief. In their theology Mormons stress the future existence of the deceased. They emphasize a time of resurrection beyond the spirit world when the spirit will be reunited with the body as it was during its earthly existence. The verses in *Doctrine and Covenants* most often quoted to illustrate this concept read:

> For man is spirit. The elements are eternal, and spirit and element, inseparably connected, receive a fullness of joy: And when separated, man cannot receive a fullness of joy.[23]

Throughout the *Book of Mormon*, the Mormon scriptures, there are many other references to this belief that the physical body and the spirit will be reunited. For example:

> I soon go to rest in the paradise of God, until my spirit and body shall again reunite.[24]

and:

> The soul shall be restored to body and body to soul; yea, and every limb and joint shall be restored to its body; yea, even a hair of the head shall not be lost; but all the things shall be restored to their proper and perfect frame.[25]

The belief in a future existence structures the Mormon attitude toward grief and death. According to Mormon theology, the deceased person remains essentially the person he was and will be reunited with family and friends at some future time. The Mormon graveside service stressing the importance of protecting the grave and body from the elements and destruction can best be understood in light of the idea of the physical resurrection of the body as a part of the future existence of the deceased.

Stevenson published detailed accounts of Zuni death practices and beliefs, including cornmeal rituals similar to that which the Zuni members of Alfred's family performed at his graveside, but the few people necessary to carry the body to the grave were the only ones who accompanied it there in the periods of time when she made her observations, and the ritual was performed in the home as the body was prepared for burial. Stevenson noted, "All hands dipped meal from a small bowl and sprinkled it through the opening [of the blanket] upon the face, the youngest child being led by the grandfather to perform this rite,"[26] and the ritual she described closely resembles the actions of Alfred's Zuni family as daughters, son and sons-in-law, grandsons and granddaughters circled past the two bowls.

White cornmeal, one of our Zuni co-researchers explained, was used symbolically because the Zunis believe that white cornmeal has "a tendency to die and spring forth a spiritual life after it dies." She further explained that the ritual meant "Alfred doesn't get buried there forever; he comes out of there."[27] This interrelatedness of death and birth is frequently expressed in Zuni culture. One of the folktales Frank Hamilton Cushing collected ends with the death of a young wife and the words "But then it is well! If men and women had never died, then the world long ago had overflowed with children, starvation, and warring."[28] In traditional thought and in Zuni traditional ceremony, death makes room for new life. The instructions given the dead emphasize a similar attitude toward death. "Do not linger with the living, accept change, become actively and fully involved in being what you now are—a spirit," is the message for the dead conveyed by the Zuni ceremonies.

In Zuni tradition the person who places the bowls of cornmeal at the head of the grave is a clan member of the deceased (related to him on his mother's side of his family). Since Alfred was Navajo and did not have Zuni clan relatives, the responsibility for arranging and overseeing the bowls of corn meal would normally have passed to his wife's clan relatives (related to her on her mother's side of her family). Since Alfred's wife's mother was a Pima-Maricopa Native American, his wife's father's clan member filled the role and served the function. Alfred's wife's father's relative acted the part of his clan sister; Zuni adapted and arranged its funerary practice to bury Alfred as a brother.

The use of plastic flowers at graveside is a relatively recent addition to Navajo ceremony. The Navajo are noted for adopting and adapting items or traits from other cultures which suit their needs and purposes. The incorporative acculturation of plastic flowers is now Navajo, may be a borrowing from Anglo-American culture, but is also striking similar to the way flowers are traditionally used in Mexican-American cultures including the Rimrock Spanish-Americans with whom the Ramah Navajo have had a long, personal relationship, suggesting that others of the people of Rimrock helped bury Alfred even if their influence was indirect.

Public funerary meals similar to the one at the Mormon Ward Building and the ones at Bertha's home and Rita's home are common in many cultures. These meals and gatherings were not in any way in opposition to each other but rather were complementary to each other. Jocelyn Drozd's comments about the functions of American funerary meals describe in general many of the functions of funerary meals at Rimrock:

> The repast component of the funeral rite functions, first and obviously, to feed and refect those who have participated in the ritual. Second, the food of the repast is a "natural" symbol around which to construct rituals to "end" bereavement activities and bring the living back to a reaffirmation of continuing life. Third, the repast component of the funeral ritual shares the functional characteristics of the entire ritual, such as the reinforcement of the sense of organic solidarity, the publicizing of this solidarity and the recognition, by the community at large, of the new roles within the family structure. Finally, perhaps a new function of the repast, would be to counterpoint alienation.[29]

The ceremony of feeding the dead held four days after Alfred's funeral was distinctly Zuni. The spirits of the dead are traditionally believed by the Zuni to linger near their homes for four days and nights after death and then travel to Kolhu/Wala:Wa, the Zuni heaven, to dwell. The ceremony of feeding the dead is to encourage and sustain them on their journey. The Zuni believe that the spirits of the dead return to the great Zuni ceremonial dances, but they do not believe that the spirits remain at Zuni. Spirits of the dead are not feared, but they are encouraged to separate themselves from the people who are still living.[30] Perhaps the most remarkable feature of the ceremony to feed Alfred's spirit was the fact that the ritual Zuni prayers which are traditionally offered during the ceremony by a male Zuni relative of the dead to hasten the spirit on its journey to Zuni heaven were prayed by one of Alfred's Navajo relatives in the ceremony held for him so that Navajos had a part in the Zuni ceremony.

Alfred's grave, his tombstone and his grave's landscaping are signs and symbols of cultures and their folklives. The spatial placement of Alfred's grave and casket follow Mormon burial customs shared with many other Anglo-American Christian traditions which bury the dead so that they may face the rising sun or Christ at the time of the second coming. This spatial arrangement is different from the traditional burial position of Zuni but is fully compatible with Navajo custom which decrees that the buried may face any of the traditional six directions but down.

Alfred's tombstone is a Christian and Mormon element of his burial. The praying hands and cross motifs are well within the boundaries of traditional Mormon iconography, and the use of a commercial stone differs from both the Navajo custom of not erecting any kind of memorial marker at a grave and the Zuni traditional use of handmade objects as memorial markers.

The iris plants which were used to outline Alfred's grave and decorate it were brought from Zuni. The placement of the iris around the edges of the grave recalls the traditional use of fences and other boundaries to enclose graves in the extensive Zuni cemetery.

The continued presence of the temporary marker from the funeral home on Alfred's grave is a feature of his burial which is shared with the other Navajo graves in this section of the Ramah Community Cemetery. Objects which have been in contact with dead bodies, burials, or graves are viewed as potentially dangerous in traditional Navajo culture and are generally not removed for any reason.

The tri-cultural funerary practices utilized by the people of Rimrock and their evincing of cultures are remarkable; the fact that they support each other is perhaps even more remarkable. This acceptance of and concern for other peoples and cultures who live nearby, typified by Alfred K. Lorenzo's burial, is made possible by Zunis' emphasis "to be courteous to those who come your way," Navajo incorporative acculturation and traditional interpretations of Mormon theology.

The people of today's Rimrock grew up together, went to school together and work together—all in the shadow of some well-known, unflattering descriptions of their cultures' interactions. Evon Vogt and Malcolm J. Arth's chapter, "Intercultural Relations" in *The People of Rimrock*[31] painted a bleak picture of intolerance, discrimination, hatred and occasional violence between the various cultures, and the people of Rimrock today are very much aware of how their parents were described. (There are, I have observed, more copies per capita of *The People of Rimrock* and of many less well-known research publications concerning the area and its interactions to be found today at Rimrock than are to be found anywhere else in the world.) The people of Rimrock today frequently report that members of one or more cultures, usually one or ones other than their own, were deeply hurt in the past by the way they were described in cultural research. The people of Rimrock today frequently describe cultures in the area other than their own with the statement, "You couldn't find a better group of people." Perhaps the most important change in the cultures of the area has been an increase in the general self awareness of the descendants of the subjects of the Harvard study of values and in their awareness of each other. The people of Rimrock today, by and large, seem to share a sense of brotherhood which is partially due to the many books and articles written about the area.

Richard M. Dorson indicated that an area's sense of itself as indicated by a special name was the most reliable clue to the existence of a folk cultural area;[32] it is also true that a folk cultural area may be called into existence by being so designated. It was a regional Rimrock folk culture or family (encompassing within it Zuni, Mormon, and Ramah Navajo cultures) which buried Alfred K. Lorenzo as a brother, and the multi-cultural ceremonies and objects which they employed were an appropriate and fitting tribute to a man who loved to observe and experience cultural differences and cultural interactions.

Notes

I wish to express my gratitude to Alfred's friends and families for sharing information about his funerary services and their meanings with me. Unless otherwise indicated, all photographs in the essay are by Kathryn Cunningham.

[1]Richard Huntington and Peter Metcalf, *Celebrations of Death: The Anthropology of Mortuary Ritual* (New York: Cambridge UP, 1979), p. 211.

[2]C. Gregory Crampton, *The Zunis of Cibola* (Salt Lake City: U of Utah P, 1977), p. 2.

[3]"Navajo," in *Perspectives in American Indian Culture Change*, ed. Edward H. Spicer (Chicago: U of Chicago P, 1961), p. 328.

[4]Arthur Woodward, *A Brief History of Navajo Silversmithing* (Flagstaff Arizona: Museum of Northern Arizona *Bulletin*, 14, 1938).

[5]Ruth M. Underhill, *The Navajos* (Norman: U of Oklahoma P, 1956), pp. 46-47.

[6]Stephen C. Jett and Virginia E. Spencer, *Navajo Architecture: Forms, History, Distribution* (Tucson: U of Arizona P, 1981).

[7]Underhill, *The Navajos*.

[8]David M. Brugge and Charlotte J. Frisbie, ed., *Navajo Religion and Culture: Selected Views* (Santa Fe: Museum of New Mexico P, 1982).

[9]John L. Landgraf, *Land-Use in the Ramah Area of New Mexico: An Anthropological Approach to Areal Study* (Cambridge, MA: Papers of the Peabody Museum of American Archaeology and Ethnology, Vol. 42, No. 1, 1954). p. 952.

[10]Evon Z. Vogt and Ethel M. Albert, ed. *The People of Rimrock: A Study of Values in Five Cultures* (New York: Atheneum, 1970).

[11]Florence Kluckhohn and Fred Strodtbeck. *Variations in Value-Orientations: A Theory Tested in Five Cultures* (Evanston, Illinois: Row, Peterson and Co., 1961).

[12]See the bibliography given in Vogt and Albert, *The People of Rimrock*, pp. 309-320.

[13]Dorothea Leighton and Clyde Kluckhohn, *Children of the People* (New York: Octagon Books, 1974), pp. 134-135.

[14]Vogt and Albert, *The People of Rimrock*, p. x.

[15]A copy of the eulogy was furnished to me by Marvin Lewis.

[16]Clyde Kluckhohn, *To the Foot of the Rainbow* (New York: Nash and Crayson, 1927), pp. 10-12.

[17](REC88-KKBC-C11), Recorded June 9, 1988, 67-year-old male interviewed by Keith and Kathryn Cunningham at Ramah, New Mexico. (Citations beginning REC refer to Arizona Friends of Folklore field tapes.)

[18]*Principles of the Gospel* (Salt Lake City: Church of Jesus Christ of Latter-day Saints, 1982), p. 95

[19]*Children of The People*, pp. 91-93.

[20]"The Zuni Indians: Their Mythology, Esoteric Fraternities, and Ceremonies," in *Twenty-Third Annual Report of the Bureau of American Ethnology, 1901-1902* (Washington: Government Printing Office, 1904), pp. 305-306.

[21]Richard Kluckhohn, ed., *Culture and Behavior: Collected Essays of Clyde Kluckhohn* (New York: The Free Press of Glencoe, 1962), p. 141.

[22]For a description of Navajo ethnopoetics see Barre Toelken, "The 'Pretty Language' of Yellowman: Genre, Mode, and Texture in Navaho Coyote Narratives," *Genre* 2 (1969), pp. 211-235. Syntactical rhythm as a poetic device in Anglo-American verse is explained and discussed by Stephen Minot, *Three Genres* (Englewood Cliffs, New Jersey: Prentice-Hall, 1971), pp. 50-52.

[23]*Doctrine and Covenants* 93:33-34.

[24]*Book of Mormon*, Moroni 10:34.

[25]*Book of Mormon*, Alma 40:23.

[26]"The Zuni Indians," p. 309.

[27](NA89-KKBC-C1), recorded 15 March 1989, 72-year-old female interviewed by Keith and Kathryn Cunningham at Zuni, New Mexico. (Citations beginning NA refer to the Arizona Friends of Folklore field tapes.)

[28]*Zuni Folk Tales* (Tucson: U of Arizona P, 1986), p. 33.

[29]Joycelyn Therese Helen Drozd, "An Investigation of the Significance of the Repast Component in American Funeral Ritual" (Master's thesis, Northern Illinois U, 1980), p. 40.

[30]Elsie Clews Parsons, "A Few Zuni Death Beliefs and Practices," *American Anthropologist*, n.s., 18 (1916), pp. 250-255.

[31]*The People of Rimrock*, pp.46-62.

[32]*Buying the Wind* (Chicago: U of Chicago P, 1964), p. 289.

Oriental and Polynesian Cemetery Traditions in the Hawaiian Islands

Nanette Napoleon Purnell

Hawai'i is often referred to as the "Melting Pot" of the Pacific because of the diversity of ethnic groups that have settled in the islands from the orient and throughout the Pacific basin.

Even though the "American/Western" culture is dominant in contemporary Hawai'i, most ethnic groups have managed to preserve and perpetuate much of the traditional belief systems and customs of their homeland and maintain a very strong sense of ethnic identity. This sense of ethnic identity is evident in the clothes people wear, the foods they eat, the social activities they attend, and even the manner in which they bury their dead.

In Hawai'i there are four ethnic groups, in particular, whose cemeteries and burial traditions mark them as some of the most fascinating and unique in America today: the Chinese, the Japanese, the Samoan/Tongan and the native Hawaiian.

The Chinese Way of Death

The name of the first person of Chinese ancestry to set foot on the shores of the Hawaiian islands is unknown, but it is believed he arrived via merchant ship in the year 1789, only 11 years after the British explorer, Captain James Cook, discovered the islands in 1778.

Although small groups of Chinese continued to come to the islands throughout the early 1800s, the first major group of immigrants did not appear until 1852, arriving as contract laborers to work on the sugar plantations which were just then emerging as the major economic industry in the Hawaiian islands. Although these laborers brought very few material goods with them in these early years, they did bring their own religious beliefs, their own cultural traditions, and their own way of burying and honoring their dead.

When these pioneer settlers arrived in Hawai'i, one of the first things they did was to form fraternal organizations, called "Societies," which served primarily as extended families that were responsible for the general social and economic welfare of its members. These responsibilities included helping with arranged marriages, supporting indigent families, and establishing "proper" burial grounds for the dead.

To fulfill this last obligation, most Societies put aside part of their membership dues to pay for a parcel of land that would be used as temporary resting places for the spirits of the departed.

Traditional religious beliefs, which were part Buddhist, part Confucianist and part Taoist, held that the spirits of the dead could not attain peace in the afterworld unless the bones of the dead could be laid to rest in the person's ancestral village in China. But because these early settlers were living thousands of miles from their homeland, they had to temporarily bury their dead in cemeteries established by the Societies.

Customarily, these bodies were left in the cemetery for a period of about seven years. After that time, if the family or Society had saved enough money, the bones were dug up, bundled, and placed in porcelain jars, wooden boxes or even suitcases to be shipped back to China (Fig. 9:1). The cost of returning the bones included not only the cost of sending the bones themselves but also the boatfare for a living family member or close friend who would attend to a proper re-burial in the ancestral village.

Many families or Societies were able to save enough money for this special voyage. Many did not. To accommodate those bones which were dug up but not sent back to China, special "bone houses" were built in the cemeteries to house the remains (See Fig. 9:1). These bone houses were intended to be temporary storage facilities for those families still saving money for the return journey, but many became permanent with the passing of time and the increasing influence of Western religious beliefs in the Chinese community.

"Feng Shui"—The Chinese Cemetery Selection System

In 1851 a small group of Chinese leaders in the community established the Lin Yee Chung Society. Its purpose was to purchase burial land, to coordinate traditional Chinese funeral rites and to arrange for the return of remains to China for permanent burial when possible. To this end the founding fathers enlisted the help of a young man named Lum Ching, who came to Hawai'i in hopes of making a living with his freshly acquired knowledge of an astronomy/geology-based concept called *Feng-shui.*[1]

Feng-shui rules dictate that, wherever possible, Chinese cemeteries should be placed on a prominent hillside overlooking a body of water—a river, the ocean, a lake—and that it should be surrounded by cliffs or mountains on at least two sides. A hillside location affords the spirits of the dead a pleasant view of nature, and of village life below, while the mountains and the water serve as boundaries for the spirits who dwell in and around the burial grounds in the afterworld of the dead. These boundaries are to stop the spirits from their natural tendency to wander away from the burial grounds in order to make trouble for the living. This protection system is further enhanced by the placement of a "spirit gate" (Fig. 9:2) at the entrance to the cemetery. This gate is not to keep the living from coming into the cemetery, but rather to keep the spirits of the dead from wandering out of it.

According to Lin Yee Chung historian, Wah Chan Tom:

Fig. 9:1. "Bone House" at the Lin Yee Chung Chinese Cemetery, Manoa Valley. Inside are approximately 100 jars, suitcases and boxes holding bones removed from their graves many years ago to await shipment back to China.

Fig. 9:2. Spirit Gate at entry functions to keep spirits of the dead from following their natural tendency to wander away from the cemetery. Lin Yee Chung Chinese Cemetery.

Lum Ching would often be seen carrying two round "magic" instruments on the outskirts of the city, studying the environment of various locales. These instruments were the "low poon," an astronomy-based compass, and the light-reflecting mirror. These were primitive instruments for measuring actual, scientific phenomena.

One morning Lum Ching and a friend hiked into Manoa Valley (on the island of O'ahu) and noticed a peculiar knoll projecting into the center of the valley, about a mile from where they were standing. They hiked to the knoll, then called "Akaka Peak," where they discovered a beautiful view from the valley to the sea.

Lum Ching then carefully set his complicated compass on a level surface following the run of the mountain range, and to his surprise, the compass needle pointed directly south. He did some further calculations and set his magic mirror alongside the compass, tilting it in several directions to catch the rays of the sun.

In astonishment, he turned to his friend and said, "We are at an extraordinary spot. It is the pulse of the watchful dragon of the valley. People from all directions will come from across the seas and gather here to pay homage. It is a haven suitable for the living as well as the dead. The Chinese people must buy this area and keep it as sacred ground.[2]

The Lin Yee Chung Society immediately bought the parcel of land, thereby establishing the first exclusively Chinese cemetery in Hawai'i (Fig. 9:2). The great natural beauty of the site in Manoa valley, and its status as the "dragon's pulse," attracted many members of the Chinese community. Today, it is not only the oldest and most historic Chinese cemetery in the state, it is also the most significant in terms of its adherence to the principles of *Feng-shui*.

"Ching Ming"—The Chinese Memorial "Season"

Every year in April the Chinese in Hawai'i, like their counterparts in China, celebrate *Ching Ming*. Literally translated as the "Clear-Bright festival," *Ching Ming* is the traditional spring "Festival of the Dead." According to Duane J.L. Pang, a Taoist Priest in Honolulu:

Ching Ming's tradition goes back as far as the early Chou Dynasty, originally associated with the idea of fertility, freedom, and love. Because it announced the advent of spring, it began as a celebration of life-renewal that coincided with spring's mating season. It was an agrarian fertility festival marking the beginning of the active outdoor period of life.

This celebration of new life also caused a craving for the blessings of the ancestors. It was the Chinese belief that the dead dwelt in the afterworld, but had a strong influence over the destinies of men. The worshipping of the dead was undoubtedly the desire to invoke their aid, or at any rate ensure that they did nothing harmful to them or the annual crop. Originally, sacrifice and homage to the ancestors were paid in ancestral halls or in homes. The practices of worshipping at the graves evolved during the Chou Dynasty, when this spring festival evolved into an annual family outing in the countryside for a day of picnicking and cleaning the graves.[3]

Anthropologist Francis L.K. Hsu has noted that the Chinese have three basic assumptions about ancestor worship: 1) that all good fortune or misfortune of (living) individuals derives from the shadows of their ancestors; 2) that all departed ancestors have needs like those they had while living; and 3) that the departed ancestors will assist their children and relatives if veneration is shown to them by taking care of their gravesites.[4]

Traditionally, *Ching Ming* begins on the 106th day after Winter solstice (December 21), and is usually placed 15 days after the Spring equinox. According to the solar calendar, then, *Ching Ming* begins on the 5th of April, varying according to the lunar calendar between the 10th and 20th days of the third moon. In Hawai'i, *Ching Ming* "officially" begins on the 5th of April, but unless the 5th happens to fall on a Saturday or Sunday, opening ceremonies, which are held individually by each cemetery, are scheduled for the first weekend in April.[5]

The most important ritual performed at the centuries-old ceremonial rites on the opening day of *Ching Ming* is the "Three Presentations Ceremony," a 34-step religious service that is usually conducted by a Buddhist or Taoist priest at the grave of the *tai-ju*, or "Grand Ancestor" (the first person to have been buried at the site) (Fig. 9:3). The actual steps in the ceremony are as follows:

1. Brief ritual of thanks for blessings of Mother Earth.
2. Call to gather and stand at attention.
3. Light three rounds of firecrackers.
4. Beat drums and sound gongs.
5. Sound loud fanfare (by Chinese band).
6. Render soft music (by Chinese band).
7. Head of Ritual (President) takes position, advancing one step.
8. Ceremonial assistants advance one step.
9. All other participants prepare to perform.
10. Present red banner and ornaments.
11. Present bamboo torches and guide strips.
12. Present large lighted incense, three times.
13. Present fresh flowers, three times.
14. Bow three times.
15. Offer tea, lifting center cup. Refill all five.
16. Offer wine, lifting center glass. Refill all five.
17. Offer rice, lifting center bowl.
18. Offer entree—fish or meat or pork.
19. Offer vegetable dish.
20. Cut up the roast pork.
21. Offer the roast pork.
22. Offer the plate of sugar buns.
23. Offer the plate of fresh fruits.
24. Bow three times.
25. Reader of eulogy steps forward.
26. Present Eulogy.
27. Present the assortment of paper images.
28. Send paper images to be burned.

29. Bow three times for final time.
30. Head of Ritual steps back and retreats.
31. Ceremonial assistants step back and retreat.
32. Reader of eulogy steps back and retreats.
33. Ceremony completed,
34. Light firecrackers.[6]

This formal ritual may be broadly divided into three major sections: preparation and decoration (step 1-13); offering of tea, wine and food (step 15-23); and reading of the eulogy and presentation, by burning, of the ceremonial money and paper images (steps 25-28). Three bows of respect by all those present are extended after each section. At the conclusion of the ceremony, a string of 10,000 or more firecrackers is set off. The main ceremony described above takes approximately one hour. Following its conclusion, a number of less elaborate services are held at various other important gravesites in the cemetery, such as the Tomb of the Unknown Chinese Soldiers, the Tomb of the Earth Mother (who protects those buried at the cemetery) and at the Bone House. When all of these ceremonies, which are conducted by the officers of the Society (who are all male) have been completed, individual families, including women and children, conduct similar rituals at specific individual gravesites (Fig. 9:4). Symbolic foods, such as rice, roasted duck, sweet buns and tea, as well as decorative materials, candles and incense are placed at the grave to provide for the dead in the afterworld. Symbolic "grave money" is also burned (Fig. 9:5), and firecrackers are set off to chase away any evil spirits that may be lurking around the graveyard.

In recent years a number of the elaborate rituals associated with *Ching Ming* have been altered or adapted to fit western values and traditions, or have been abandoned altogether in favor of more "Christian" burial rites. Still, it is interesting to note that while many Chinese today are Christian, adherence to traditional Chinese burial customs are still being practiced in some quarters, although sometimes without the full understanding or acceptance of the traditional meaning of such rituals.

Japanese Plantation Graveyards

The second major group of immigrants to arrive in the Hawaiian islands to work as contract laborers were the Japanese, in 1885.[7] Like the Chinese before them, the Japanese brought with them very little in the way of material goods but held fast to their traditional religious beliefs and cultural practices.

When these first immigrants arrived, they were assigned to live in plantation-owned and operated camps, located in the immediate vicinity of the sugar mills, which dominated the landscape as well as the economic status of Hawai'i in the 19th century. The camps were spartan yet self-sufficient communities which included a number of one and two-room bungalows, a general store, a "bath house" and a cemetery. These plantation cemeteries were owned by the plantations, but maintained by the residents of the camps.

Even though laborers worked in the fields up to 12 hours a day, six days a

Fig. 9:3. Officers of the Lin Yee Chung Chinese Cemetery perform the "Three Presentations Ceremony" which officially begins *Ching Ming*, the Chinese memorial season.

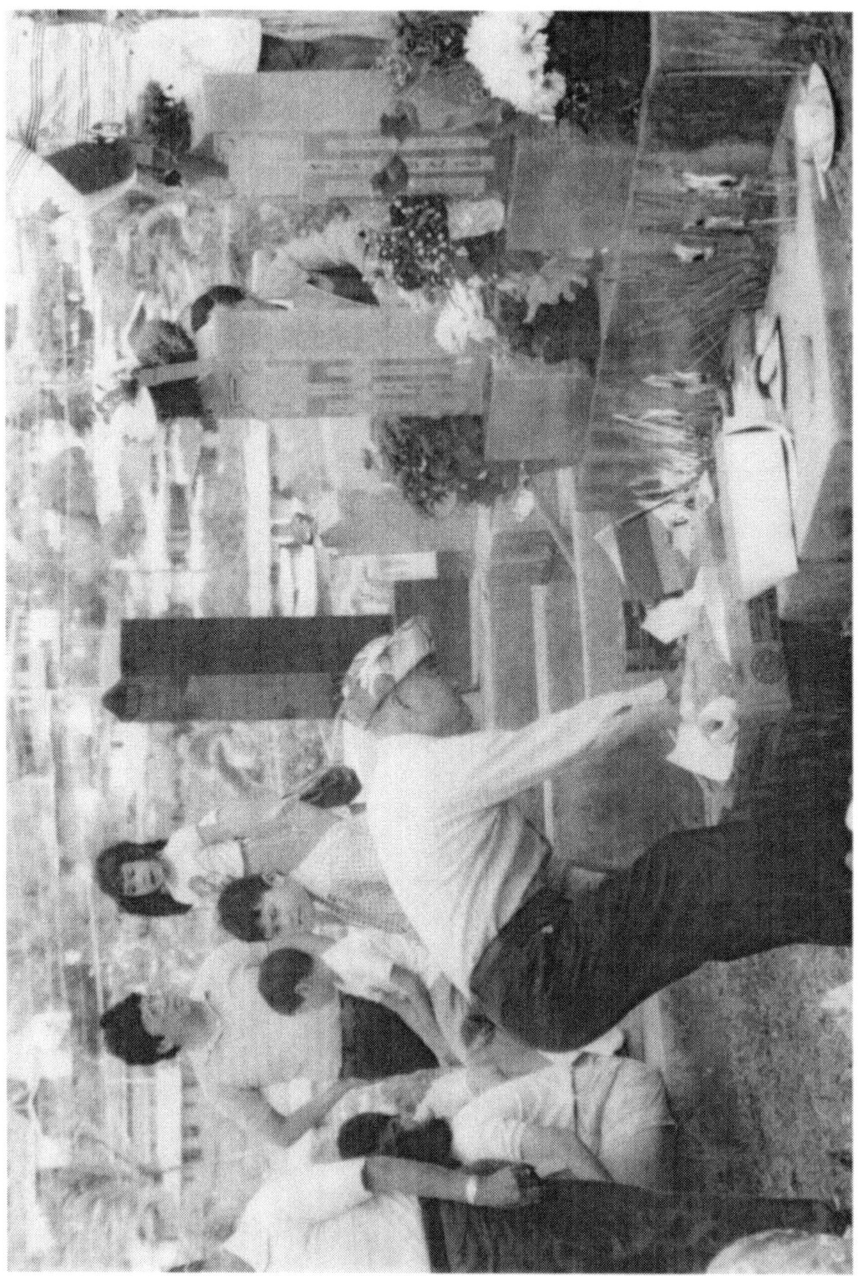

Fig. 9:4. Individuals provide offerings of food and other items at a family gravesite in the Lin Yee Chung Chinese Cemetery during *Ching Ming*.

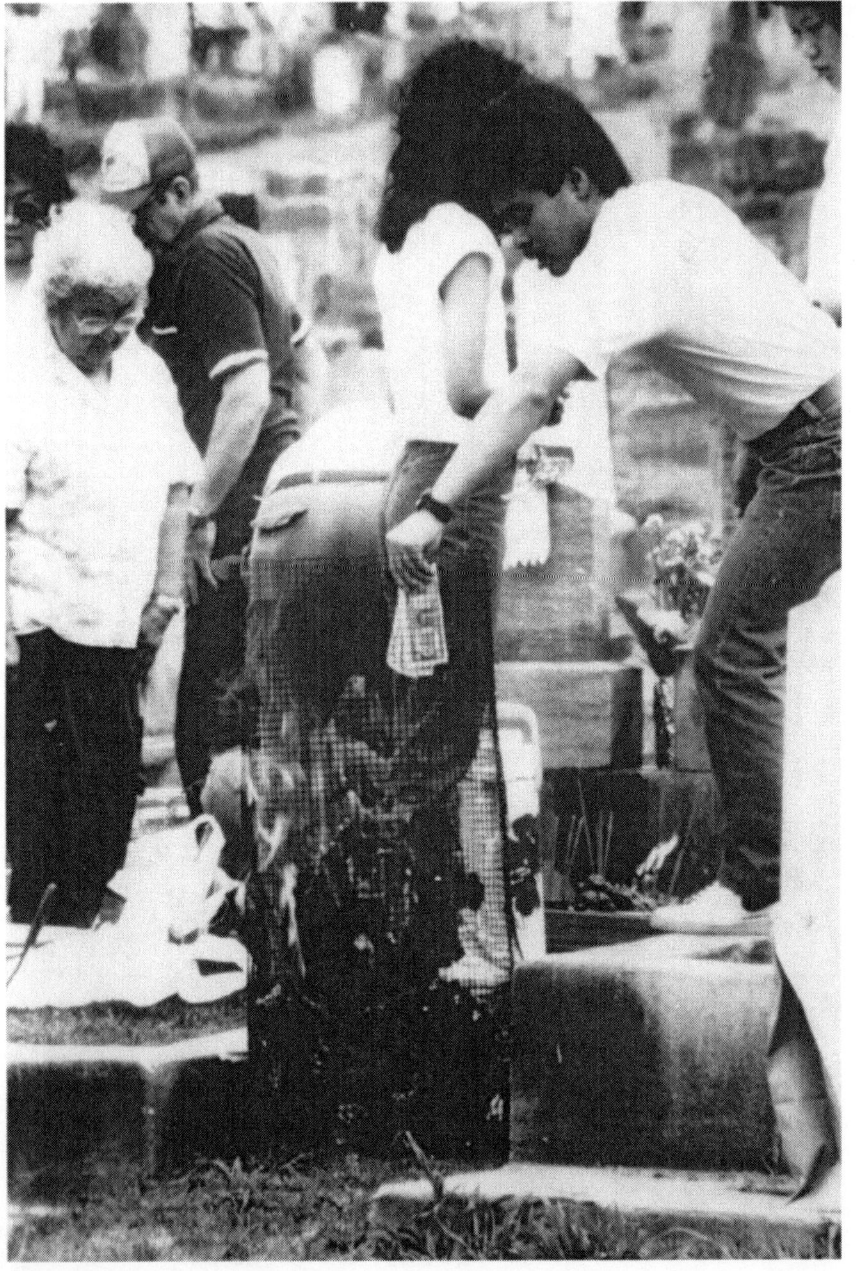

Fig. 9:5. Burning of "Grave Money" for the spirits of the dead during *Ching Ming*. Lin Yee Chung Chinese Cemetery.

week, their monthly income amounted to no more than about $15 for men and $10 for women. These wages were barely enough to feed and clothe the workers and their families, much less pay for luxury items, such as commercially available marble and granite tombstone markers for the dead. Thus, most early plantation markers were made of basalt rock, which was plentiful for the taking and soft enough to sculpt and inscribe with the few tools available in the camps. These markers (See Fig. 9:6) are generally about two to three feet high and about 18-24 inches wide, with an almost pointed crown. They were either placed directly into the ground or mounted on a 3-tiered concrete pedestal. Usually, only the front of the marker is smoothed-out to bear a surname, while the rest of the stone is left roughly carved.

While all of these physical characteristics are typical of the Japanese plantation-style marker, none can be traced to any specific religious or cultural traditions. They seem to be a style that is unique to Japanese plantation cemeteries in Hawai'i, their evolution owing in large part to the particular conditions of plantations life which prevailed at that time and in that place.

Even though most *issei* (first generation) settlers were traditional Buddhist, thereby believing in cremation rather than body burials, there were no crematory facilities available in rural areas where the plantations were located. For this reason, most late 19th century burials were in fact body burials. In time, small crematories were built at the cemetery sites or at nearby Buddhist temples to accommodate traditional cremations.

The usual duration of a laborer's contract was about three years. After this obligation was fulfilled, most workers left the plantations to seek their fortunes elsewhere, which usually meant in the nearest urban area. While this process was certainly beneficial to the immigrants, enhancing economic mobility and social integrations, it also insured that many plantation camps, along with their graveyards would, in time, become abandoned. Eventually, all the houses, stores and bath houses would physically disappear. Only the cemeteries would remain. Today, although most frequently neglected or forgotten altogether, they stand as unique symbols of the hardship, poverty and courage of those original settlers.

Modern Japanese Burial Traditions and Tombstone Styles

In accordance with modern-day Buddhist and Taoist religious traditions, cremation is still the preferred form of burial, although not all Japanese subscribe to this practice. After cremation the urns are either placed in below-ground vaults, which can hold up to eight urns, or in large above-ground vaults, which can hold up to 15 urns (Fig. 9:7).

The Japanese term for a gravesite is *hakka*, meaning "grave" (in the case of a single inurnment), or "grave house" (in the case of multiple inurnments). In either case, most *hakka* are usually topped with black or grey granite tombstones bearing inscriptional data and various religious symbols.

Japanese tombstones are unique in this area because there is not only inscriptional data on the face of the stone, but on all other sides of the marker as well. If written in *kanji* (Japanese characters), the face of the stone will bear the

Fig. 9:6. Early Japanese "plantation style" gravemarkers. 'Aiea Plantation Cemetery, 'Aiea.

Fig. 9:7. Japanese *Hakka*, or family "burial houses." Honolulu Memorial Park, Nu'uanu.

family surname (which reads from top to bottom on the marker) with the image of a "mon" or "crest" which is usually found just above the top of the surname (Fig. 9:8). This "mon" is usually a family crest, but can also be a temple crest or even a company or business crest. In addition, many markers commonly have carved on the face of the stone the image of a lotus blossom motif, which is a religious symbol for eternal life in the afterworld (Fig. 9:8). Most inscriptions and religious motifs are filled-in with gold or white paint to make them more readable.

The reverse side of the marker will usually have the first names, birth and death dates of all those inurned in the *hakka*. In addition, inscriptional data can also be found on both sides of the marker. This data usually describes where the first person buried came from in Japan, (e.g.,) the prefecture (state) he or she came from, the district (county) within the prefecture and sometimes even the village within the county.

For persons of Japanese ancestry who today are tracing their genealogy, this inscriptional data is invaluable since most *issei* (first generation immigrants) who came to Hawai'i provided little or no written documentation about their former residences in Japan. The only difficulty results from the fact that this data is usually written in *kanji* (characters), which very few contemporary Japanese-Americans can read.

In Hawai'i there are numerous old Japanese cemeteries, but very few have plots left to purchase. Therefore, most burials today are in modern, western, memorial parks, which have separate Buddhist sections set aside for inurnments. Because of space limitations, these inurnments are usually restricted to the smaller, below-ground vaults, although in a few cemeteries the traditional above-ground grave "houses" can be found.

The "Jizo" and The "Pagoda" Style Markers

Two of the most unique grave marker designs to be found in Hawai'i are restricted to Japanese graveyards. These are the *Jizo* markers (Fig. 9:9) and the Pagoda style markers (Fig. 9:10).

The *Jizo*, one of the most popular Buddhist deities in Japan, is commonly regarded as the guardian of both children and farmers. In Hawai'i, the *Jizo* is only found in early plantation cemeteries, and usually indicates the grave of a child, although a few adult graves have been associated with this image. Though striking, this form of marker is relatively rare, with only 25-30 having been identified in the state.

Another culturally significant but rather rare Japanese marker type is the "Pagoda" marker. The Pagoda marker comes in five separate pieces placed one on top of the other in the form of a Pagoda or temple, and symbolizing the five elements of the universe—Earth, Water, Fire, Wind and Air (See Fig. 9:11). This style of marker can be found in both plantation and contemporary Japanese cemeteries, but is not commonly used because of the cost of such monuments.

"O Bon"—Japanese Veneration of the Dead

The Japanese, like the Chinese in Hawai'i, do not have a single memorial

Fig. 9:8. "Mon" (family crest) and lotus blossom motif, two commonly used images on Japanese gravemarkers. O'ahu Cemetery, Nu'uanu.

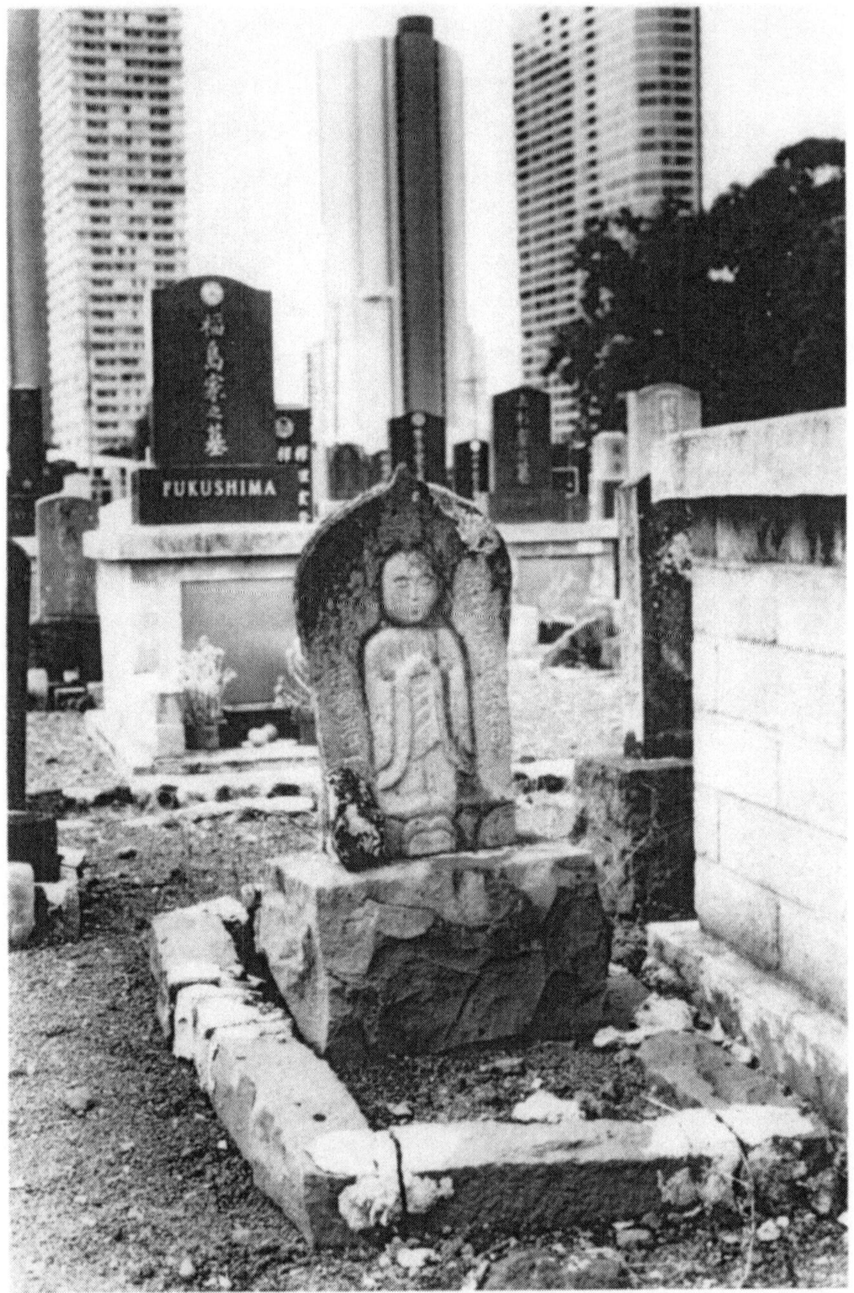

Fig. 9:9. Japanese *Jizo* is a minor Buddhist deity whose image usually indicates the grave of a child. Mo'ili'ili Japanese Cemetery, Mo'ili'ili.

Fig. 9:10. Japanese Pagoda marker (see Fig. 9:11 for breakdown of symbolism). O'ahu Cemetery, Nu'uanu.

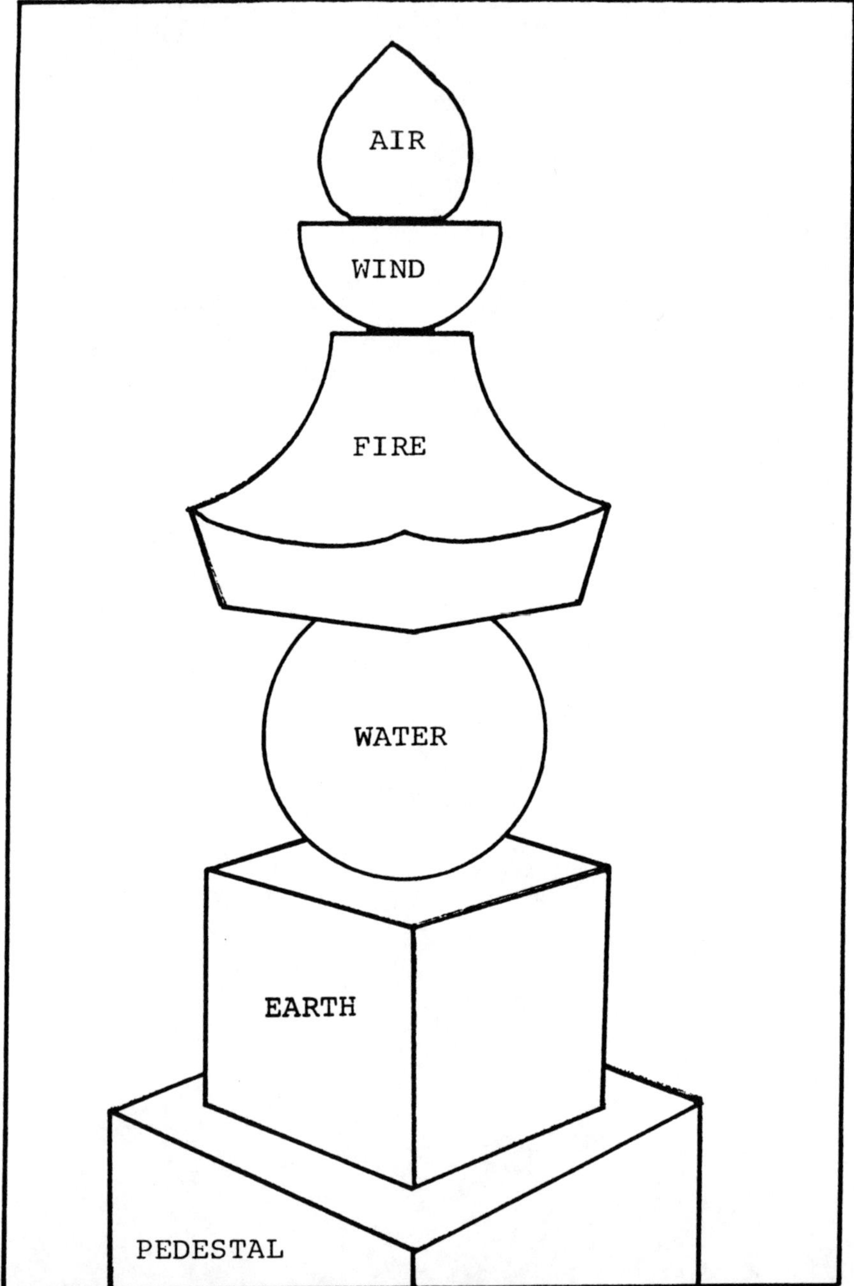

Fig. 9:11. A Japanese Pagoda marker is constructed in five pieces, representing the five elements of the universe—Earth, Water, Fire, Wind and Air.

day which is devoted to honoring the dead, but instead have a memorial "season" which is celebrated in July and August.

This traditional festival is known as *O Bon* or *Urabon*, from the Sanskrit word *ullambana*, meaning "to be suspended upside down." The origin of the *O Bon* tradition is commonly attributed to a moralistic legend that came to Japan from China, and ultimately from India, in several slightly different versions. This legend:

> ...has it that one of Buddha's disciples attained deep insight, which enabled him to look into the depths of existence. To his horror he saw that his deceased mother had been reborn among the Hungry Ghosts of Hell. Because of her past offense of eating meat and then denying the misdeed, she was eternally condemned to hang upside down, famished and emaciated, suffering a punishment akin to that of Tantalus, for in the moment that she tried to take in food or water they turned to fire. By practicing compassion and charity to an extraordinary degree, Buddha's disciple accumulated enough merit to rescue his mother from the nether world and bring her to the shores of Nirvana, whereupon, enraptured by her deliverance, she danced for joy, holding a bon "round tray" heaped with food. Her son too was overjoyed, as were his friends, and all joined in a happy celebration with music, dance, and offerings to express their gratitude for this rewarding of good deeds by deliverance of the dead and reunion with the living.[8]

For contemporary Japanese, *O Bon* is the time of year when the spirits of the dead return to earth to commune with the living. In Hawai'i, this festival, one of the most important of the year, is celebrated in three parts.

The first part calls for the living to pay homage to the dead by visiting and adorning their graves with various symbolic foods, such as rice, oranges, sake (rice wine) and tea. In addition, incense is burned to welcome the spirits, and paper lanterns are hung on each grave to symbolize the lighting of the way to the world of the living (Fig. 9:12). It is not believed that the spirits physically come out and eat the foods presented at the gravesites, but rather that they absorb the essence of each item.

The second part of *O Bon* is the more festive, more secular element of the season and is celebrated with a traditional Japanese-style community dance held at the temple or community hall. In Hawai'i, "Bon Dance" is a popular event for both the young and the old, but for most it is celebrated as a strictly secular, social event with very little attention paid to the more traditional significance of venerating the dead.

The third and final part of the *O Bon* trilogy comes at the close of the season when it is time for the spirits to return to the afterworld. To symbolize this event, the living purchase floating paper lanterns which are illuminated by candles and set afloat upon the ocean at the close of a evening "Bon" dance session. Each lantern has the name of a deceased person written upon it. This colorful event is know as the *Toronagashi*, or "Floating Lanterns Festival," and is one of the most beautiful of all the Japanese festivals.

Of all the ethnic groups in Hawai'i, the Japanese seem to spend the most time in the cemeteries worshipping at the tombs of the dead—not only during *O*

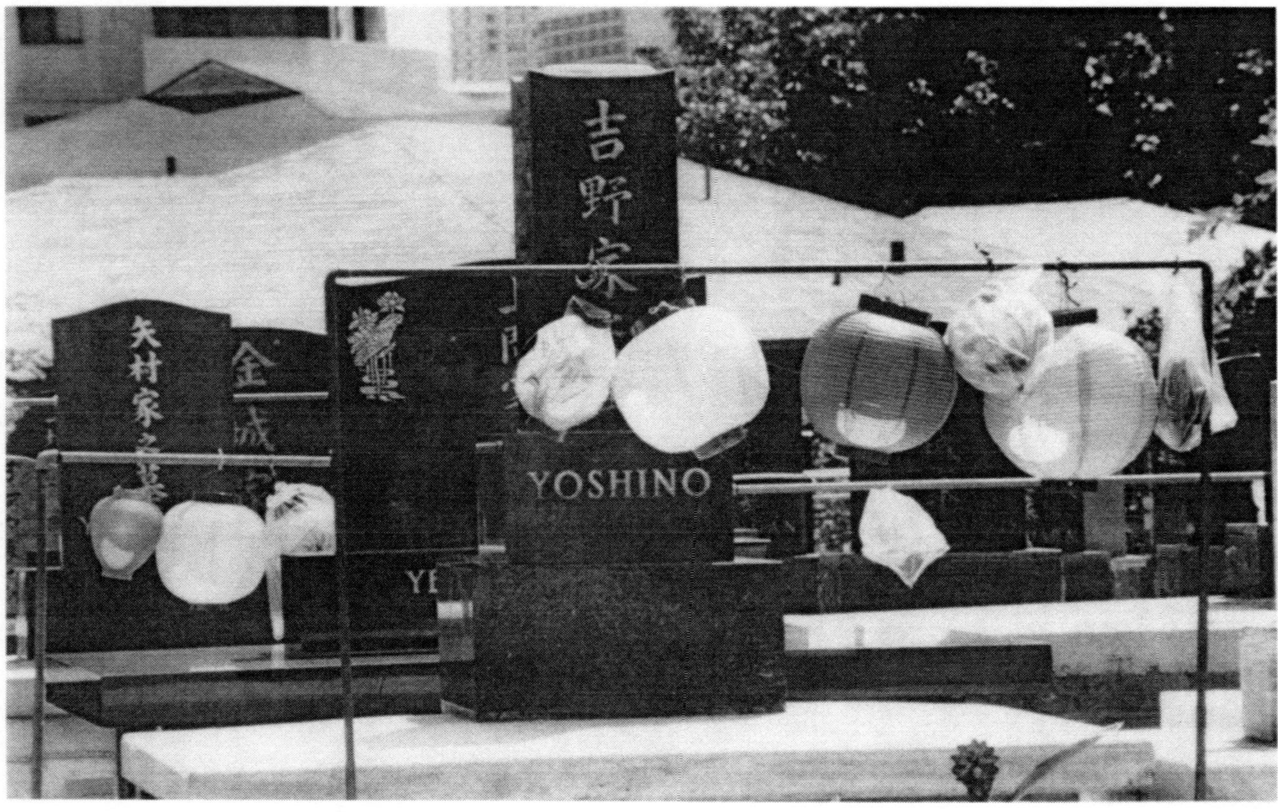

Fig. 9:12. Paper lanterns strung on gravemarkers symbolize the lighting of the way for the spirits of the dead during *O Bon*, the annual Japanese memorial season. Mo'ili'ili Japanese Cemetery, Mo'ili'ili.

Bon, but at many other times of the year, such as Christmas, Easter, Memorial Day, family anniversaries, birth and death days, and on other auspicious occasions.

Samoan and Tongan Marker Types

Together, the Samoan and Tongan population in Hawai'i comprises less than one percent of the total population. It is not surprising, then, that there are no exclusively Samoan or Tongan graveyards in Hawai'i such as in the case of the Chinese or the Japanese. However, in terms of visual imagery, the gravemarkers of this ethnic group are amongst the most unique in Hawai'i.

There are generally two types of markers which stand out as typically Samoan/Tongan in nature. The first type, which is the most common, looks like a three-tiered "cake" design, usually painted white, but oftentimes painted in bright pastel shades of yellow or blue (Fig. 9:13). Most of the cake style markers are topped with a traditional granite or marble marker, though a number are not. The origins or symbolism of the three-tiered marker style are unknown, but the colors are typical of those used to paint household dwellings in both Samoa and Tonga.

The second type of Samoan/Tongan marker which can be found in Hawai'i is quite rare. In fact, there is only one cemetery in the state where they have been located so far: the Sunset Memorial Park on O'ahu. This design is referred to as a house or *fale* marker, owing to its graveshelter type configuration which resembles the traditional open-walled house design typically found in both Samoa and Tonga (Fig. 9:14).

In both Samoa and Tonga, western-style "cemeteries" are a relatively new phenomenon. There are a few sites designated as official graveyards, usually associated with churches, but traditionally the deceased are buried in the front yard of the family home. Also, in both cultures it is customary to plant many types of plants and flowers around the gravesite, which then become a permanent part of the decorative motif. Judging from the examples seen in Sunset Memorial Park, Samoan/Tongan burial practices in Hawai'i attempt, at least in some instances, to recreate symbolically these traditions of the home islands.

Ancient Hawaiian Burial Traditions

Prior to the arrival of the first missionaries in 1820, native Hawaiians did not have western-style cemeteries or gravemarkers as we know them today.[9] There were two major reasons for this. The first was because native Hawaiians did not have a written language, and therefore did not have any use for tombstones which would bear inscriptional data. The second reason they did not have many marked burials was because of the common practice of grave robbing.

In pre-western contact Hawai'i, the deceased were often buried with valuables or cherished personal items such as cooking bowls, hand-woven mats, jewelry or weapons. Sometimes graves would be plundered to obtain these items. More importantly, however, graves were dug up specifically to obtain the

Fig. 9:13. Samoan/Tongan three-tiered “cake” marker. Sunset Memorial Park, Pearl City.

Fig. 9:14. Samoan/Tongan *fale*, or open-house markers. Sunset Memorial Park, Pearl City.

bones of the deceased because it was believed that the *mana* or spiritual power of a person dwelt in his bones—even after death. Therefore, if one were able somehow to obtain a deceased person's bones they would then have that person's *mana* or power in addition to their own. This would, in essence, double their spiritual power, an asset of great significance in times of battle or hardship. Bones obtained in this fashion and for this purpose were often made into fish hooks, jewelry and weapons.

The ancient Hawaiian social and political system was defined and dominated by a caste system consisting of five major status groups. Your ranking in this system (which you were born into) determined the power and status of your *mana*. If you were a member of the *Mo'i* class (Kings and Queens who ruled each island) or the *Ali'i* class (Chiefs), your bones, an obvious target for grave robbers coveting such immensely powerful *mana*, would have been hidden secretly in the night by one or two trusted warriors who were sworn to secrecy. If they were to reveal this unmarked burial place they would have been immediately put to death. By way of contrast, if you were of the lowest ranking class, called the *kauwa* or "outcast" class, your *mana* would be of little consequence and such precautions would have been virtually unnecessary.

In many instances the preferred burial places of high ranking classes were large caves which would be big enough to hold sacred items such as war canoes, feather capes and helmets, or hundreds of other grave goods associated with royalty. Some were entombed in special dwellings at the *heiau*, or temple, which were guarded day-and-night by specially selected guards.

Burial of all social classes might take place in one of several types of locations—in caves, in the ground, or even at sea. Cremation was not a common practice. It was usually reserved for those who broke the religious *kapus*, or prohibitions, which governed everyday life, and was generally considered a shameful fate. Wherever the burial took place, only immediate family members would be in attendance, and instead of marking the gravesite with tombstones, trees and shrubs were subtly planted to mark the burial spot. It then became each family member's sacred responsibility to remember this burial place and to pass on the knowledge of its location to younger generations through oral histories and chants. Today, many of these oral histories and chants which documented family histories for many generations have been lost, and thereby also the knowledge of many burial places.

Although Western influence in Hawai'i officially began with the arrival of Captain James Cook in 1778, it was not until 1820 that Western values and traditions would significantly influence native Hawaiian burial customs. This was the year that the first group of missionaries (New England Calvinist) arrived in the Hawaiian islands. Their influence, and that of the other religious missionaries from throughout the world in later years, would ultimately change the course of Hawaiian culture and history. One consequence of this influence can be clearly seen in the burial patterns of Native Hawaiians, which from this time forward would increasingly adopt the flavor of more Westernized traditions.

"Mauna Ala"—The Only Royal Mausoleum in the United States

Hawai'i has the unique distinction of having the only royal mausoleum in the United States. Today, *Mauna Ala*, which literally means "fragrant mountain," is more commonly known as "The Royal Mausoleum" (Fig. 9:15).

The current mausoleum, which is located in the Nu'uanu Valley on the island of O'ahu, was built in 1865 to alleviate the overcrowded condition of the original royal mausoleum—known as *Pohukaina*—which had been constructed in 1825 to house the remains of King Kamehameha II and his wife Kamamalu. This large, windowless crypt was designated as a sacred royal burial ground which had the added status of having King Kamehameha II buried there. Soon the remains of royalty from other islands were transferred to *Pohukaina* because of this status.[10]

By 1864 *Pohukaina* had become overcrowded and plans for a newer and larger mausoleum were initiated. In 1865, a Gothic-style mausoleum was built in Nu'uanu, only a mile away from the *Pohukaina* site, which today is part of the grounds of the Iolani Palace in downtown Honolulu. Within a few years even this new structure had become to small to house the many members of royalty being deposited there. Through funds provided by the estate of the late Princess Bernice Pauahi Bishop (the last descendant of the Kamehamehas), a new underground crypt was eventually built to house the remains of all the members of the Kamehameha dynasty. A short time thereafter, the Hawaiian legislature authorized the construction of yet another underground crypt to house the remains of the descendants of the Kalakaua dynasty, the last ruling monarchs of the Kingdom of Hawai'i. Today, the mausoleum at Nu'uanu has been restored to its original condition and is used as a chapel for special occasions honoring the monarchs buried on the grounds.

Hawaiian "Decoration Day"

Before World War II Memorial Day in Hawai'i, as in many parts of the country, was known as "Decoration Day" and was not merely an occasion to honor veterans but a day to visit all family burial sites and participate in a number of traditional rituals. Many families, especially those of Hawaiian ancestry, celebrated this occasion by bringing to the cemetery bags and boxes of freshly cut tropical flowers to make elaborate floral decorations for adorning the gravesites. The day was considered one of the most colorful and festive events of the year, and many families would spend the entire day in the cemetery decorating the graves of family members with a profusion of bright flowers and foliage, having a picnic lunch, and telling numerous tales of the lives and times of the dead. Thus, for many, the cemetery on Decoration Day became the site of extensive family reunions.

Today, a large number of Hawaiian cemeteries present a colorful mixture of Christian gravemarkers surrounded by traditional trees and shrubs such as the beautiful and fragrant plumeria tree, which is also known as "graveyard plumeria." One of the more common decorative designs found on contemporary Hawaiian graves is the *kahili*, or royal standard motif (Fig. 9:16). In ancient times the *kahili*, fashioned of red, yellow, or blue feathers from rare

Fig. 9:15. *Mauna Ala*, in Nu'uanu, the only Royal mausoleum in the United States, houses the remains of many chiefs and monarchs of the Hawaiian Kingdom.

Fig. 9:16. Hawaiian *Kahili*, or Royal Standard grave decorations. Hawaiian Memorial Park, Kane'ohe.

and exotic birds, were a distinctive symbol of royalty. Today, in cemeteries at any rate, they are frequently used to mark the grave of any person of Hawaiian ancestry, regardless of his or her lineage. However, instead of using feathers of birds which are now extinct or endangered, most contemporary *kahili* are made of chicken feathers which have been colored to match the plumage of their more exalted ancient brethren.

Conclusion

In Hawai'i, the mixing of Polynesian, Oriental and Western cultures and religions has had a profound impact upon the traditional forms in which the dead are buried, memorialized through gravesite markers and other decorations, and honored and remembered through annual memorial celebrations. Many material forms remain in Hawaiian cemeteries to remind the visitor to these islands of the important role ethnic groups have played in their historic and cultural development. And though the vibrant mortuary customs associated with such events as the Chinese *Ching Ming*, Japanese *O Bon*, and Native Hawaiian Decoration Day festivals are without doubt on the decline, these too maintain enough of their vitality to provide strong images of the fascinating ethnic diversity which is so distinctive a feature of modern Hawaiian culture.

Notes

All photographs in this essay are by Nanette Napoleon Purnell and feature material from the Island of O'ahu.

[1]Chuen-Yuen David Lai, "A *Feng-shui* Model as a Locational Index," *Annals of the Association of American Geographers* 66:4 (1974), pp. 505-513.

[2]*The Story of Manoa Chinese Cemetery-With a Discussion of Ancestor Worship* (Honolulu: Lin Yee Chung Association, 1988), p. 5.

[3]"The *Ching Ming* Festival of China" (Honolulu: Unpublished Paper, U of Hawaii, 1973), p. 1.

[4]*Under the Ancestor's Shadow* (New York: Columbia UP, 1948), p. 178.

[5]*Traditions for Living: A Booklet of Chinese Customs and Folk Practices in Hawai'i*, ed. May Lee Chung, Dorothy Jim Luke, and Margaret Leong Lau (Honolulu: Associated Chinese Women, 1979), n.p.

[6]In Wah Chan Thom, *The Story of Manoa Chinese Cemetery*, p. 27-A. This translation of the ceremony into English, done by the Lin Yee Chung Cemetery Association in 1988, is thought to be the first since its inception over 2,000 years ago.

[7]For additional information concerning Japanese immigrants in Hawai'i see Franklin Obo and Kazuko Sinoto, *A Pictorial History of the Japanese in Hawai'i 1885-1924* (Honolulu: Hawai'i Immigrant Heritage Preservation Center, Bishop Museum, 1985).

[8]John De Francis, *Things Japanese in Hawaii* (Honolulu: The UP of Hawaii, 1973), p. 45.

[9]For additional information on ancient Hawaiian burial practices see the following: E.S. Craighill Handy *et al.*, *Ancient Hawaiian Civilization* (Rutland,

Vermont: Charles E. Tuttle Co., 1965); John Papa Ii, *Fragments of Hawaiian History* (Honolulu: The Bishop Museum P, 1959); Samuel Kamakau, *Ka Po'e Kahiko: The People of Old* (Honolulu: The Bishop Museum P, 1964).

[10]It is commonly believed that the remains of King Kamehemeha I were hidden secretly in a burial cave somewhere on the island of Hawai'i (the "Big" Island), and they have never been found. The mausoleum built at *pohukaina* to house the remains of King Kamehameha II was a major break from traditional ancient Hawaiian burial practices.

The Literature of Necroethnicity in America: An Annotated Bibliography

Richard E. Meyer

For those wishing to pursue additional reading on ethnic funerary practices in America, I have prepared the following, somewhat eclectic, list of suggested sources. Each of the individual entries is followed by a brief—phrase to sentence length—parenthetical annotation designed to give a somewhat more complete notion of the work's scope and content than the title alone might be capable of suggesting. Insofar as possible, I have endeavored to keep these comments descriptive rather than evaluative, though I would hasten to point out that I have only included items which, to my mind at least, are of clear value in broadening our understanding of this varied and complex area of human activity. The focus of the bibliography is admittedly limited to this book's specific concerns: for a more comprehensive listing of works relating to the overall study of funerary traditions in America see the bibliography at the conclusion of my *Cemeteries and Gravemarkers: Voices of America Culture* (Ann Arbor, Michigan: UMI Research P, 1989; rpt. Logan, UT: Utah State UP, 1992). The literature on general ethnicity in America is immense, and I have not attempted to address that issue here, though the reader interested in some useful standard works is directed to the notes which accompany my introductory essay for this volume. It should be mentioned that extremely useful brief pieces treating ethnic cemeteries and gravemarkers appear with relative frequency in such publications as the quarterly *Newsletter of the Association for Gravestone Studies* and in a number of the standard monthly trade journals which serve the various funerary industries—e.g., *Stone in America* (American Monument Association), *American Cemetery* (American Cemetery Association), and *MB News* (Monument Builders of North America). In the interests of space, I have listed only a few of the more extensive examples from these periodicals. Finally, I have appended a list of conference papers on topics relevant to this book's scope which have been presented in recent years at meetings of the Cemeteries and Gravemarkers Section of the American Culture Association (ACA), the Association for Gravestone Studies (AGS), and the American Folklore Society (AFS). These are identified by author, title, year and sponsoring organization, and—in instances where the title is not sufficiently self-explanatory—a brief note as to relevant content.

Books and Articles

Adams, Robert H. "Markers Cut by Hand." *The American West* 4:3 (1967), pp. 59-64. (Focus on wooden, concrete, and metal markers in the Hispanic Southwest.)

Alverson, Fred. "Ramojus Mozoliauskas." *Stone in America* 98:9 (1985), pp. 30-37. (Feature on Chicago Lithuanian-American monument designer and his ethnically oriented products.)

Babba, Preston A. *Pennsylvania German Tombstones: A Study in Folk Art.* Allentown, Pennsylvania: Schlecters, 1954. (The earliest of many studies of this folklorically rich ethnic group's gravemarkers.)

Baird, Scott. "Language Codes in Texas German Graveyards." *Markers* 9 (1992), pp. 216-255. (Linguistic approach to analyzing retention and assimilation as reflected by gravemarkers.)

Bell, Edward L. "The Historical Archaeology of Mortuary Behavior: Coffin Hardware from Uxbridge, Massachusetts." *Historical Archaeology* 24:3 (1990), pp. 57-78. (Considers comparative data from representative Black cemeteries and offers observations on the interplay of deathways, ethnicity, and economy.)

Bolton, H. Carrington. "Decorating of Graves of Negroes in South Carolina." *Journal of American Folk-Lore* 4 (1891), p. 214. (Very brief early study of African survivals in Black American deathways.)

Bronner, Simon J. "Elaborating Tradition: A Pennsylvania-German Folk Artist Ministers to his community." *In Creativity and Tradition in Folklore: New Directions*. Edited by Simon J. Bronner. Logan, Utah: Utah State UP, 1992, pp. 277-325. (Documents the work of 19th century minister and gravestone carver Isaac Stiehly, whose extant markers demonstrate vividly the social and expressive purposes of folk art.)

Brunvand, Jan. "The Merry Cemetery of Transylvania." *North Carolina Folklore Journal* 21:3 (1973), pp. 83-88. (Tradition of intensive personalization on gravemarkers in remote Romanian Village.)

Burgess, Frederick. *English Churchyard Memorials*. London: SPCK, 1963. (Classic study of British mortuary traditions, invaluable in understanding early American counterparts.)

Cannon, Aubrey. "The Historical Dimension in Mortuary Expressions of Status and Sentiment." *Current Anthropology* 30:4 (1989), pp. 437-447. (Contains a section on historic and contemporary mortuary practices amongst members of Northeast Iroquoian cultures.)

Clark, Edward W. "The Bigham Carvers of the Carolina Piedmont: Stone Images of an Emerging Sense of American Identity." In *Cemeteries and Gravemarkers: Voices of American Culture*. Edited by Richard E. Meyer. Ann Arbor, MI: UMI Research P, 1989; rpt. Logan, UT: Utah State UP, 1992, pp. 31-59. (Following one family of Scotch Irish stonecarvers through several generations, study traces the gradual shift in emphasis on gravestone imagery from Scotch Irish to American nationalistic symbolism.)

Clark, Lynn. "Gravestones: Reflectors of Ethnicity or Class?" In *Consumer Choice in Historical Archaeology*. Edited by Suzanne M. Spencer-Wood. New York: Plenum Press, 1987, pp. 383-395. (Studies size, form, and decoration of gravestones from several ethnic groups—Italians, Slovaks, Jews, and Irish—in Broome County, New York.)

Clark, Sara. "The Decoration of Graves in Central Texas with Seashells." In *Diamond Bessie and the Shepherds*. Edited by Wilson M. Hudson. Publications of the Texas Folklore Society, no. 36. Austin: Encino Press, 1972, pp. 33-43. (Examines this decorative practice shared by several ethnic groups.)

Clarke, Rod. *Carved in Stone: A History of the Barre Granite Industry*. Barre, Vermont: Rock of Ages Corporation, 1989. (Historical focus, with some useful material on the various ethnic groups who have worked in the Barre quarries and stonecarving shops.)

Combes, John D. "Ethnography, Archaeology and Burial Practices Among Coastal South Carolina Blacks." *Conference on Historic Site Archaeology, Papers* 7 (1972), pp. 52-61. (Emphasis upon African survivals.)

Cozzens, Arthur B. "A Cherokee Graveyard." *Pioneer America* 4:1 (1972), p. 8. (Very brief; largely photographs.)

Cunningham, Keith. "Navajo, Mormon, Zuni Graves: Navajo, Mormon, Zuni Ways." In *Cemeteries and Gravemarkers: Voices of American Culture*. Edited by Richard E. Meyer. Ann Arbor, MI: UMI Research P, 1989; rpt. Logan, UT: Utah State UP, 1992, pp. 197-215. (Separation and blending of cultural deathways in a remote New Mexico community.)

De Sola Pool, David. *Portraits Etched in Stone: Early Jewish Settlers, 1682-1831*. New York: Columbia UP, 1952. (Contains some material on early Jewish cemeteries and gravemarkers in America.)

Dewhurst, C. Kurt, Betty MacDowell and Marsha MacDowell. *Religious Folk Art in America: Reflections of Faith*. New York: E.P. Dutton, 1983. (Contains brief treatments of gravemarkers of rural southern Blacks and certain European immigrant groups.)

Erwin, Paul F. "Scottish Gypsies and Their Burial Customs: Facts and Folklore," *Urban Resources* 4:3 (1987), pp. C1-C4. (Preliminary findings on burial practices of Scottish Travellers in Cincinnati.)

Farber, Daniel and Jessie Lie Farber. "Early Pennsylvania Gravestones." *Markers* 5 (1988), pp. 96-121. (Photo essay contains numerous examples of Pennsylvania German gravemarkers; intended as companion piece to article by Thomas E. Graves, "Pennsylvania German Gravestones: An Introduction," in same issue.)

Fenn, Elizabeth A. "Honoring the Ancestors: Kongo-American Graves in the

American South." *Southern Exposure* 8 (1985), pp.42-47. (Interpretive data on African survivals amongst southern rural Blacks.)

Fenza, Paula J. "Communities of the Dead: Tombstones as a Reflection of Social Organization." *Markers* 6 (1989), pp. 136-157. (Contains brief section dealing with Gypsy gravesites in suburban Chicago's Forest Home Cemetery.)

Ferri, J. Michael. "Deaths, Wakes, Funerals: Italian American Style." In *Dominant Symbols in Popular Culture*. Edited by Ray B. Browne, Marshall W. Fishwick, and Kevin O. Browne. Bowling Green, Ohio: Bowling Green State University Popular Press, 1990, pp. 224-230. (Covers both pre- and post-burial practices within Italian communities in Boston, Philadelphia, and Providence, Rhode Island.)

Graves, Thomas E. "Liebster Kinder und Verwandten: Death and Ethnicity." *Keystone Folklore* (New Series) 2: 1-2 (1983), pp. 6-14. (Emphasis on 19th-century Pennsylvania-German gravemarkers as indicators of ethnic separateness; some treatment also of Slovaks, Italians and Ukrainians.)

_____. "Pennsylvania German Gravestones: An Introduction." *Markers* 5 (1988), pp. 60-95. (Thoroughgoing analysis of both visual and verbal components of these distinctive ethnic artifacts.)

Grider, Sylvia Ann and Sarah Jarvis Jones. "The Cultural Legacy of Texas Cemeteries." *Texas Humanist* 6:5 (1984), pp. 34-39. (Examines, amongst others, cemeteries of rural Blacks, Mexican-Americans, and several central European immigrant groups.)

Griffith, James S. *Southern Arizona Folk Arts*. Tucson: The U of Arizona P, 1988.) (Much of this book's focus is ethnically oriented, with some attention paid to gravesites of Mexican-Americans and Serbians.)

Gosnell, Lynn and Suzanne Gott. "San Fernando Cemetery: Decorations of Love and Loss in a Mexican-American Community." In *Cemeteries and Gravemarkers: Voices of American Culture*. Edited by Richard E. Meyer. Ann Arbor, MI: UMI Research P, 1989; rpt. Logon, UT: Utah State UP, 1992), pp. 217-236. (Grave decorating practices in a major San Antonio cemetery are shown to be an important symbolic process by which members of this ethnic group express a sense of ongoing relationship with departed family members.)

Hanks, Jacqueline. "St. Casimir Cemetery." *Stone in America* 101:11 (1988), pp. 28-37. (Feature on Lithuanian cemetery in Chicago emphasizes how these immigrants demonstrate love for their native country and culture through mortuary practices.)

Hannon, Thomas J. "Western Pennsylvania Cemeteries in Transition: A Model for Subregional Analysis." In *Cemeteries and Gravemarkers: Voices of American Culture*. Edited by Richard E. Meyer. Ann Arbor, MI: UMI Research P, 1989; rpt. Logan, UT: Utah State UP, 1992), pp. 237-257.

(Demonstrates, amongst other things, how cemetery study may help document historic ethnic settlement patterns in a frontier region.)

Hawker, Ronald W. "In the Way of the White Man's Totem Poles: Stone Monuments Among Canada's Tsimshian Indians, 1879-1910." *Markers* 7 (1990), pp. 213-231. (Study demonstrates cross-cultural accomodation in the wake of missionary contact with native groups in British Columbia.)

Hitchcock, Ann. "Gods, Graves, and Historical Archaeologists: A Study of Chinese Gravestones." *AFF Word* 2:2 (1972), pp. 11-19. (Chinese funerals and gravemarkers in Tucson, Arizona's Evergreen Cemetery.)

_____. "Gods, Graves, and Historical Archaeologists: A Study of a Mexican-American Cemetery in Harshaw." *AFF Word* 3:3 (1973), pp. 1-10. (Mexican-American burial customs and gravemarker styles in a small southern Arizona community.)

_____. "Gods, Graves, and Historical Archaeologists: A Study of Two Papago Cemeteries in Southern Arizona." *AFF Word* 1:2 (1971), pp. 7-17. (Intensive study of funerary traditions of Papago Indians in cemeteries at Mission San Xavier and Santa Rosa Francisco, Arizona.)

Huber, Leonard V. *Clasped Hands: Symbolism in New Orleans Cemeteries.* Lafayette, Louisiana: The Center for Louisiana Studies, 1982. (Contains section on 19th century tombs and monuments erected by mutual benevolent societies of various immigrant groups.)

Ingersoll, Ernest. "Decoration of Negro Graves." *Journal of American Folk-Lore* 5 (1892), pp. 68-69. (Another very early study of African survivals.)

Jackson, Kenneth T. and Camilo José Vergara. *Silent Cities: The Evolution of the American Cemetery*. New York: Princeton Architectural P, 1989. (General survey of American cemeteries contains several very useful sections on ethnicity, with particular attention directed to Italian, German, Irish, Jewish, and Hispanic groups.)

Jansen, Lee. "The New Ethnic Symbolism." *Stone in America* 104:10 (1991), pp. 32-39. (Concentrates on gravestone symbolism amongst Asians and Hispanics, the fastest growing ethnic communities in contemporary America.)

Jeane D. Gregory. "Folk Art in Rural Southern Cemeteries." *Southern Folklore* 46:2 (1989), pp. 159-174. (As in several of his works, the author provides valuable insights into the debate concerning varying ethnic origins for southern American cemetery traits.)

_____. "The Upland South Cemetery: An American Type." *Journal of Popular Culture* 11:4 (1978), pp. 895-903. (See annotation for previous entry.)

_____. "The Upland South Folk Cemetery Complex: Some Suggestions of Origin." In *Cemeteries and Gravemarkers: Voices of American Culture*. Edited by Richard E. Meyer. Ann Arbor, Michigan: UMI

Research P, 1989; rpt. Logan, UT: Utah State UP, 1992), pp. 107-136. (Argues forcefully for the predominance of European over Native American and African influences on southern rural cemetery traits.)

Jordan, Terry G. " 'The Roses So Red and the Lilies So Fair': Southern Folk Cemeteries in Texas." *Southwestern Historical Quarterly* 83 (1979-80), pp. 227-258. (Postulates various ethnic origins, including African, Native American, and European, for a number of southern cemetery cultural traits.)

_____. *Texas Graveyards: A Cultural Legacy.* Austin: U of Texas P, 1982. (Major Sections on Mexican-American and German-American groups, in addition to various others.)

Kelley, Thomas E. "German-Russian Graves Marked by Iron Crosses." *American Cemetery* 57:7 (1984), 23-26; 38. (Focus on German-Russian immigrants in North Dakota, ca. 1880s-1940s; uses some material from Vrooman/Marvin, *Iron Spirits*, but supplements with additional information.)

Kleinberg, S.J. "Death and the Working Class." *Journal of Popular Culture* 11:1 (1977), pp. 193/55-208/71. (Study of mourning and funerary traditions amongst the working classes of late 19th century Pittsburgh deals briefly with Slovak and Welsh groups.)

Kloberdanz, Timothy J. "Iron Lilies, Eternal Roses: German-Russian Cemetery Folk Art in Perspective." *Journal of the American Historical Society of Germans from Russia* 6:3 (1983), pp. 27-31. (Wrought iron grave cross designs and other funerary traditions amongst German-Russian immigrants in North Dakota; also printed in Vrooman/Marvin, *Iron Spirits.*)

Knapp, Ronald G. "The Changing Landscape of the Chinese Cemetery." *The China Geographer* 8 (1977), pp. 1-14. (Study of traditional cemetery in Taiwan sheds light on Chinese-American mortuary practices.)

Kremenak-Pecotte, Beverly. "At Rest: Folk Art in Texas Cemeteries." In *Folk Art in Texas*. Edited by Francis Edward Abernethy. Publications of the Texas Folklore Society, no. 45. Dallas: Southern Methodist UP, 1985, pp. 53-63. (Heavily illustrated essay features many examples of gravemarkers displaying ethnic design characteristics: unfortunately, it rarely defines or discusses them in this context, remaining essentially descriptive.)

Krüger-Kahloula, Angelika. "Tributes in Stone and Lapidary Lapses: Commemorating Black People in Eighteenth and Nineteenth Century America." *Markers* 6 (1989), pp. 32-100. (Revealing study of the socio-cultural implications behind the erecting, by Whites, of memorials for slaves and other Blacks in early America.)

Lai, Chuen-Yan David. "A Feng Shui Model as a Location Index." *Annals of the Association of American Geographers* 27 (1974), pp. 506-513.

(Important to the understanding of desired spatial configurations in traditional Chinese-American Cemeteries.)

Levy, B.H. "Savannah's Old Jewish Community Cemeteries." *The Georgia Historical Quarterly* 66:1 (1982), pp. 1-20. (Historical Study of early 18th century Jewish congregations and burial grounds.)

Little, M. Ruth. "Afro-American Gravemarkers in North Carolina." *Markers* 6 (1989), pp. 102-134. (Study of markers found in 32 Black cemeteries in North Carolina, with special focus on the work of two Black folk craftsmen.)

MacLean, Douglas. "The Origins and Early Development of the Celtic Cross." *Markers* 7 (1990), pp. 232-275. (Though concentrating on native Irish and Scottish examples, study has important implications for the continued popularity of this form of gravemarker in American cemeteries.)

Marquardt, Lewis B. "Metal Grave Markers in German-Russian Cemeteries of Emmons County, North Dakota." *Journal of the American Historical Society of Germans from Russia* 2:2 (1979), pp. 18-26. (Supplements work of Sackett, Kloberdanz, Vrooman/Marvin, and others.)

Mathias, Elizabeth. "The Italian-American Funeral: Persistence Through Change." *Western Folklore* 33:1 (1974), pp. 35-60. (Traces funerary customs from origins in southern Italy through immigrant burials and up to contemporary practices in South Philadelphia's Italian-American community.)

Maynard, Juliane. "Wisconsin's Wrought Iron Markers." *Markers* 1 (1980), pp. 76-79. (Brief consideration of these artifacts as found in immigrant Catholic cemeteries.)

McDonald, Frank E. "Pennsylvania German Tombstone Art of Lebanon County, Pennsylvania." *Pennsylvania Folklife* 25:1 (1975), pp. 2-19. (Emphasis on visual symbols found on 18th century markers.)

McDowell, Peggy. "J.N.B. de Pouilly and French Sources of Revival Style Design in New Orleans Cemetery Architecture." In *Cemeteries and Gravemarkers: Voices of American Culture*. Edited by Richard E. Meyer. Ann Arbor, Michigan: UMI Research P, 1989; rpt. Logan, UT: Utah State UP, 1992, pp. 137-158. (Argues that the mausoleum style in New Orleans cemeteries was strongly influenced by cultural tastes of the city's predominant French population and by architectural trends popular in contemporary France.)

McGann, Tom. "Chicago's Bohemian National Cemetery." *American Cemetery* 63:6 (1990), pp. 22-25; 52-54 and 63:7 (1990), pp. 25-29. (Two-part article on Chicago's *Ceskonarodni Hrbitov*, or Bohemian National Cemetery, which since 1877 has served Czech immigrants of the area.)

McGrath, Robert L. "Death Italo-American Style: Reflections of Modern Martyrdom." *Markers* 4 (1987), pp. 107-113. (Brief examination of the self-designed monument of an Italian immigrant stonecutter in Barre, Vermont.)

McGuire, Randall H. "Dialogues with the Dead: Ideology and the Cemetery." In *The Recovery of Meaning: Historical Archaeology in the Eastern United States*. Edited by Mark P. Leone and Parker B. Potter, Jr. Washington, D.C.: Smithsonian Institution P, 1988, pp. 435-480. (Another study of cemeteries in Broome County, New York—see L. Clark, "Gravestones: Reflectors of Ethnicity or Class?"—with considerable emphasis on a variety of immigrant groups.)

Milbauer, John A. "Cemeteries of Mississippi's Yazoo Basin." *The Mid-South Geographer* 5 (1989), pp. 1-19. (Some attention devoted to Black cemeteries.)

_____. "Folk Monuments of Afro-Americans: A Perspective on Black Culture." *Mid-America Folklore* 19:2 (1991), pp. 99-109. (Based on Fieldwork in Mississippi, Arkansas and Oklahoma).

_____. "Southern Folk Traits in the Cemeteries of Northeastern Oklahoma." *Southern Folklore* 46:2 (1989), pp. 175-185. (The area of study contains numerous Cherokee burials, and some attention is given to the tradition of gravehouses within that culture.)

Milspaw, Yvonne J. "Segregation in Life, Segregation in Death: Landscape of an Ethnic Cemetery." *Pennsylvania Folklife* 30:1 (1980), pp. 36-40. (Examination of old cemeteries in Steelton, Pennsylvania offers evidence that the community's 19th century European immigrants were segregated in death as in life.)

Nichols, Elaine, ed. *The Last Miles of the Way: African-American Homegoing Traditions, 1890-Present*. Columbia, South Carolina: South Carolina State Museum, 1989. (73-page exhibition catalog contains much information on African-American [South Carolina] burial, funerary, mourning, and gravesite practices; four articles by separate authors, many photographs.)

Norris, Darrell A. "Ontario Gravestones." *Markers* 5 (1988), pp. 122-149. (Contains a section on "Ethnicity and Status".)

Parrington, Michael and Janet Wideman. "Acculturation in an Urban Setting: The Archaeology of a Black Philadelphia Cemetery." *Expedition* 28:1 (1986), pp. 55-62. (Excavation of early 19th century Black burial grounds indicates significant survival of African burial practices despite pressures to assimilate.)

Pitchford, Anita. "The Material Culture of the Traditional East Texas Graveyard." *Southern Folklore Quarterly* 43 (1979), pp. 227-290. (Some attention given to traits derived from Black, Native American and European traditions.)

Roberts, Warren E. "Tombstones in Scotland and Indiana." *Folk-Life* 23 (1984-85), pp. 97-104. (Traces the southern Indiana practice of depicting tools on gravemarkers to antecedent practices in Scotland.)

Rose, Jerome C., ed. *Gone to a Better Land: A Biohistory of a Black Rural Cemetery in the Post-Reconstruction South.* Arkansas Archaeological Survey Research Series no. 25. Fayetteville, Arkansas: Arkansas Archaeological Survey, 1985. (Extensive document records findings of archaeological survey team who excavated an abandoned Black burial site in Lafayette County, Arkansas in 1982.)

Ruth, Kent and Jim Argo. *Here We Rest: Historic Cemeteries in Oklahoma.* Oklahoma City: Oklahoma Historical Society, 1986. (Contains a chapter on Native American graves and another—"The Melting Pot"—on a variety of immigrant graves.)

Sackett, Samuel J. "Steel Crosses in Volga German Catholic Cemeteries in Ellis, Rush, and Russell Counties, Kansas." *American Historical Society of Germans from Russia Work Paper* 21 (1976), pp. 20-24. (Pioneering study on the use of these distinctive gravemarkers indicates steel was an American substitute for the wood crosses used by these immigrants in their homeland.)

Sanborn, Laura Sue. "Camposantos: Sacred Places of the Southwest." *Markers* 6 (1989), pp. 158-179. (Cemetery and gravemarker styles in Hispanic New Mexico, with some attention to Native American influences.)

Schulyer, Robert L., ed. *Archaeological Perspectives on Ethnicity in America.* Farmingdale, New York: Baywood Publishing Co., 1980. (Essays on mortuary practices of various ethnic groups.)

Sexton, Rocky. " 'Don't Let the Rain Fall on my Face': French Louisiana Gravehouses in an Anthro-Geographical Context." *Material Culture* 23:3 (1991), pp. 31-46. (Provides an interesting contrast to the studies of gravehouses conducted in upland south areas by Jeane and others.)

Stone, Gaynell. "Material Evidence of Ideological and Ethnic Choice in Long Island Gravestones, 1670-1800." *Material Culture* 23:3 (1991), pp. 1-29. (Study of 164 Long Island cemeteries examines markers of Dutch and English Quaker groups.)

Tashjian, Ann and Dickran Tashjian. "The Afro-American Section of Newport, Rhode Island's Common Burying Ground." *In Cemeteries and Gravemarkers: Voices of American Culture.* Edited by Richard E. Meyer. Ann Arbor, MI: UMI Research P, 1989; rpt. Logan, UT: Utah State UP, 1992, pp. 163-196. (Black community life in an 18th century commercial center is reconstructed through documentary study of the Black section of this important early American cemetery.)

Thompson, Robert Farris. *Flash of the Spirit: Africian and Afro-American Art and Philosophy.* New York: Random House, 1984. (Important background material for an understanding of Black American memorials and other burial traditions that derive from African art and customs.)

Trask, Deborah. *Life How Short, Eternity How Long: Gravestone Carving and Carvers in Nova Scotia*. Halifax: The Nova Scotia Museum. 1978. (Contains sections on "French and Indians," "German Stones," and "Scottish Stones".)

Vidutis, Ricardas and Virgina A.P. Lowe. "The Cemetery as a Cultural Text." *Kentucky Folklore Record* 26 (1980), pp. 103-113. (Intensive study of a German Catholic cemetery in southern Indiana.)

Vlach, John Michael. *The Afro-American Tradition in Decorative Arts*. Cleveland: Cleveland Museum of Art, 1978. Reprint. Athens, GA: U of Georgia P, 1990. (Chapter on "Graveyard Decoration" remains classic study of rural Black cemetery traditions in the American South.)

_____. "Arrival and Survival: The Maintenance of an Afro-American Tradition in Folk Art and Craft." In *Perspectives on American Folk Art*. Edited by Ian M.G. Quimby and Scott T. Swank. New York: Norton, 1980, pp. 177-217. (Contains section on "Grave Decoration," a briefer treatment of some of the material Vlach covers in other sources.)

_____. *By the Work of Their Hands: Studies in Afro-American Folklife*. Ann Arbor, Michigan: UMI Research P, 1991. (Of particular interest is Chapter 4, "From Gravestone to Miracle: Traditional Perspective and the Work of William Edmondson," providing important insights into Black funerary practices in general as well as the work of this celebrated folk stonecarver.)

_____. "Graveyards and Afro-American Art." *Southern Exposure* 5 (1977), pp. 161-165. (Material covered more fully in *The Afro-American Tradition in Decorative Arts*.)

Vrooman, Nicholas Curchin and Patrice Avon Marvin, eds. *Iron Spirits*. Fargo, North Dakota: North Dakota Council on the Arts, 1982. (Heavily illustrated study of the blacksmith-created iron grave crosses, originally prevalent in the Black Sea area of southern Russia, which form so impressive a part of the cemetery landscape of German Russians in North Dakota and other areas of the Great Plains.)

Waring, Mary A. "Mortuary Customs and Beliefs of South Carolina Negroes." *Journal of American Folk-Lore* 7 (1894), p. 318. (Brief early commentary supplements the work of Bolton and Ingersoll.)

Warren, Nancy Hunter. "New Mexico Village Camposantos." *Markers* 4 (1987), pp. 115-129. (Mexican-American funerary traditions over several centuries in New Mexico.)

Weiser, Fredrick S. "Baptismal Certificate and Gravemarker: Folk Art at the Beginning and End of Life." In *Perspectives on American Folk Art*. Edited by Ian M.G. Quimby and Scott T. Swank. New York: Norton, 1980, pp. 134-161. (Interesting correlation of folk art motifs on a variety of Pennsylvania German forms.)

West, John O. "Folk Grave Decoration Along the Rio Grande." In *Folk Art in Texas*. Edited by Francis Edward Abernethy. Publications of the Texas Folklore Society, no. 45. Dallas: Southern Methodist UP, 1985, pp. 47-51. (Descriptive account of Mexican-American funerary traditions in southwest Texas.)

_____. *Mexican-American Folklore*. Little Rock, Arkansas: August House, 1988. (Section contains material on *grutas*, grave decoration, and *descansos.)*

Whitlock, Susan Opt. "The Celtic Cross." *Stone in America* 98:3 (1985), pp. 24-31. (Origins and contemporary uses of this well known memorial artifact, with some attention to its continuing appeal to those of Irish descent.)

Willsher, Betty. "The Green Man As an Emblem on Scottish Tombstones." *Markers* 9 (1992), pp. 58-77. (Also treats some North American examples of this Scottish motif.)

_____. "Scottish Tombstones and the New England Winged Skull." *Markers* 2 (1983), pp. 105-114. (Traces this most characteristic of Puritan New England gravestone motifs to its Scottish antecedents.)

Willsher, Betty and Doreen Hunter. *Stones: 18th Century Scottish Gravestones*. New York: Taplinger Publishing Co., 1978. (Important resource for understanding Scottish sources of numerous American gravestone motifs and designs.)

Winkler, Louis. "Pennsylvania German Astronomy and Astrology IV: Tombstones." *Pennsylvania Folklife* 22:2 (1972), pp.42-45. (Sun, moon and star motifs in Pennsylvania German folk art generally and as depicted on gravemarkers.)

Wright, Robert. "Lithuanian Legacy." *Stone in America* 100:12 (1987), pp. 16-23. (Monuments created for members of Chicago's extensive Lithuanian community.)

Conference Papers

Alexander, James R. "Hope for the Future, Reflections of a Past: The Gravemarkers of Hope Cemetery, Barre, Vermont." ACA/1993. (Italian).

Baird, Scott. "From Territory to Tombstone: Language, Culture, and Rites of Passage." ACA/1990. (English; Hispanic; German.)

Barber, Russell J. "The Agua Mansa Cemetery as an Indicator of Ethnic Identity." ACA/1989. (Hispanic.)

_____. "*Cerquitas* in Cemeteries of the Mexican Folk Tradition." ACA/1991.

_____. "Structural Relationships Between Ethnicity and Cemetery Layout in California Cemeteries." ACA/1993. (Various ethnic groups).

Blake, Fred. "The Chinese of Valhalla: Patterns of Assimilation and Identification in a Midwest American Cemetery." ACA/1992.

_____. "Occasional Gravemarkers and Sociocultural Identities in Hawaii's Cemeteries." ACA/1993. (Chinese; Japanese; Filipino; various other groups).

Chittenden, Varick. "Laid to Rest?: Cross Cultural Differences in a Mohawk Indian Graveyard." ACA/1993.

Clark, Edward. "The Bigham Family Carvers: Gravestone Symbols of an Emerging National Identity in the Carolina Piedmont." ACA/1987. (Scotch-Irish).

Coggeshall, John M. "Ethnic Architecture: The Concrete Expression of Identity." AFS/1986. (Various ethnic groups; some consideration of monuments.)

Coleman, Edwin, II. " 'Go Down Death': Expressions of Black Funerals in the Northwest." AFS/1984.

Cunningham, Keith, "Mormon, Navajo, Zuni Graves: Mormon, Navajo, Zuni Ways." ACA/1987.

_____. "The People of Rimrock Bury Alfred Lorenzo: Tri-Cultural Funerary Practice." ACA/1989. (Zuni, Navajo, Mormon.)

Darlington, James. "Cultural Assimilation Among Eastern Europeans in Western Canada: The View from the Graveyard." AGS/1992. (Ukrainian; Polish; Rumanian).

Decoster, Jean-Jacques. "Death Doeth Us Part: Processes of Separation and the Production of Social Identity in the Funerary Practices of a Quechua Community." ACA/1993.

Dobkins, Rebecca. "'Ancestor Days' as Ritual Response to Indian Grave Desecration: Folk Traditions Converge in Reburial Ceremonies in Western Kentucky." AFS/1990.

Erwin, Paul F. "Funeral and Burial Customs of Rom Gypsies in Cincinnati Cemeteries." ACA/1990.

_____. "Irish Gypsies or Tinkers' Funeral and Burial Customs in Cincinnati Cemeteries." ACA/1989.

_____. "Burial Customs of Scottish Travelling People and Irish Tinkers in Cincinnati Cemeteries." ACA/1987.

Eula, Michael J. "Working Class Culture and Italian-American Gravemarkers in New Jersey and New York, 1880-1980." ACA/1993.

Fannin, Minxie Jensvold. "St. Augustine's Chapel and Cemetery in South Boston, Massachusetts." AGS/1989. (Irish.)

Farber, Dan and Jessie Lie Farber. "The Tulip, the Fez, and the Turban on Turkish Gravemarkers." AGS/1986.

Franks, Herschel A. and Jill-Karen Yakubik. "African-American and Euro-American Cemeteries in Southeastern Louisiana." ACA/1993.

Gambone, Robert L. "Prairie Piety: Ethnic and Religious Associations Evidenced on 19th Century Minnesota Gravemarkers." ACA/1993. (French; German; Irish; Scandinavian).

Garman, James C. "'Faithful and Loyal Servants': The Reflections of Pre- and Post-Emancipation Attitudes in Newport, Rhode Island's Material Culture of Death." AGS/1990.

_____. "Problems of Attribution Amongst the Stevens Family and Their Slaves, 1745-1810." AGS/1988.

Gosnell, Lynn. "Contemporary Grave Decoration in an Urban Mexican-American Context." AFS/1987.

Gosnell, Lynn and Suzanne Gott. "Grave Decoration in an Urban Mexican-American Community." ACA/1987.

Gott, Suzanne. " 'Affective Display': The Evocation of Emotional Experiences Through Foregrounded Visual Presentation." AFS/1987. (Mexican-American)

Gradwohl, David M. "Intra-Group Variations in the Jewish Cemeteries of Lincoln, Nebraska." ACA/1991.

_____. "The Jewish Cemeteries of Louisville, Kentucky: Mirrors of Historical Processes and Theological Diversity Through 150 Years." ACA/1992.

Graves, Thomas E. "Keeping Ukraine Alive Through Death: Ukrainian-American Gravestones as Cultural Markers." ACA/1989.

_____. "Liebster Kinder und Verwandten: Death and Ethnicity." AFS/1982

_____. "The Multiethnic Cemetery: Melting Pot or Tossed Salad?" ACA/1992.

_____. " 'On foreign Land I Will Die': Contemporary Ukrainian-American Gravemarkers." AFS/1990.

_____. "Pennsylvania German Gravestones: An Introduction." AGS/1985.

_____. "Silent Witnesses: Decorated but Textless Gravestones of the Pennsylvania Germans." AGS/1987.

_____. "Trees-of-Life—Stones-of-Deaths: The Folk-Cultural Context of Pennsylvania-German Gravestones." AGS/1988.

_____. " 'We Bow to Thee, O Lord, on High': Pennsylvania German Mennonite Gravestones." AGS/1986.

_____. "Work, Politics, and Art in Contemporary Ukrainian Gravestones." ACA/1990; AGS/1990.

Hannon, Thomas J. "A Comparison of Monumentation in the Republic of Ireland and Ethnic Irish Monumentation in Pennsylvania." ACA/1992.

_____. "Here and There, Then and Now: Hungarian Monumentation in Trans-Danubia and the Penn-Ohio Area." ACA/1991.

_____. "Here Lies our Ethnicity: Surnames in Stone." ACA/1988. (Various ethnic groups.)

Hardy, Sandra J. Hammond. "Pennsylvania Germans and Their Gravestones: Lancaster County, 1770-1810." ACA/1991.

Hawker, Ron. "The White Man's Totem Poles: Stone Grave Monuments Among the Tsimshian Indians of the Canadian Northwest Coast, 1885-1930." ACA/1988

Hildenbrant, Daniel R. "Grave Painting in Southwest Louisiana." ACA/1991.

(Cajun; Video.)

_____. "The Tongan Way in Burial Customs and Grave Decorations." ACA/1992. (Video.)

Hunt, Melinda. "The Nature of New York's Hart Island: Social Structure and the City Cemetery." ACA/1993. (Various ethnic groups).

Jeane, Gregory. "The English Lych Gate: Origin of the Southern Rural Graveshelter." ACA/1991.

_____. "The Upland South Folk Cemetery Complex: Some Suggestions of Origin." ACA/1987. (European; African-American; Native American.)

Kiest, Karen. "Lasting Marks on the Prairie: Bohemian Immigrant Cemeteries in Nebraska." ACA/1989.

Kloberdanz, Timothy J. "Prairie Cross Markers: German-Russian Blacksmiths of the Great Plains." AGS/1988.

_____. " 'We Can Even Beat the Devil': German-Russian Blacksmiths of the Great Plains." AFS/1985. (Treats gravemarkers.)

Kürti, Laszlo. "Hungarian Immigrant Gravemarkers in North America: A Work in Progress." AGS/1985.

Lemmon, Alfred. "The Cemeteries of New Orleans: Preserving the Past for the Future." ACA/1993. (Various ethnic groups).

Little, M. Ruth. "The Last Generation of Traditional Stonecutters in Piedmont Carolina: 1830-1870." AGS/1989. (German Lutherans and Moravians.)

Matternes, Hugh B. "Modern Expectations and Prehistoric Reality in Western Kentucky: Historic Cemetery Modification at Wickliffe Mounds." ACA/1992. (Native American.)

Matturri, John. "Uncommon Grounds: American Burial Memorials and the Relationship Between the Living and the Dead." AGS/1989. (Several groups, primarily Italian.)

McDonald, Mary. "Symbols from Ribbons: Afro-American Funeral Ribbon Quilts in Chatham County, North Carolina." AFS/1986.

McDowell, Peggy. "J.N.B. de Pouilly and French Sources of Revival Style Architecture in New Orleans Funerary Arts." ACA/1987.

Meyer, Richard E. "Markers Made of Wood." ACA/1985. (Various ethnic groups.)

Milspaw, Yvonne J. "The Doctrine of Stone: Religion in the Folk Tombstones of German Pennsylvania." AFS/1985.

Miniaci, Michael A. "Yorba Cemetery: From Rural Rancho to County Historical Site." AGS/1988. (Hispanic.)

Mires, Maynard. "Grave Sheds of Chippewa/Objibway 19th Century Christian Indians on Western Lake Superior." AGS/1991.

Nelson, Malcolm A. and Elizabeth Hoffman. "Flowers in the Desert: Gravemarkers, Decorations and Offerings in the American Southwest." ACA/1993. (Mexican-American; Native American).

Olson, Ted. "Buried Alive: Cultural Assimilation in Kentucky Graveyard Folklore." ACA/1992. (Several ethnic groups.)

Patterson, Daniel W. "Early Stone Carving in Piedmont North Carolina." AFS/1975. (Scotch-Irish; German.)

Pearson, Charles E. "The Cemetery and Material Culture: St. Louis II Cemetery, New Orleans." ACA/1993. (African-American; French and Spanish Creole; various immigrant groups).

Pocius, Gerald. " 'Even in Death': Religious Conflict and the Location of Gravestones in Eastern Newfoundland Communities." AFS/1975. (English; Irish.)

Purnell, Nanette. "Cemetery Markers of the Hawaiian Isles." AGS/1986. (Chinese; Japanese; Filipino; Polynesian.)

Richardson, Milda. "Lithuanian-American Cemetery Art: Visual and Verbal Imagery." ACA/1993.

Riley, Thomas J. "Burial Units in Nineteenth Century America: Reflections of Ethnic Differences in Social Organization." ACA/1988. (Various ethnic groups.)

Rotundo, Barbara. "Who Controls the Product, Artist or Patron?" ACA/1991. (African-American.)

Sarapin, Janice. "Cultural Movements and Customs in New Jersey's Old Burial Grounds." ACA/1993. (Native American; African-American; Moravian; Jewish).

Schildknecht, Calvin E. "Folk Art of Gravestones of Western Maryland and Adjacent Pennsylvania." AGS/1988. (German; Scotch-Irish.)

Sclair, Helen. "Chicago's Ethnic Cemeteries." ACA/1992. (Many ethnic groups.)

Sexton, Rocky. "Cultural Variation in Southwest French Louisiana as Reflected in the Cemetery Landscape." ACA/1993. (Cajun).

Sherman, Susan C. "The Maplewood Jewish Cemetery of Malden, Massachusetts: A Source for the Study of Boston's Early Jewish Community." ACA/1990.

Sheumaker, Helen. "The Ties Between Us: Gravestones of Georgetown, Kentucky and Nicodemus, Kansas." ACA/1993. (Africian-American).

Shoupe, Catherine A. "Tools of Their Trade: Craft Insignia on 18th Century Scottish Headstones." AFS/1987.

Stone, Gaynell. "Ethnicity and Ideology in Material Culture: Colonial Long Island Gravestones, 1680-1820." AGS/1988. (Dutch; English.)

Strangstad, Lynette. "Conservation of Gravestones in the Southeastern United States." AGS/1988. (Native American; Spanish; French; African-American.)

Sze, Corrine. "The Dawson Cemetery: The Legacy of a Vanished Coal Mining Company Town in Northeastern New Mexico." ACA/1993. (Various ethnic groups).

Tashjian, Dickran and Ann Tashjian. "Afro-American Gravestones in Newport, Rhode Island." ACA/1987.

Trask, Deborah. " 'Hier Ruhet in Gott': German Tombstones in Nova Scotia." AGS/1988.

van Lent, Peter. " 'Je me souviens': Gravemarkers as Cultural Sustainers in the French-American Communities of Northern New York." ACA/1993.

Watters, David. "Folk Elements of New Hampshire Graveyards." AGS/1990. (Scotch-Irish.)

Weaver, William Woys. "Pennsylvania-German Funeral Foods: Symbols and Customs Before 1900." AGS/1988.

Weissler, Chava. "Cemetery Prayers and Rituals Among Ashkenazic Jewish Women." AFS/1985.

West, John O. "Folk Grave Decoration Along the Rio Grande." AFS/1984. (Mexican-American.)

Willsher, Betty. "Heads in Stone: The Devil Mask, the Portrait, and the Green Man on Scottish Gravestones." AGS/1989.

Young, Bradley J. "The Ellis County Volga-German Gravemarkers, 1876-1920." ACA/1991.

Zeitlin, Steven J. "The Performance of Grief: Death and Stories." AFS/1985. (Jewish.)

Contributors

Russell J. Barber is Professor of Anthropology at California State University-San Bernardino. His research and publications have focused on studies of prehistoric and historic archaeology, principally in North America. He heads a multidisciplinary team of scholars undertaking a long-term study of the Agua Mansa community in Southern California.

Keith Cunningham is Professor of English and Folklore at Northern Arizona University. For many years the editor of *Southwest Folklore*, his scholarly interests range from material culture studies to Native American oral narratives. His two most recent books are *The Oral Tradition of the American West* and *American Indians' Kitchen-Table Stories.*

Paul F. Erwin is Professor Emeritus of History at the University of Cincinnati and an ordained Methodist minister. In addition to his interest in Gypsy folkways, he was authored a large number of corporate histories and a textbook on Ohio history, *Round on the Ends.*

Thomas E. Graves is a professional folklorist and independent scholar with a particular interest in ethnically-based material culture. In addition to several published works on Pennsylvania German gravemarkers, he is the co-author (with folklorist Don Yoder) of the book *Hex Signs.*

Roberta Halporn is the Director of the Center for Thanatology Research and Education, a non-profit organization disseminating information in the areas of aging, dying and death. A member of the Board of Directors of the Association for Gravestone Studies, she has recently produced the re-issue of Harriette Forbes' long out-of-print seminal work in gravestone studies, *Gravestones of Early New England and the Men Who Made Them.*

Karen S. Kiest is a practicing landscape architect with the firm of Wallace, Roberts and Todd in San Francisco. Holder of an advanced degree in Landscape Architecture from Harvard University, her scholarly interests combine nineteenth and twentieth century cemetery design in Europe and the United States with the study of cultural settlement patterns in America.

John Matturri is a professional writer whose interest in the cultural history of cemeteries is part of a larger concern with the nature and cultural functions of visual objects. In addition to publishing work on photography, film and painting, he is currently completing work on a Ph.D. in Philosophy at the Graduate Center of the City University of New York.

Richard E. Meyer teaches Literature and Folklore at Western Oregon State College. His eclectic research interests and publications range from the 18th century poetry of George Crabbe to contemporary horror fiction and from the folklore of American outlaws to the gravemarkers of Oregon pioneers. Chairman of the Cemeteries and Gravemarkers Section of the American Culture Association, he has edited the book *Cemeteries and Gravemarkers: Voices of American Culture* and is editor of *Markers: The Journal of the Association for Gravestone Studies.*

Nanette Napoleon Purnell is Director of the Cemetery Research Project, Kailua, O'ahu, Hawai'i. Her work with the Project has led to the systematic identification and cataloging of all cemeteries in the State of Hawai'i. She has lectured widely throughout the Islands and elsewhere on the cultural and historical significance of Hawaiian cemetery sites.

CPSIA information can be obtained at www.ICGtesting.com
Printed in the USA
BVOW01*0212310816

460708BV00006B/13/P